Mountaincraft and Leadership

A Handbook for Mountaineers and Hillwalking Leaders in the British Isles

Eric Langmuir

THE SCOTTISH SPORTS COUNCIL

Mountainwalking Leader Training Board

Langmuir, Eric
  Mountaincraft and Leadership
  1. Mountaineering   2. Leadership
  I. Title
  796.5'22   GV200

Seventh Reprint with Amendments 1993
Eighth Reprint 1994

ISBN 0-903908-75-1

Published jointly by:

  The Scottish Sports Council, copyright © 1984
  Caledonia House,
  South Gyle,
  Edinburgh EH12 9DQ
  Telephone 031-317 7200
  Fax 031-317 7202

  The Mountainwalking Leader Training Board,
  Crawford House, Precinct Centre, Booth Street East,
  Manchester M13 9RZ
  Telephone 061-273 5839

Trade distribution by Cordee
3a De Montfort Street,
Leicester LE1 7HD

Filmset by Advanced Filmsetters (Glasgow) Ltd
Printed by Brown, Son & Ferguson, Glasgow
Bound by James Gowans, Glasgow

Contents

Foreword

I make no apology for beginning this Foreword on a personal note. My first involvement in mountain training goes back over 40 years to the second year of the war, when I ran a course at Helyg in North Wales for officers and other ranks of an armoured brigade; later, I became Chief Instructor at a Commando Mountain and Snow Warfare Centre in the Cairngorms. For ten years I was involved in setting up the first national centre for mountain activities established by the Central Council for Physical Recreation in the former Royal Hotel at Capel Curig: later to be taken under the wing of the Sports Council. I refer to those far-off years in order to testify to the huge strides in the skills and resources acquired since then, for the task of initiating newcomers into the lore of mountaincraft; and to contrast the military training manuals which we drafted at Braemar for the War Office, with this excellent re-written version of *Mountain Leadership*.

Those of us who were involved in those early courses had little notion of the dimensions to which mountain training would be developed in the years ahead, to the point it has reached today. Yet even then it was apparent that something exciting was astir; there was an urge for adventure in post-war Britain for which the mountains could provide an outlet. There was a feeling abroad of a dynamic new age, at the end of this conflict and the beginning of a new era.

But this soon gave rise to anxiety about safety. There were far too many groups of young people, too large in number, unsuitably equipped and led by too few adults with too little experience and skill. The need to establish a code of standards and to draw up schemes for the certification of adult leaders—though frowned upon by some mountaineers at the time—became essential in the interest of safety. This demand for qualifications as a safeguard for youthful parties in the mountains led, for a while, to unfortunate misapprehensions over the title of the Mountain Leadership Certificate. It seemed to imply a greater degree of experience than any limited training course could provide. Today, these courses are better understood, while their value is widely accepted.

Looking back over all this span of time, I marvel at what has been achieved in giving so much pleasure and satisfaction to so many people—especially young people—within reasonable parameters of safety. I say 'reasonable' purposely, for safety in mountains is, and should be, a relative term. If you seek to eliminate it altogether, you remove the magnet of adventure, in which an element of risk is an essential ingredient; risk is the honey-pot which lures us to the mountains. Most of the satisfaction in every 'risk' sport lies, not in courting hazards unprepared, but in matching danger with your skills, and in extending your experience in order to step up, with impunity, the degree of risk which you seek.

The title of this book is *Mountaincraft and Leadership*. The fascination of mountaincraft is that it has so many facets. It can range from climbing the gritstone edges in Derbyshire to scaling an ice-clad mountain face of Himalayan proportions; from a day's trek through the Lairig Ghru to a journey across the Greenland Icecap. In every situation, no matter what the scale, the scene and the problem can be changed dramatically by weather conditions. For the young, there is an endless vista of progress and new experience ahead; for the elderly there is the delight in returning to first beginnings.

A word about leadership. I won't attempt to improve on Ken Ogilvie's excellent chapter, but I hope that all who, with the help of this book, set out to qualify as mountain leaders will also learn the skills and the pleasures of teaching those whom they lead over the mountains and moorlands; giving them responsibilities under their guidance and not acting as mere conductors. I say this with feeling, for in my own boyhood I spent six seasons in the European Alps, both in winter and summer, climbing many big peaks with professional guides, yet learning very little and missing much of the fun and satisfaction of graduating as an all-round mountaineer.

I especially welcome Mark Hutchinson's chapter on Access and Conservation. The mountains in our English and Welsh National Parks and, to a lesser extent, the Scottish Highlands—even the bigger ranges around the world—are in danger of suffering irreversible damage from the sheer numbers of people who visit them. It is up to us, who derive so much benefit and pleasure from the mountain scenery and all else that mountains have to offer, to play our part in safeguarding these precious assets for future generations.

I hope that all of you who study this book and apply its teaching to your own knowledge of the mountains will find as lasting a joy in them as I have over the last sixty years or so, since I first started as a ten-year-old, walking in the Alps.

JOHN HUNT

Patron
The British Mountaineering Council

Acknowledgements

Rewriting a book is probably the most difficult assignment an author may have to undertake and this book has proved no exception. I have retained the general format of the former handbook, *Mountain Leadership*, which is to a large extent circumscribed by the content of the ML Training Schemes. Much of the material in the old handbook is as relevant today as it was when the book was originally published in 1969. As far as possible I have retained this material and, where appropriate, added to it. I have taken the opportunity of standardising the approach so that the leadership aspects are directed at the mountain leader rather than the instructor responsible for his training. This, together with the wealth of new material and illustrations for the general mountaineer, has resulted in a substantial increase in the content of the book. The task has been made possible through the help of many people and in particular the members of the editorial board appointed by the MLTB and the SMLTB to oversee the production: David Atherton, Robin Campbell, Chris Dodd, Allen Fyffe, Peter Hodgkiss, Wally Keay, Charles McLennan, Ken Ogilvie, Reg Popham, Roger Putnam and Duncan Ross. Their sterling work has ensured that the contents meet the requirements of the Boards and are therefore applicable throughout the British Isles. The illustrations were drawn by Phil Alder, David Mason, Susan Nuttgens, David Simon and Archie Sinclair. I am greatly indebted to Ken Ogilvie for the chapter on Leadership and to Mark Hutchinson for the chapter on Access and Conservation, both important aspects of mountain training which are now receiving the attention they deserve. Others have assisted me by reading the text and making suggestions which I have included in the final manuscript: Roger O'Donovan, Rod Pashley, John Brown, Graham Tiso, Rod Ward, Ken Oldham and others too numerous to mention. My grateful thanks to them all. It is fitting to remember that it was Lord Hunt, who has written the foreword to this book, who chaired the original meeting in 1962 which laid the foundations of the mountain leader training schemes.

1 Navigation

Navigation is fun! It is an intensely interesting, indeed fascinating, aspect of mountain craft, the proper practice of which brings considerable personal satisfaction. It is one of the most important keys which unlocks a whole new world of adventure and discovery. It is a skill which you ignore at your peril. Far too many accidents are caused by original errors in route finding. It is not enough just to follow a set course in fine weather at low level. Experience of blind navigation in the most severe weather conditions is essential if you wish to aspire to the freedom of the hills.

There is a popular myth about having a good or bad 'sense of direction' which must be scotched at the outset. How often one hears the expression that someone has no sense of direction. Nonsense! They are either resigned to being labelled in this way or they have not tried. Even mice can be trained to find their way out of a maze—provided the motivation is there! The ancient peoples of the world learned to navigate through the meticulous observation of natural phenomena; the sun, the moon and stars, the migration of birds, the wave patterns in the oceans, the behaviour and signs of other species and so on. Observation is still the keynote to successful navigation today although this is sometimes obscured by our increasing tendency to rely on gadgets or the recorded experience of other experts, such as the map makers themselves.

There is perhaps one further lesson to learn from the navigators of old and that is to keep track of a journey as a whole rather than as a series of disconnected sections. It is quite possible to complete a route successfully without ever knowing where you are in relation to your starting point or even to the country immediately outside the narrow corridor of your route. From time to time you should stand back from the absorbing detail and think of where you are in a wider context. This self-orientation will not only help you to anticipate what lies ahead but will enable you to respond positively should some mishap occur requiring a change of plan.

One final word of advice. Do not leave it to someone else to do all the navigating. Even the best can make a mistake and you may be asked to pick up the threads at a moment's notice. Keep involved and in touch with all that is going on.

Map Symbols

Most maps contain hundreds of thousands of bits of information about the ground, not all of which are relevant to the mountaineer. Indeed, most maps in general use are a compromise to the sometimes conflicting demands of different groups and interests. The selection of information to portray is one problem for the map makers; another is the actual presentation of that information on the map. Because of the severe limitation of space a system of shorthand is used by which means a great deal of information is conveyed by 'conventional signs'. With a little practice these signs are easily recognised and if in doubt you can refer to the key which is given in the margin of the map. Of particular interest to the hillwalker is the convention which is used to represent relief and associated signs such as those depicting outcrops and cliffs. These are dealt with in more detail later. Footpaths and boundaries of various kinds can be easily confused and you would do well to familiarise yourself with the appropriate map symbols. On 1:50,000 maps a stream is shown by a single blue line gradually increasing in thickness as the distance increases from the source up to the point at which the stream is 8 metres wide. From this point downstream it is shown by a double line.

While it is important to be able to extract the maximum amount of information from the map, it is just as important to know what the map does not tell you. In the first place maps are not produced just for the benefit of the fraternity of mountaineers, although this is an assumption too readily made by many of us. They do not, for example, tell us very much about the nature of the terrain and how easy or difficult it is to walk over. There is no map symbol for knee-high heather or for a dissected peat hag! The special maps produced for orienteering do go some way towards providing the kind of information which is particularly relevant to the hillwalker, but their use is generally confined to lowland and forest areas. Next time you have the opportunity, try navigating with the aid of air photographs. Although the technique of 'reading' air photographs is a specialised art, you will be surprised how much additional information you can learn from one and it will serve to illustrate some of the limitations of conventional maps.

Which Map?

The first thing you have to decide is what scale of map is suited to your purpose. The scale of a map is always printed on the front cover and is expressed as the ratio between a unit of length on the map and the equivalent distance on the ground. A scale of 1:25,000 means that one unit of length on the map is equivalent to 25,000 units on the ground, or, to put it into actual units, one centimetre is equivalent to 25,000 centimetres or 250 metres. In the same way 1:50,000 means that 1 cm on the map is equivalent to 50,000 cm or 500 metres on the ground.

Some common map scales and their use:

Scale	Meaning	Use
1:10,000	1 cm = 100 m	Orienteering
1:25,000	1 cm = 250 m	Ideal for walking, but you may require more than one map to cover your area
1:50,000	1 cm = 500 m	The most popular map for walking
1:63,360	1 in = 1 mile	Now replaced by 1:50,000 maps
1:100,000	1 cm = 1,000 m	Cycling, hostelling, holidaying, route selection
1:250,000	1 cm = 2,500 m	Cycling, motoring, etc.
1:1,000,000	1 cm = 10 km	Map of UK

For the hillwalker the choice seems to be between the 1:50,000 and the 1:25,000 published by the Ordnance Survey.

Obviously it is possible to show a great deal more detail on the larger scale map, but this advantage is offset by the fact that you have to carry four times as much map. Your final choice is inevitably a compromise between the two. Additional information about these two scales is provided at the end of this chapter.

Measuring Distance

Once you know the scale of a map it is a relatively simple matter to measure the length between any two points in centimetres and convert this into distance along the ground. Nearly all compasses are provided with a centimetre scale. The grid lines on all Ordnance Survey maps are spaced 1 km apart so it is possible to estimate distance quite quickly, simply by

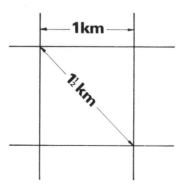

Fig. 1. *The grid lines on Ordnance Survey maps are 1 km apart. The diagonal is approximately 1·5 km.*

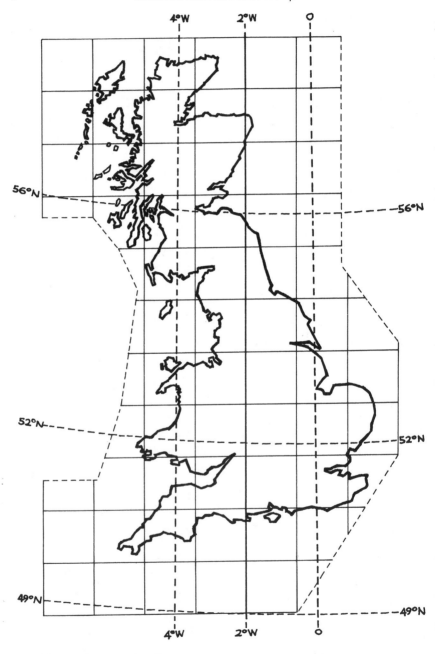

Fig. 2.   *The National Grid.*

counting the number of grid squares separating the points. It is useful to know that the diagonal from corner to corner of a grid square is approximately $1\frac{1}{2}$ km.

Looking after your Map

Only a few maps, such as some of the 1:25,000 leisure maps, are provided with any protection against the weather. The ideal arrangement is to cover the map completely, and preferably on both sides, with a transparent adhesive film such as 'transpaseal'. The treated map should then be refolded in the manner which allows any part of it to be viewed by a single opening of the folds. The expense of protecting a map in this way is probably only justified if it is in fairly constant use. A clear plastic envelope or bag serves well enough and the map should be prefolded so that the route for the day is exposed. Some people favour map cases and boards, but it should be remembered that such items can become unmanageable in high winds.

The National Grid

If you look at any Ordnance Survey map you will see that it is overprinted with a network, or grid, of lines. These grid lines are 1 km apart and form part of a larger National Grid which covers the whole of mainland Britain. The system was introduced as a sort of index system so that every point in the country could be given a unique reference number which would enable it to be identified. Indeed, it was once suggested that such a system could provide a postal code for every home in the land.

Figure 2 shows how the country is divided into a series of larger squares, 100 km × 100 km, each of which is further divided into smaller squares 1 km × 1 km. The grid is based on two axes selected from convenient lines of latitude and longitude, 49°N for the horizontal axis and 2°W for the vertical. Being a rectilinear pattern this grid differs from the lines of latitude and longitude, the difference increasing as the distance from the axes increases. You will appreciate, therefore, that there is only one grid line which actually points to true north and that is the one which coincides with the line of longitude 2°W. The remaining vertical grid lines differ slightly from true north, and this difference is recorded in the map margin for each corner of the sheet. It is never more than about 3°. As we shall shortly see it is grid north which we use as our reference for navigating with the compass so that the difference between true north and grid north is of academic interest only.

Since the grid lines are numbered, it is possible to refer to a particular 1 km square by giving the number of the two lines which bound it on the west and south. The vertical grid lines, known as eastings because they are numbered eastwards, are always given first, followed by the horizontal lines, known as northings because they are numbered northwards. By further subdivision, co-ordinates can be given for individual 100 m squares. So it is important to realise that a grid reference refers to an area 100 m × 100 m, not a point. You should also appreciate that any six-figure grid reference is duplicated in each one of the larger 100 km squares. To make it unique you need to add the two grid letters which identify the particular 100 km square. The appropriate letters are to be found in the map margin.

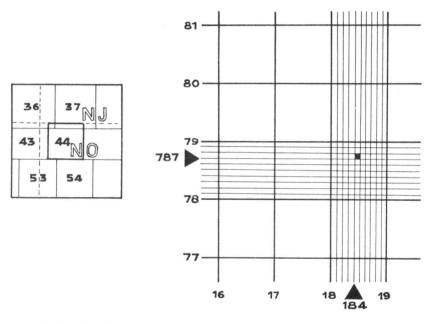

Fig. 3. *The grid reference for the 100 m square is 184 (eastings) 787 (northings). To make the reference unique you must add the grid letters appropriate to your position, in this case NO. The complete reference is therefore NO 184787.*

Setting the Map in relation to the Ground

Since the map is a plan representation to scale of the actual ground, it should be possible to turn the map in such a way that with your own position as the central point all the features that you can see around you are in their correct relative positions. This is called setting or orientating the map and is one of the first and most important techniques of map reading. You may also use the compass to set the map if identifiable features are not visible. This technique is described later (see p. 23). Once the map is set, you can identify all the features which can be seen and most importantly select a route across country to reach an unseen objective.

Fig. 4. *Setting the map by reference to identifiable features on the ground.*

If you are following a linear feature such as a path it is usually unnecessary to identify other features. Simply turn the map until the path lines up with the real path you are walking on. You can then anticipate changes in direction, junctions and the appearance of features which will confirm your actual position along the path.

Get into the habit of walking with the map set. If you do this (and it takes a bit of getting used to because the place names and so on may be upside down) the features that you see on the map match those that you see around you. This correct orientation is far more useful in relating the map to the ground than being able to read the place names. Try to think of the map as a three-dimensional model, rather than a book which has always to be held the right way up. The right way up for a map is when it is set.

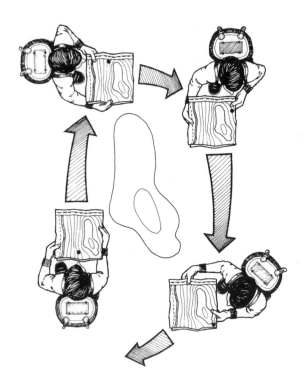

Fig. 5.   *Get into the habit of walking with the map set.*

Relief

It is one thing to represent the ground surface on a horizontal plane; this basic technique of map making has been used from the earliest times. It is quite another to depict the ups and downs, the shape of the ground, on such a plane. It is a problem that map makers have wrestled with for long enough without success. That is until the contour line was invented.

Curiously enough, the contour principle was first used in 1730 to show the shape of the sea bed, but it was not until much later that contour lines made their appearance on maps in general use.

It is important to appreciate that a contour line represents the inter-section of a horizontal plane with the surface of the ground. The coast line is a good starting point since, in a way, it is the only 'real' contour line and is the one from which all others are derived. Raise the level of the sea in increments of 10 m and you have a succession of new shore lines or contour lines, each one 10 m vertically above the other. When you are looking at a map the arrangement of the contour lines should allow you to build up a 3-D picture in your mind of what the ground actually looks like. The closer the contour lines are packed together, the steeper the slope.

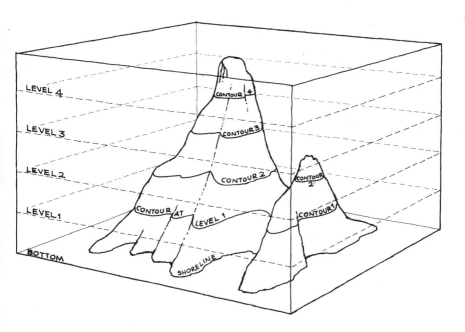

Fig. 6. *Contour lines can be visualised as successive shore lines formed by raising the level of the sea in a series of equal vertical steps.*

There is a limit to the amount of information which can be conveyed by contour lines because they only give the shape of the ground at certain predetermined intervals. They do not tell you what is happening in between. It is quite possible, therefore, for small features to be completely missed because they fall within two contour lines.

With practice you will quickly learn to associate certain characteristic arrangements of the contour lines with particular mountain forms, such as ridges, valleys, cols, concave and convex slopes and so on.

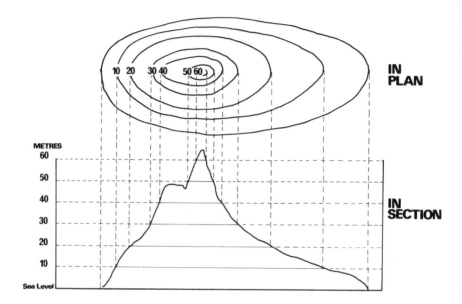

Fig. 7.   *The vertical and horizontal aspects of contour lines. In this example the vertical, or contour interval is 10 m.*

How Steep?

It follows from what has been said that it is the density of contour lines in a particular area on the map which gives a measure of the steepness of the ground in that area. But how steep? This is not an easy question to answer and yet it is one of considerable importance to the mountaineer.

Steepness can be measured in two ways:

(a) By measuring the angle of the slope from the horizontal. It is surprising how few of us think in terms of angles and there is a general tendency to overestimate the steepness of slopes, even amongst climbers and skiers, two categories of outdoor sportsmen to whom such information is critical. The truth of the matter is that there is no easy way for measuring slope angles in the field without the aid of a clinometer, itself a simple enough instrument, but not one which is commonly available.

(b) By measuring the gradient. In other words the ratio of the vertical to the horizontal component of the slope, where the vertical component is taken to be one unit of length. This is rather easier to visualise than angular measurements and on the hill it is quite possible to estimate the gradient with the aid of an ice axe or ski stick to act as a measuring rod.

Nowadays gradients are frequently expressed as 'so many per cent' and it is important to realise just what this means. A gradient of 30% means 30 units up for every 100 units along.

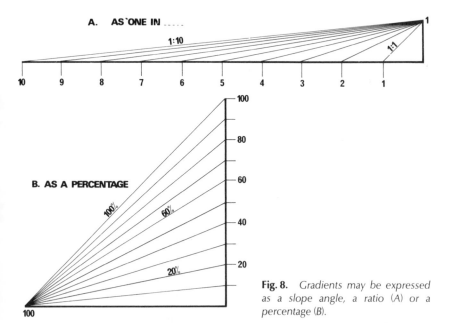

Fig. 8. *Gradients may be expressed as a slope angle, a ratio (A) or a percentage (B).*

It can be seen that the two ways of expressing gradients are readily convertible. To find the percentage gradient simply divide 100 by the ratio gradient, e.g.

If the ratio gradient is 1:10, the percentage gradient is

$$\frac{100}{10} = 10\%.$$

To convert the other way from percentage gradient to ratio gradient divide 100 by the percentage gradient, e.g.

If the percentage gradient is 20%, the ratio gradient is

$$\frac{100}{20} = 1:5.$$

Mountaincraft and Leadership

Table 1 will help you to compare gradients and angles and to relate these to slopes with particular characteristics.

Table 1.   Slopes and gradients

Slope angle	Gradient 1:___ (approx.)	Gradient percent (approx.)	Description of slope
5°	1:11	9%	gentle slope—normal walking—equivalent to a fairly steep road
10°	1:6	18%	walk directly up—very steep road gradient—easy ski slope angle
15°	1:4	27%	good ski-ing terrain—limit of road gradient
20°	1:3	36%	route selection and care in placing feet—if hard snow/ice care is required, especially in descent
25°	1:2	47%	probably start zigzag walking—steep ski slopes
30°	1:1·7	58%	zig-zag up, but go straight down—into avalanche country
35°	1:1·4	70%	start to pick way up and down—rock scrambling
40°	1:1·2	84%	care required in descent—near max. angle of repose for scree
45°	1:1	100%	graded snow/ice climbing
50°	1:0·8	119%	angle of 'scarp' slope below cornice—near limit of friction on rock
55°	1:0·7	143%	steep snow/ice pitch
60°	1:0·6	173%	extremely steep climbing on rock or ice
70°	1:0·4	275%	hands touch rock/ice when held horizontally in front

Fig. 9. *Fading out contour lines. Note how the intermediate contour lines are left out when the space becomes too constricted.*

Obviously it is extremely important to develop an awareness of the steepness of slopes as represented by the density of the contour lines. In practice, with the map scales in common use, it quickly becomes impossible to include all the contour lines, because there is just not enough room for them. It is very rarely that the thicker contour lines are faded out, so it is best to get used to judging steepness on the spacing of these lines. Take for example the 2nd Series 1:50,000 maps with a vertical interval (v.i.) of 10 m and a thicker contour line every 50 m. At a slope angle of approximately 27°, or 1:2, the intermediate 10 m lines start to be faded out. In the case of First Series maps where the v.i. is greater (50 ft) the contours are not so tightly packed and fading out is not necessary until a slope angle of about 37°. This fading out does not imply a loss of detail: in fact, the shorter v.i. and larger horizontal scale result in a wealth of new detail. Nevertheless, account must be taken of the general effect that slopes in the range 20°–30° appear to be very steep because of the overcrowding of contour lines.

Steepness of Slope from Contour Lines

Table 2. For use with 1:50,000 maps (Landranger Series)

Number of thick contour lines in 1 cm of map	Horizontal distance between thick contours on map in millimetres	Vertical interval 50 m between thick contours		Vertical interval 250 ft between thick contours	
		Gradient	Slope angle	Gradient	Slope angle
1	10·0 mm	1:10	6°	1:6·6	9°
2	5·0 mm	1:5	11°	1:3·3	17°
3	3·3 mm	1:3·3	17°	1:2·2	25°
4	2·5 mm	1:2·5	22°	1:1·6	31°
5	2·0 mm	1:2	27°	1:1·3	37°
6	1·7 mm	1:1·7	30°	1:1·1	42°
7	1·4 mm	1:1·4	35°	1:0·9	47°
8	1·25 mm	1:1·25	39°	1:0·8	51°
9	1·1 mm	1:1·1	42°	1:0·7	55°
10	1·0 mm	1:1	45°	1:0·6	57°
12	0·8 mm	1:0·8	51°	1:0·5	62°
14	0·7 mm	1:0·7	55°		
16	0·6 mm	1:0·6	59°		

Table 3. For use with 1:25,000 maps

Number of thick contours per cm of map	Distance between thick contour lines on map	Vertical interval 50 m between thick contours		Vertical interval between thick contours = 100 ft (30·5 m)	
		Gradient	Slope angle	Gradient	Slope angle
1	10 mm	1:5	11°	1:8	7°
1·5	6·7 mm	1:3·3	17°	1:5·5	10°
2	5 mm	1:2·5	22°	1:4·1	13°
2·5	4 mm	1:2	27°	1:3·3	17°
3	3·3 mm	1:1·7	31°	1:2·7	20°
4	2·5 mm	1:1·25	39°	1:2	26°
5	2 mm	1:1	45°	1:1·6	31°
6	1·7 mm	1:0·8	50°	1:1·4	36°
7	1·4 mm	1:0·7	54°	1:1·2	40°
8	1·25 mm	1:0·6	58°	1:1	44°
9	1·1 mm	1:0·6	61°	1:0·9	48°
10	1 mm	1:0·5	63°	1:0·8	51°

On steeper slopes it is unrealistic to expect details of individual gullies and smaller cliff features to show up. Here we are at the mercy of the artistic licence accorded to the cartographer. For this reason and also because of fading out, it is best to rely on the thicker contour lines when estimating the steepness of slopes from the map. Get used to judging slope angles from the density of the thicker lines. Unfortunately, you also have to get used to dealing with different maps, the most common being the 1:50,000 first series with a v.i. of 50 ft, the 1:50,000 second series with a v.i. of 10 m and the 1:25,000 series with v.i. of 10 m and 5 m. The effect of these variations in scale and v.i. is to alter the density of the contour lines for any given slope. This takes a lot of getting used to. Study Fig. 10 which illustrates the difference between two types of map in common use.

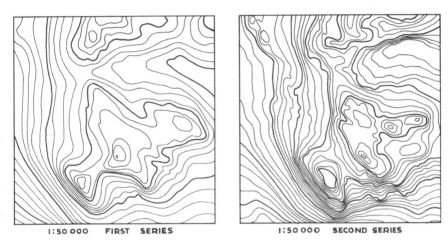

1:50 000   FIRST   SERIES   1:50 000   SECOND SERIES

Fig. 10.   *Notice the improvement in the second series map. The first series, 1:50,000 map is simply a scaled-up version of the old seventh series, 1 inch to 1 mile map. Note the increase in the density of contour lines in the second series due to the reduction in the v.i. from 50 ft to 10 m.*

In attempting to interpret the hieroglyphics which are used to depict outcrops of rock and cliffs it is prudent to refer to the contour lines. The main change in the newer maps is that outcrops are now shown with a continuous line at the bottom of the rocks, in contrast to cliffs which are shown with a continuous line at the top. The distinction between the two features is not always clear and many a cliff is shown as an outcrop and vice-versa.

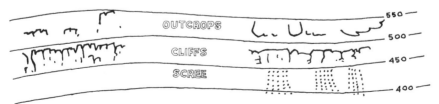

Fig. 11.   *Symbols used to denote outcrops and cliffs. Left, older maps; right, newer.*

Foreshortening Effect

Remember that a map is really a projection of the landscape on a horizontal plane. Imagine looking down onto the ground from an aircraft; a cliff will appear as a single line or perhaps a narrow band whereas in fact it may be 1,000 ft high. Similarly, a steep slope will appear to be shorter than it actually is because of this foreshortening effect. Under normal circumstances it does not amount to much and can be discounted but on steeper slopes the actual distance along the ground can be considerably more than the horizontal distance indicated by the map. The table below gives a rough guide to the relationship between slope angle, horizontal (map) distance and the actual distance. It can be seen that on a slope of say 30° the extra distance travelled to that shown on the map is only 15%. In other words if you measure the distance from the map as 200 m the actual distance to be walked on the ground will be 230 m.

However, beyond this slope angle, the extra 'hidden' distance is considerable. For instance, a horizontal distance of 200 m becomes an actual distance of 280 m on a 45° slope and 400 m on a 60° slope.

Table 4.   Showing the additional distance travelled to that shown on the map as a result of the foreshortening effect

Slope angle	Additional distance travelled
10°	1·5%
20°	6%
30°	15%
40°	31%
45°	41%
50°	56%
60°	100%

The effect of this is relatively slight on the sort of slopes normally frequented by hill walkers. It is taken into account in the various formulae used to estimate time and distance. Nevertheless, it is important to be aware of the problem. It not only seems longer when you are slogging up a steep hillside: it actually is longer. It's a comforting thought!

Introducing the Compass

It is said that the Chinese discovered the principle of the compass more than 5,000 years ago. It has retained its essential simplicity over the centuries and even today it is nothing more than a magnetised bar of metal suspended in the earth's magnetic field. It has been and remains the mainstay of the explorer and an essential tool of the mountaineer. It is when conditions are at their most severe that the compass becomes an indispensable aid to safe navigation.

The Compass

It is true to say that there is a compass available for almost every specialist requirement from deep sea diving to rally driving. Whatever the use, it is a precision instrument on which the success or failure of an enterprise may depend. For the hillwalker the range of models is bewildering and it is perhaps worthwhile to look for a moment at the features which help to make a compass suitable for use on the hill. There is no doubt that the Silva range is the most popular and we shall use this as our model.

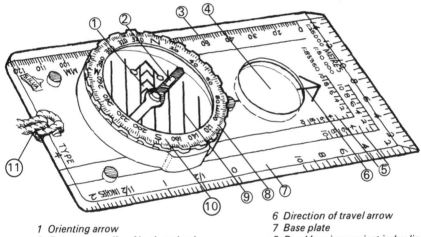

	6 *Direction of travel arrow*
1 *Orienting arrow*	7 *Base plate*
2 *Compass needle—North end red*	8 *Read bearing against index line*
3 *Scale*	9 *Orienting lines*
4 *Magnifying lens*	10 *Compass housing*
5 *Romer for grid references*	11 *Carrying cord*

Fig. 12.   *The parts of a compass.*

In the first place the compass should be compact, robust, light in weight and easy to handle and to operate in adverse conditions when you may have to use it with gloves on. The needle should settle down quickly when the compass is rotated and for this the capsule which holds the needle must be liquid filled. The compass should be able to be used as a protractor to measure angles on the map as well as giving a clear indication of the direction of travel when used to follow a bearing across country. Some models are specially adapted for sighting by incorporating a mirror or prism. To a certain extent this is a matter for individual preference but any more advanced gadgetry is inappropriate. It should have at the very least a scale marked out in millimetres and centimetres and it is useful to have a romer which facilitates taking accurate grid references.

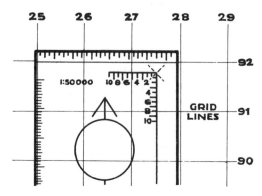

Fig. 13. *Using a romer to find a grid reference. In this example the grid reference is 275918.*

The rim of the housing is usually marked off in 360°, although models are available with other scales. The figures and subdivisions must be clearly visible and it is useful to have some means of keeping the compass orientated in the dark without having to use a torch. Few compasses are equipped to do this satisfactorily and rely on spots of luminous paint on the north end of the needle, the orientating arrow and the direction of travel arrow.

One of the drawbacks of the conventional compass is the fact that constant adjustments have to be made to take account of magnetic variation. On certain models, such as the Silva Ranger, the dial can be adjusted to allow for this so that the figure shown against the direction of travel arrow is always the magnetic bearing. This can save a lot of mental arithmetic. Naturally, you have to readjust the dial when you move to a different country where the magnetic variation may be significantly different.

Like all precision instruments the compass requires careful handling. Try not to drop it and when you are not using it put it away in its case. If you do not have a proper case an old sock or a section of tubular bandage will serve equally well. Store apart from other compasses and electrical equipment such as TV sets, telephones, doorbells, etc. After a period of time some compasses develop an air bubble inside the capsule. Provided it is not too large this does not interfere with the functioning of the compass.

Deviation

Since the compass needle is a magnet it will respond to magnetic fields other than the earth's. Any object containing ferrous metal, if large enough or close enough to the compass, will distort the earth's magnetic field in its vicinity. This distortion causes the compass needle to 'deviate' from its true orientation. Even quite small objects can have a disproportionate effect: a metal badge, a watch, a camera, a wire fence and so on. On a larger scale there are certain types of rock that cause compass deviation, notably the rough gabbro of the Cuillin of Skye, but fortunately this is the exception rather than the rule. Normally, if you keep your compass well clear of metal objects you should have no problems.

True North

True north and south are at the geographical poles, the points at which the earth's axes meet the surface. In the northern hemisphere the direction of the north pole is indicated by the Pole Star which can be found by following the pointers in the constellation of the Plough, or Great Bear as it is more properly known.

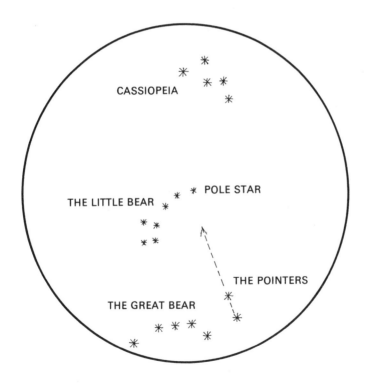

Fig. 14. *Finding true north by the stars. The Great Bear is also known as the Plough or the Big Dipper.*

If you can see the sun it is also possible to orientate yourself, provided you have a watch. Hold the watch horizontally and point the hour-hand towards the sun. Now bisect the angle between the hour-hand and 12 o'clock. This line will point due south. When using British Summer Time (April–October) bisect the angle between the hour-hand and one o'clock. If you have a digital watch you can still find south by drawing a conventional clock in the margin of your map and using that instead of a watch.

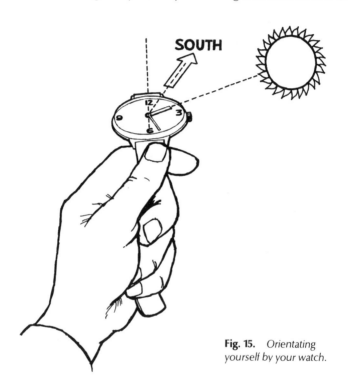

Fig. 15.   *Orientating yourself by your watch.*

Grid North

As has been shown earlier in this chapter, O.S. maps are orientated to grid north which differs slightly from true north except along longitude 2°W.

Magnetic North

The earth behaves just like a gigantic magnet creating its own magnetic field within which a suspended magnetised object, such as a compass needle, will align itself. Unfortunately for map users, the magnetic north pole does not coincide with the geographical north pole; in fact it is to be found in Canada, somewhere north of Hudson Bay. From the British Isles the magnetic north pole is currently some 7° west of the geographical pole. In other parts of the world this magnetic variation, as it is called, may be different. In the Alps for example, it is two or three degrees west. In some areas of the world magnetic north is east of grid north. Since maps are orientated to the National Grid rather than to true north it is customary for the angle between grid north and magnetic north to be given in the map margin. Naturally, this 'magnetic variation' has to be allowed for when converting a map bearing (angle from grid north) to a compass bearing (angle from magnetic north) or vice versa. Since magnetic north is to the west of grid north in this country, the compass or magnetic bearing is always the greater of the two.

Fig. 16.   *North points.*

Magnetic north about 8°W of grid north in 1976 decreasing by about $\frac{1}{2}$° in five years.

There is a further complication due to the fact that magnetic north is not a fixed point. It changes its position over a period of years. Fortunately, the movement can be predicted and an appropriate adjustment made to the magnetic variation. At the present time magnetic north is moving in a direction which reduces the westerly variation from locations within the British Isles by approximately $\frac{1}{2}$° in 5 years.

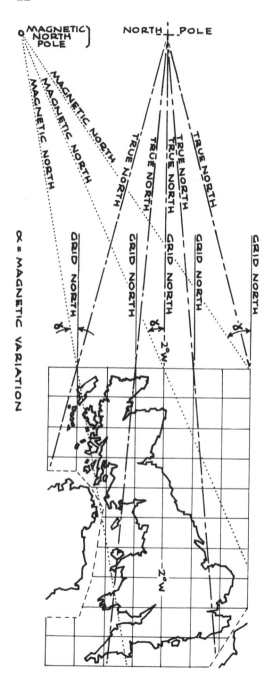

Fig. 17. *The relationship between the three norths: magnetic north, true north and grid north. For the purpose of illustration the north poles are shown much closer to the British Isles than they really are. Note particularly the decrease in the magnetic variation, 'α', as you move westwards.*

Setting the Map with the Compass

In poor visibility it is useful to be able to set the map quickly using the compass. To do this simply place the compass on the map and turn both compass and map until the red end of the needle points to north on the map.

Fig. 18. *Setting the map 'roughly' with the compass.*

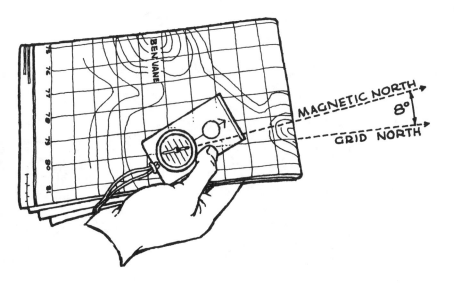

You can allow for magnetic variation if you wish, either by turning map and compass that little bit more so that the needle points just to the west of grid north or by setting the actual variation on the dial, matching the edge of the compass with the N–S grid lines and then turning both map and compass until the needle falls inside the orienting arrow. Your choice of method will depend on the circumstances and the need or otherwise for accuracy. As far as possible the map should remain 'set' as you follow your route. Only in this way can the features you see on the map be identified with their real counterparts without the necessity for complicated mental gymnastics.

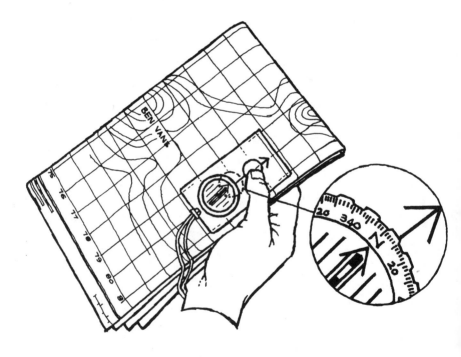

Fig. 19. *Setting the map 'accurately', by setting the magnetic variation on the compass dial.*

To take a Compass Bearing from the Map and follow it on the Ground

The first task is to measure on the map the angle between grid north and your intended direction of travel. You can use an ordinary protractor to do this or alternatively, use the compass as a protractor, if it has this facility.

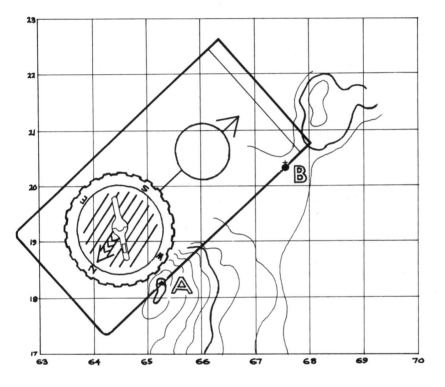

Fig. 20. *Taking a compass bearing from the map*
Stage I. *Align your compass with your direction of travel on the map.*

Place the compass with one of the long edges along the line joining your present position, A, with your objective, B, making sure that the direction of travel arrow on the compass plate is pointing in the direction you want to go, i.e. from A to B.

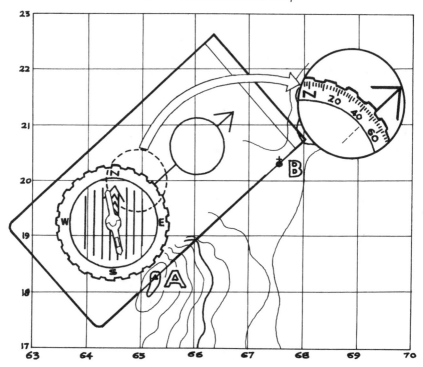

Fig. 21. *Taking a compass bearing from the map.*
Stage II. *Turn the housing so that the orienting arrow is lined up with the N–S grid lines.*

Now hold the compass plate firmly in this position on the map and rotate the compass housing so that the lines engraved on it are parallel to the north–south grid lines which can be seen through the housing. Make sure that the north arrow on the housing is pointing towards north on the map.

The number of degrees between grid north and your intended direction of travel is shown on the rim of the compass housing against the direction of travel arrow (see inset, Fig. 21). This is the bearing of your objective and at this stage it is worth making a visual check against the map that the figures are of the right order and not 180° out, as can all too easily happen.

To find out what this direction is on the ground you need to refer to the compass needle. But the compass needle does not in fact point to grid north, but towards the magnetic north pole. Therefore, you have to make an allowance for this. Since magnetic north is to left or west of grid north and since bearings are measured in a clockwise direction you will readily appreciate that for any given direction of travel the angle between that direction and magnetic north will always be greater than that between the direction of travel and grid north. And it will be greater by the number of degrees that magnetic north is to the west (left) of grid north—i.e. the magnetic variation.

There are all sorts of rhymes and tricks to help you remember whether to add or subtract the magnetic variation, e.g. 'Add for mag, get rid for grid.' However, if you understand why the compass bearing is different from the map bearing you will always be able to work out whether to add or subtract.

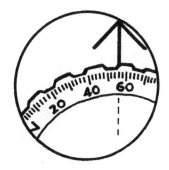

Fig. 22. *Taking a compass bearing from the map.*
Stage III. *Now lift the compass off the map and add the magnetic variation to the grid bearing, i.e. 48° +7° = 55°. This is your magnetic bearing.*

To recap: in order to find the direction of travel from the map you use the compass as a protractor and measure the number of degrees between the N/S grid lines and that direction. You then have to add the magnetic variation to get the angle between magnetic north and your chosen direction. This is the bearing which you must set on your compass and use to follow your chosen course.

B

You now have to follow the magnetic bearing set on your compass.

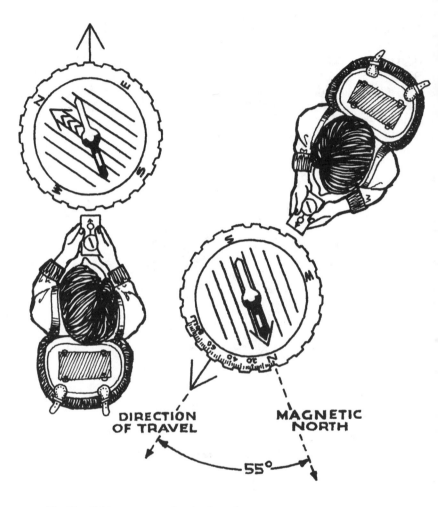

Fig. 23. *Taking a compass bearing from the map.*
Stage IV. *Walking on the magnetic bearing.*

Hold the compass in front of you with the direction of travel arrow pointing directly away from you (Fig. 23, left). Turn your whole body, still holding the compass in front of you, until the compass needle falls within the arrow engraved on the bottom of the compass housing, with the red end of the needle towards the arrowhead (Fig. 23, right). Walk in the direction indicated by the direction of travel arrow.

Compass to Map

It is sometimes necessary to take a compass bearing and convert it to a map bearing. It may simply be to put a name to a peak or some other feature you can see or it may be to help you to pinpoint your own position by taking compass bearings to visible features which you can identify on the map. Whatever the reason the technique is the same.

1. Point the direction of travel arrow at the feature.
2. Holding the compass in this position, turn the housing until the orientating arrow lies directly underneath the north end of the compass needle.
3. The figure which is given at the base of the direction of travel arrow is the angle between the line to the feature and magnetic north, i.e. the magnetic bearing to the feature.

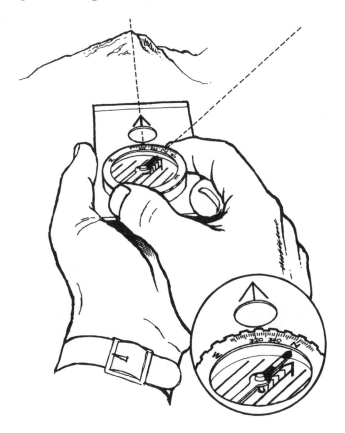

Fig. 24.   *Taking a compass bearing to a distant peak.*

4. Now subtract the magnetic variation for your locality to arrive at the grid bearing and set this figure on your compass, e.g. $322° - 7° = 315°$.

5. Place the compass on top of the map in such a position that the orienting arrow and lines are parallel to the N–S grid lines, making sure that the arrow is pointing to the top (north) of the map.

6. Now move the compass on the map into a position so that one of its long sides intersects the feature or your own position, whichever is known, making sure that the direction of travel arrow is pointing away from your own position and towards the feature.

7. If you are trying to identify the feature, you know that it is somewhere along the edge of the compass or an extension of it. What, of course, this exercise does not tell you is the distance to the feature.

In just the same way, if you are trying to find your own position from a known feature, you know that it will be somewhere along the line indicated by the edge of the compass, but in the opposite direction from that indicated by the direction of travel arrow.

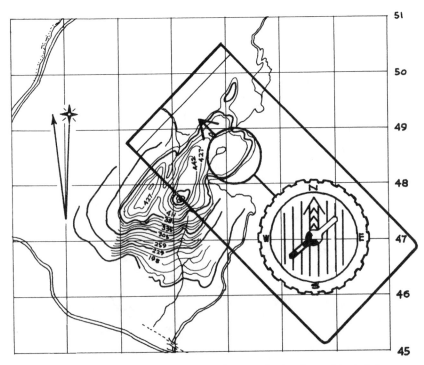

Fig. 25. *Transferring the compass to the map having first subtracted the magnetic variation.*

Finding Your Position from Known Features

It is sometimes possible to pinpoint your position by reference to a feature or features which you can identify on the ground. Take for example a situation where you are following a path across a featureless plateau. In the distance to one side you can see a peak which you can identify on the map. You take a bearing to the peak. Since it is a magnetic bearing it will be greater than the grid bearing. You therefore subtract the magnetic variation of say, 8° to arrive at the true bearing and set this on your compass. Place the compass on the map in such a way that the engraved lines on the housing are parallel to the N–S grid lines on the map with the arrow pointing to the top of the map and slide it into a position where one of the long sides of the compass plate crosses the peak. Your position on the path is where the extension of this side intersects the path. This technique assumes, of course, that you know which footpath you are on.

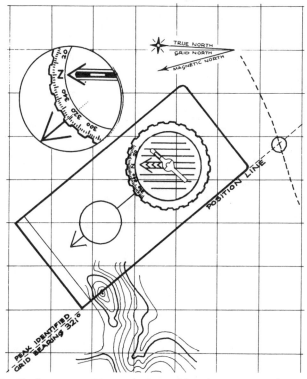

Fig. 26. *Finding your position on the footpath by taking a compass bearing to a feature which can be identified on the map.*

In this example the magnetic bearing to the peak from the path was 329°. The grid bearing is therefore 321°.

Resection

In some circumstances you may be in open country with only a very general idea of your position. In this event you require at least two and preferably three identifiable features. Repeat the procedure previously described for each of the features. Your position will be at the intersection of the lines representing the bearings to them. It is unlikely that the three lines will meet at a point and in this case you take your position to be the mid-point of the triangle so formed. This procedure is sometimes known as 'resection'.

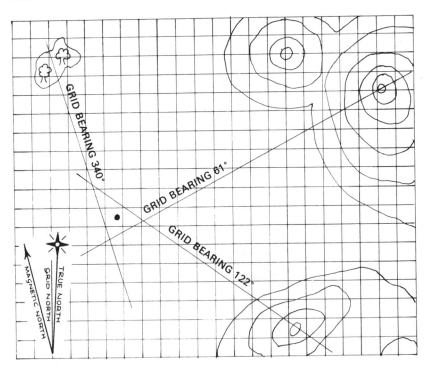

Fig. 27. *Finding your position by resection. Note the 'cocked hat' or triangle, within which your position must lie.*

Resection is a fairly time-consuming procedure, and in adverse conditions you are unlikely to be able to identify the three features required for an accurate 'fix'. You are much more likely to catch a brief glimpse of the way ahead or a sight of some landmark which you can identify on the map. The art of navigation lies in piecing together these various clues with all the other information which is available.

How Do I Keep on Course?

In reasonably good visibility: pick out features along your line of travel and simply walk to them. The ideal is to have the actual line indicated by the alignment of two features. In this way you avoid drifting to one side of your course.

In good visibility you may hardly have to refer to the compass, especially if you are following the advice given earlier and are taking note of features as you go along. The advantage of this approach is that you do not become the slave of the compass, but can make allowances for terrain by contouring round obstacles, following the line of least resistance and yet sticking to your overall course. One of the hallmarks of the good navigator is that he uses his compass only when it is necessary.

In poor visibility it is, of course, much more difficult to hold a line. In some circumstances two navigators can sometimes be better than one, with the one behind checking up on the navigation of the leader and calling out corrections as required.

Fig. 28. *Keeping on course.*

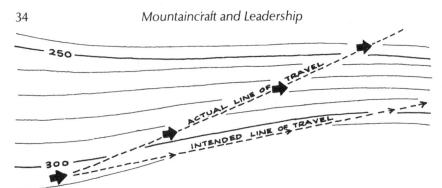

Fig. 29. *Drifting. Even following a compass bearing it is easy to drift downhill. This can happen if you try to follow a bearing on your compass without relating it to features on the ground. It is especially easy to drift downwards when traversing a hillside.*

You know now the direction you want to proceed in, but it would be asking too much, both of your equipment and your expertise, to be able to hit the target spot on. So you must know when to stop. In other words, you must answer the question...

How Far Have I Come?

Well, if you know where you started and you know where you are and can identify these two positions on the map then it is a simple matter to measure the distance between them, using the scale on your compass to find out exactly how far you have come. But what happens when you set out from a known position and are trying to get to a point which is hidden from you, perhaps because it's buried in a forest, or out on a featureless moor, or simply because the mist is down and visibility is reduced to a few yards? Your compass will tell you that you are going in the right direction, but unless you are lucky enough to walk straight into your objective, how do you know when to stop? Obviously, you have been following the shape and pitch of the ground as you went along, but if this does not provide sufficient clues then you must rely on your estimation of the distance travelled since your last check point. You can estimate the distance in one of two ways: timing and pacing. Timing is dealt with below, and pacing on page 41.

Estimation of Distance Travelled by Timing

If you know, or can at least guess, how fast you are walking you can work out how long it is going to take you to walk from your starting point to your objective.

Let us say you are at stream junction A and you want to get to the Bothy B. The distance between the two points as measured on the map is 1·5 km.

You reckon you will walk at a speed of 3 km per hour. Well, if it takes 1 hour to travel 3 km, it will only take half the time to travel half the distance, 1·5 km. In other words it will take you half an hour. So, after half an hour of walking, you stop, look around, and lo and behold there is the Bothy. It sounds easy, but there are a few possible snags which are considered below.

First of all it is not so easy to estimate how fast you are likely to walk over a given stretch of country. All sorts of factors affect your speed over the ground.

Height Climbed

Perhaps the most obvious of these is the amount of climbing you have to do. You are likely to go a lot faster downhill than slogging up a steep mountain side. So, you have to make some allowance for these variations in terrain. It is useful to have some basic formula for working out your speed over the ground and then adjust it as necessary. The traditional formula was that proposed by the Scottish climber, Naismith, back in 1892. He advocated an allowance of 3 m.p.h. plus $\frac{1}{2}$ hour for every 1,000 ft of climbing. In metric terms this becomes 5 k.p.h. plus $\frac{1}{2}$ hour per 300 m. It is just as valid today as it ever was, provided one appreciates that it is an average time for a day's expedition undertaken by reasonably fit hill walkers.

Naismith's Rule:

5 km per hour plus $\frac{1}{2}$ hour for every 300 m of ascent.

Going Down

Going downhill poses a bit of a problem. Most walkers naturally increase their speed going down fairly gentle slopes of between about 5° and 12°. There comes a point, however, at which the time taken is more than would be taken walking the same distance on the level, because of the extra care that is required. Over a day's journey it is normal practice to discount descent, on the assumption that increased speeds on the gentle descents will be compensated by slower speeds on the steep ones. However, for individual sections it may be necessary to make some allowance as follows:

Corrections for short distances:

> going gently downhill: − 10 min/300 m of descent
> very steeply downhill: + 10 min/300 m of descent

Fitness

The question of fitness is important particularly where a group of young-sters is concerned and due allowance must be made for this. Remember, too, that a party can only progress at the speed of its slowest member. A speed of 4 k.p.h. plus 1 hour for every 450 m of climbing is a more realistic estimate for such a party. See Tranter's corrections to Naismith's Rule.

Load

Another factor which affects your speed is the load carried. A heavy pack can reduce progress by 50% of the unladen speed, taking into account additional rest periods as well as speed over the ground. It is best to allow for this by simply estimating a slower speed, say 3 k.p.h. or even 2 k.p.h. in some circumstances.

Terrain

One thing over which you have no control and which can reduce your speed to a snail's pace is the nature of the ground. It is not always possible to tell from the map just how rough the ground will be. A boulder field, an unthinned plantation of conifers, breakable snow crust, boggy ground, and a host of other factors can reduce your performance dramatically. Here again, you must allow for slower progress across such terrain. In extreme conditions the estimated time can be exceeded by as much as 400%. It is worth noting that orienteering maps provide much more relevant information about the nature of the ground than do O.S. maps.

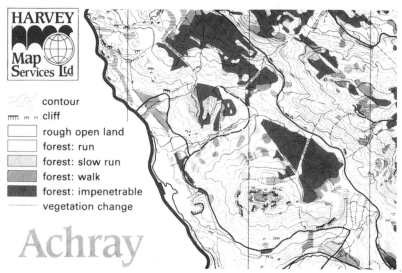

Fig. 30. *Extract from the orienteering map of Achray Forest, Stirlingshire. The scale is 1:15,000 with a 5 m contour interval. The original is printed in five colours. Reproduced with the permission of Harvey Map Services, Doune (Tel: 0786 841202). (Notice the additional information provided by the orienteering map.)*

Weather Conditions

Another factor outside your control is the weather. Adverse conditions can play havoc with the most carefully worked out route plan. A strong headwind, with or without rain or snow, can reduce your speed on the flat to less than 2 k.p.h. Conversely, a following wind can greatly increase your speed, sometimes dangerously so! Modify your estimate of speed in the light of experience for each leg of your journey and always keep in mind the fact that it can be a hard fight if the homeward leg is against the wind in the gathering darkness.

With all these factors to take into account, you could be forgiven for thinking that it is a near hopeless task to arrive at a realistic estimate. Not a bit of it! It is largely a matter of common sense and you will get a lot better with practice. It should also be borne in mind that the technique of using time to estimate distances is inevitably somewhat inaccurate. If you manage to get within 10% of the actual distance you are doing quite well. For this reason you must always be aware of the terrain as you go along, mentally checking off features as you pass them and comparing your actual time with your estimated time.

Tranter's Corrections

It is probable that on a given day's outing there will be a number of isolated 'bad patches' and these are best allowed for on the spot once you know what you are up against. General corrections, such as Tranter's corrections to times calculated on the basis of Naismith's rule, are not applicable to

Table 5.   Corrections to Naismith's Rule

Individual fitness in minutes	\multicolumn{16}{c}{Time taken in hours calculated according to Naismith's rule}
	2	3	4	5	6	7	8	9	10	12	14	16	18	20	22	24
15	1	1½	2	2¾	3½	4½	5½	6¾	7¾	10	12½	14½	17	19½	22	24
20		1¼	2¼	3¼	4½	5½	6½	7¾	8¾	10	12½	15	17½	20	23	
25			1½	3	4¼	5½	7	8½	10	11½	13¼	15	17½			
30				2	3½	5	6¾	8½	10½	12½	14½					
40					2¾	4¼	5¾	7½	9½	11½						
50						3¼	4¾	6½	8½	\multicolumn{7}{l}{Too much to be attempted}

Limit Line

separate legs of the route, but only to the route as a whole. In other words
they are useful for estimating the total time of an expedition, not in
working out the distance travelled over individual sections of it.

The fitness level is the time in minutes taken to climb 300 m in 800 m
distance at your normal pace. It should be determined for each individual
by timed trials. Allowance can be made for other factors by adopting a
higher or lower fitness level as appropriate:

> 20 kg load carried   —drop one fitness level.
> Conditions underfoot—drop one or more levels according to
> conditions.
> Conditions overhead —drop one level for journey at night or if wind
> is against you.

Errors

The question of error is significant because it is perfectly evident that an
error of 10% is unacceptable unless you do something about it. When you
combine this with a possible error in direction of, say, plus or minus four
degrees, you find that with increasing distance the area of uncertainty
within which your objective must lie becomes very large indeed. As you
can see from Fig. 31 the area of uncertainty is approximately 3 hectares at
1 km, 11 hectares at 2 km and a staggering 25 hectares at 3 km (1 hectare =
100 m × 100 m). The area of a football pitch is 0·8 hectares. The moral is
surely obvious. Keep individual sections of the route as short as possible.
When conditions are tricky and it is vital that you locate your objective
without too much casting about, use a more accurate method, such as
pace counting, to estimate distance travelled.

Homing in on the Target

Let us say that you are following a compass bearing to an objective 1 km
distant. You estimate your speed to be 3 k.p.h. and there are no further
corrections. In 20 min you know you are in the target area and at this point
you must take stock of the situation. Refer to the map for clues, but failing
such, you must set about a systematic search of the area to locate your
objective. Wherever you happen to be in the area of uncertainty, provided
your error is no greater than ±4° in direction and ±10% of distance
travelled, a search of a rectangle 200 m × 140 m is certain to lead to its
discovery. Well, almost certain! You should resist the temptation to dash
off in what you consider to be the most likely direction. If you happen to be
wrong it greatly complicates the subsequent systematic search. The most
effective method is to work outwards in a rectangular spiral from where
you expected the objective to be.

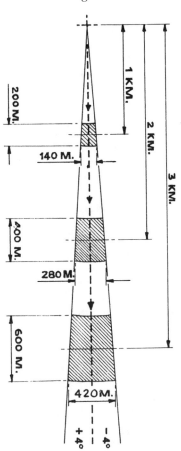

Fig. 31. *The effect of errors. The shaded areas represent the combined effect of a maximum error of plus or minus 10% in the estimation of distance travelled and a maximum angular error of plus or minus 4°.*

Mountaincraft and Leadership

Expanding Spiral Search

The steps are as follows:

(a) Search on a bearing for a distance equal to the visibility.

(b) Turn 90° to the right and search for a distance equal to twice the visibility.

(c) Turn 90° to the right and search for a distance equal to three times the visibility.

(d) And so on, turning to the right by 90° at the end of each leg and increasing the length of the next leg by a distance equal to the visibility, until the objective is found.

The route followed in this search pattern is such that no matter where the objective may lie it will be visible from some point on the expanding spiral. To simplify matters the initial bearing should be magnetic north, south, east or west. This also makes it easier to retrace one's steps to the original position should the objective not be found within a reasonable period. The method has the merit of simplicity and the advantage over other methods that the smaller the original error the quicker the objective will be found.

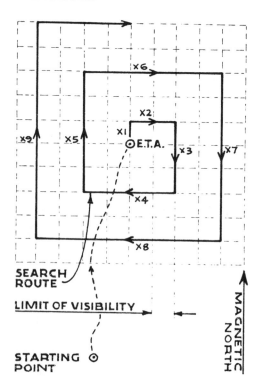

Fig. 32. *Searching for your objective at night or in poor visibility. The grid represents the limit of visibility and the heavy line the route which should be followed from your position at your expected time of arrival (E.T.A.). Note that every point within the grid is visible from somewhere along the search route.*

Sweep Search

One of the drawbacks of the spiral search is that it is difficult to take advantage of having a number of experienced mountaineers in the party. Using the sweep search method it is a relatively simple matter to space the party out so that they are still within visual contact and sweep back and forward across the area to be searched until the objective is found.

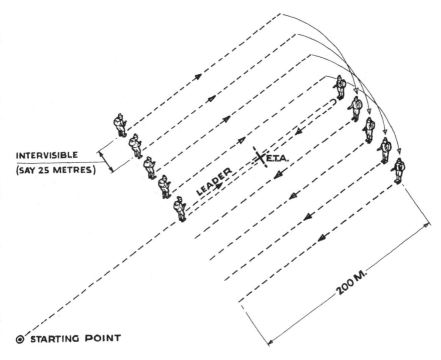

Fig. 33. *Sweep search.*

Estimation of Distance Travelled by Pace Counting

The trouble with calculating distance travelled on the basis of average speed and time taken is that it is at best a rough estimate. Such an estimate is permissible when conditions and visibility are reasonable, but in adverse conditions a mistake, or even a delay, caused by having to conduct a search, could have serious consequences. At such times it is necessary to use a more accurate procedure; in fact to measure distance by counting the number of paces from your starting point. The technique is well-known to orienteers, the best of whom achieve an almost phenomenal degree of accuracy. Obviously, the length of a single pace varies not only between individuals, but also as a result of variations in terrain and slope angle. This is something that can only be arrived at for each individual by practice and experience. As a general rule, count double paces (i.e. each time the same foot hits the ground) and as far as possible keep the distances which have to be measured in this way as short as possible. As a very rough guide an average double pace count for 100 m of flat straightforward terrain would be 65. As a general rule therefore your double pace count will be two thirds of the distance in metres.

Work out for yourself what your pace count is across a variety of terrain and different slope angles.

One hopes that in the mountains you will not have to rely on pace counting too often. Intelligent use of the map, particularly in selecting a line which minimises the possibility of error (even though it may be a longer way round) pays dividends in the end. There are one or two techniques, also derived from the sport of orienteering, which are worthy of special mention:

Tick-off Features
This is something that many will do instinctively, but it is well worth making a mental note of various features which you will come across en route and tick them off as you actually pass them on the ground. If a feature does not appear on schedule you will know immediately that something is wrong.

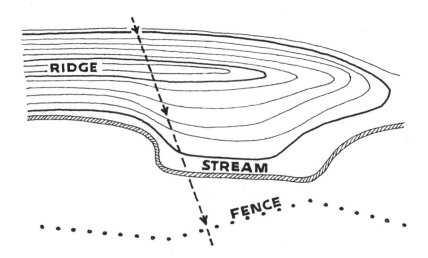

Fig. 34.   *Tick-off features: 'RIDGE, STREAM, FENCE'.*

Guide-line Features

Common sense dictates that it is sensible to follow any well marked feature if it is leading in the general direction that you wish to go, such as fences, footpaths, streams, in fact anything that is fairly easy to identify and follow.

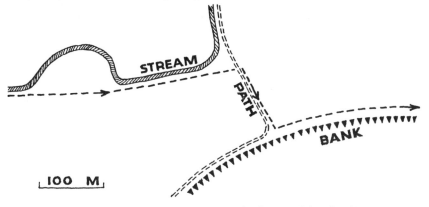

Fig. 35. *The line of the stream, footpath and bank is a useful guide taking you in the general direction of your objective.*

Aiming Off

Let us say you are walking across country and are aiming for a particular point on a stream. If you go straight for it and luck is on your side you may find the point first time. The likelihood is that you will hit the stream either upstream or downstream of the point. The question is, which? If you deliberately aim off slightly to one side you will know which way to turn when you get to the stream. The technique can be applied to any linear feature, a footpath, a ridge, a wall, etc.

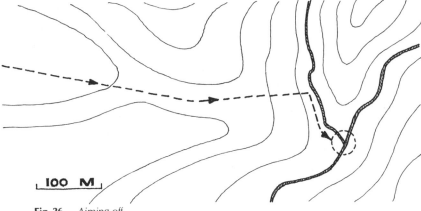

Fig. 36. *Aiming off.*

Attack Point

This is an easily identified feature which is close enough to your objective to enable you to home in on it with some degree of certainty. In other words it makes good sense to go slightly off course to hit a definite target from which you can make a successful assault on your objective. The final leg is usually accomplished by pace and compass.

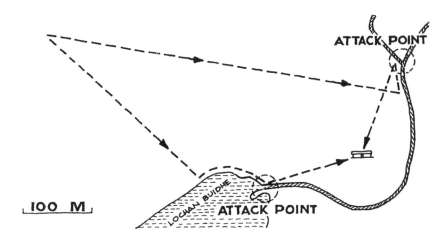

Fig. 37.   *Attack points.*

Contouring

Should we go over the top or contour round? This is a problem which all hillwalkers have to grapple with from time to time and it is not an easy one to answer. It is difficult to hold a constant height and even more difficult to keep track of your course when contouring. An altimeter will help with the former, but it is an expensive piece of equipment and few people carry one in the British hills. It is usually safe to contour when visibility is good or when you are heading for some catching feature, such as a stream in the next valley which will prevent you from going too far. Provided that you can maintain a truly horizontal course (and that takes a lot of practice) an accurate estimate of distance travelled should establish your position without too great an error. If accuracy is at a premium, as it would be in the dark with no collecting feature, it may be necessary to contour in a series of straight lines using the well-tried method of pace and compass.

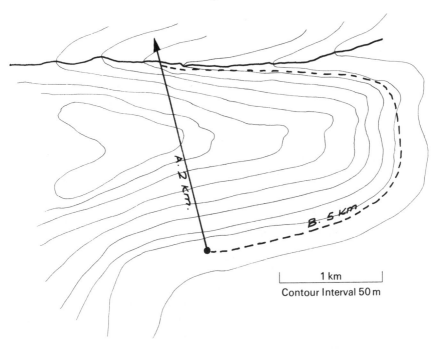

Fig. 38. *Going round or over the top? Assuming a walking speed of 5 k.p.h., route B would take 1 hour. Route A would take 24 minutes plus an allowance of 30 minutes for the height climbed, i.e. 54 minutes.*

Route A: 2 km + 300 m of climbing
          Estimated time ... 24 + 30 = 54 minutes

Route B: 5 km
          Estimated time ... 1 hour.

Navigating at Night or in Bad Weather

Navigating in reasonable conditions and good visibility should present no great problems to the mountaineer. In bad weather it is not new techniques which are required, but a more skilful and determined application of those already learned. Nevertheless it is worthwhile drawing attention to certain aspects of navigation which require special consideration in such conditions.

Be Prepared!

Your route card should not only take note of possible escape routes, but it should also record compass bearings, distances, and estimated times for any sections which might prove difficult in bad conditions. A little advance planning at this stage can forestall a lot of potential trouble later on.

Check through your equipment and make sure it is all in working order and readily accessible. Have you got a couple of spare batteries for your torch?

'Transpaseal' is a good protective cover for your map. Cover both sides and then fold the map so that the area of your route is exposed.

Be prepared to modify your route should conditions justify a change of plan.

Party Discipline and Organisation

Keep the party together and impress on each person that it is his or her responsibility to keep in touch with the person immediately in front and behind.

Appoint a responsible member of the group to bring up the rear.

Appoint another to check the navigation and in particular to ensure that the correct compass bearing is followed without drifting to one side. Obviously you must be within sight and hearing of each other so that corrections can be made from time to time as necessary.

Morale can fall to a low ebb under severe conditions with confidence in the leader being sapped by fear, ignorance and unexplained delays. Proceed at a steady pace and keep the party well-informed and involved, with everyone feeling that they have a job to do.

Techniques

Have the map correctly orientated at all times and be thoroughly aware of the disposition of features and slopes as you go along.

As far as possible keep your compass legs short, moving from one easily identifiable point to the next even if this involves a detour. Play safe and use the techniques of aiming off, attack points, catching features to full advantage.

Continual reference to the map at night using a powerful torch can seriously impair your night vision. Use your torch sparingly. It takes almost 1 hour for your eyes to become fully acclimatised to the dark after exposure to bright light. To a certain extent you can protect the night vision in one eye by closing it when you use your torch. Another useful tip is to use a red filter in your torch or your goggles. Red light does not bleach out the pigment in the eyes on which night vision depends. Unfortunately, brown contour lines tend to disappear in red light. Glare from a head torch can also affect night vision. If you use one make sure that it is set at the correct angle and if necessary use insulating tape to adjust the beam.

In extreme conditions, which most commonly occur during the winter months, it may occasionally be necessary to rope the party together, particularly in the vicinity of cliffs or cornices. In some circumstances it may be sufficient just to hold the rope without actually tying on. Allow plenty of margin for error in taking your compass bearing and choose a route well back from potential danger.

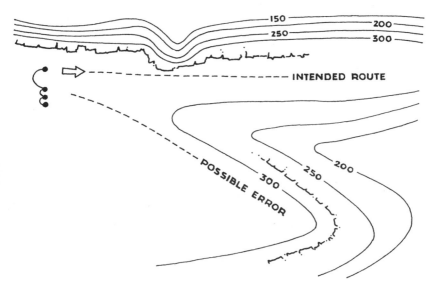

Fig. 39. *The party is lined up correctly in relation to the cliff edge, but note how a slight error can lead to a dangerous situation, disguised by the fact that they still have a cliff edge to their left.*

If roped together in this situation, align the party at right angles to the cliff edge. The leader should adopt the position nearest the edge on a long length of rope from the second and third men.

In white-out conditions it is impossible to judge scale, distance and the steepness of slopes. Throwing a snowball ahead can sometimes provide a focal point for the eye and reveal the true nature of the terrain.

Take advantage of any break in the weather or improved visibility to check on your position and to take a compass bearing along the route ahead.

A Word of Warning

Lest it be thought that all problems of bad-weather navigation can be solved by use of map and compass techniques, it should be pointed out that there are certain bad-weather problems where map and compass are of limited use. One particularly awkward case is the traverse of a narrow and complex ridge in thick weather. Not even 1:25,000 maps indicate sufficient detail of such ridges to allow accurate 'blind' navigation. For sure and reasonably rapid movement over such ground it is necessary to know the structure of the ridge from clear weather experience. Otherwise, large amounts of time may be spent in pursuing side-buttresses and missing tiny cols between minor tops or pinnacles. Lacking clear weather knowledge, party leaders would be well advised to consider alternative courses of action. Though more circuitous, they may save time and lessen anxiety.

Teaching Navigation

No person is entirely safe in the mountains if he cannot use map and compass, no matter how knowledgeable and experienced the leader. For reasons outside their control the members of a party can become separated and therefore it is important that each individual should be given sufficient basic instruction to enable him to find his way to safety. In the field of navigation the party leader must be able to give such basic instruction. Considerations of safety apart, it is surely important to encourage the less experienced to strive for a level of competence which will enable them to undertake expeditions without being led.

It is not easy to teach map reading as an 'extra' to be slotted in at odd moments during a day's hillwalking. Avail yourself of every opportunity of doing some preliminary ground work. Try not to turn these lessons into extra geography lessons. After all, this is the real thing.

Simple navigation courses can be great fun if intelligently laid out. They should if possible encircle the base so that a bad mistake can always be rectified by a quick return for further instructions. Courses should not be too long and should become progressively more difficult towards the finish. In safe country it is best to travel singly or in pairs. In larger groups, most of the navigation tends to be done by one person.

Problems of all kinds may be set on route, anything in fact which will encourage the pupil to practise the skills previously learned indoors. In the early stages concentrate on the use of the map before introducing the compass.

Orienteering is not only a fine sport in its own right, it is also a superb way of developing the skills of navigation. It has all the excitement of a treasure hunt and there is tremendous satisfaction to be had in finding a control buried in the forest. Courses can be set to cater for all levels of ability and it is one of the most attractive features of the sport that you will find the young and the not-so-young, the fit and the not-so-fit all competing together and enjoying themselves.

Some Ideas for Making Map Reading More Fun

1. Walk blindfold to estimate your tendency to drift to one side.
2. Blindfolded navigator talked through miniature course by accompanying guide.
3. Draw a map of your home-town from memory to see if you are aware of the wider relationships.
4. 'Mappo,' an adaptation of the game 'Bingo' using map symbols.
5. Place code letters at a series of fixed points. These can be used in different combinations to provide courses of varying degrees of difficulty.
6. Map reading crossword games.
7. Find your fitness level. How long does it take you to climb 300 m in 800 m horizontal distance?
8. Draw a map of an area incorporating your own system of symbols and shading to give the maximum amount of helpful information to someone following a route across it.
9. Indoor orienteering. Follow a series of compass bearings round the building. A box can be placed over the head of such a size that it allows the navigator to see his feet and avoid obstacles, but no more.
10. Treasure hunt with clues involving pace counting, recognition of features, compass bearings, etc.
11. Use maps of different scales; 1:10,000, 1:25,000, 1:50,000, etc.
12. Compare old maps with new to see how the countryside has changed over the years.
13. Measure your pace count over different terrain, e.g. path, heather, uphill, downhill, etc.
14. Follow as closely as possible a route marked on the map with a continuous line. Unmarked controls may be placed at any point on the route.
15. Improve your map memory. Set a course with a map at each control showing the route to the next control point which has to be memorised.
16. Follow a route marked on an air photograph.
17. Draw a route on a map and then cover over or cut out appropriate sections. Try to follow the route.
18. Night navigation exercise. This must be carefully prepared and supervised.

There are many other games and courses which can be devised. They are fun in themselves, but remember that they are a preparation for finding your way across the high tops where conditions may be much more severe and the margin for error considerably smaller. As with most aspects of mountain training it is experience and practice which tell in the end.

Ordnance Survey Maps

1:50,000   Land Ranger Series in lavender coloured cover
The 1:50,000 map is perfectly adequate for most purposes and indeed the second series at this scale represents a substantial improvement on the old 1-inch to 1-mile map which was used mostly by hillwalkers for many years in the past. It has the advantage of including on a single sheet of manageable proportions an area within which many walks may be accomplished without straying onto adjacent sheets. Special editions have been published for popular localities to ensure that the maximum area of interest is included on one sheet.

First Series—
Basically this map is an enlargement of the old 1:63,360 (1-inch to 1-mile) map. Covers an area 40 × 40 km. Complete UK cover. Contours and heights are given to the nearest metre, although the contour interval remains at 50 ft, with thicker lines every 250 ft.

Second Series—
This is a completely rescribed edition with additional tourist and recreational information. Complete UK cover in 204 maps by 1990. Contours are at 10-m intervals with thicker contour lines every 50 m where available, otherwise at 50 ft with heights given to the nearest metre. A metric contour survey of the whole country with thicker contour lines every 50 m will be available by the mid-1980s.

1:25,000
1. Complete UK cover is available but not as a uniform series.
2. Half the country is covered by Second Series 'Pathfinder' maps in a green cover. This map is based on adapted 1:10,000 survey. The remainder is covered by First Series maps in a blue cover. Complete coverage by the Second Series is expected by 1990.
3. Irregular availability of Pathfinder maps except in N.W. Scotland.
4. Pathfinder maps include information on:
   Rights of way (England and Wales only).
   Field boundaries.
   Most contours are at 10 m (5 m on lowlands) intervals.
5. Outdoor leisure maps are available for a limited number of areas. These

are based on the Second Series, some with water resistant yellow Polyart covers. Some are based on First Series or mixture of First and Second and these are coloured brown.

There is no doubt that this is the ideal map for mountain walking and the 'Pathfinder' Series provides additional information which is of particular interest to hillwalkers. Inevitably, because of the large scale (a Pathfinder map covers an area of 10 km by 20 km), it is sometimes necessary to use two or more maps to cover a single expedition. Special outdoor leisure maps have been published of popular areas. Those based on the Second Series are coloured yellow and may be protected by water resistant Polyart. The remainder are based on First Series surveys or a mixture of First and Second and are coloured brown.

2 Hillwalking

Preparation and Planning

Careful preparation can make all the difference to the success of an outing, whether it be a short afternoon stroll or a two-week camping expedition into the mountains. Clearly, the amount of time which should be devoted to advance planning must be related to the nature and duration of the trip, but the principle remains the same; the more thought and care you put into your planning, the more likely you are to enjoy a successful experience. Most local education authorities and many of the voluntary organisations have their own set of guidelines for teachers and leaders who intend to take groups of children into the hills. To some these rules may seem somewhat restrictive and there is no doubt that if too onerous they can inhibit the spontaneity and excitement of outdoor education. However, if pitched at the right level they provide a useful check list of tasks to be accomplished, they ensure an adequate level of communication between the party leader and those involved, including headmaster, pupils, parents and so on and they provide a very necessary assurance to parents and those in authority that the enterprise, whatever it may be, will be conducted according to agreed procedures by someone with an appropriate level of experience.

What follows is a necessarily brief summary of what is required by way of advance preparation for an expedition of several days duration involving a group of young people under the auspices of some official organisation, such as a local education authority.

Consultation	Initially with controlling authority, e.g. the headmaster and later on with pupils and parents. It is vital that all should be aware of exactly what is involved in the expedition.
Objectives	It is important to articulate the objectives right at the start so that the programme can be arranged in a way which will help them to be achieved.
Choice of area, route, etc.	This should be selected to suit the experience and capability of the group. The temptation always to choose areas of national reputation should be resisted.

Sources of information	The more information you can find out about the area and the people who live there, the better. Visit your local library, obtain copies of appropriate reference books and guides and talk to people who know the area.
Maps	Obtain sufficient copies of the 1:50,000 O.S. map of the area and allow all the group to be involved in the selection of routes.
Familiarity with area	With a party of inexperienced youngsters it is a considerable advantage for the leader to know the area beforehand. It may be possible to arrange a visit in advance of the expedition.
Fitness	The enjoyment of the whole group will be greatly enhanced if there is a general level of fitness which all can attain. For the longer expeditions some pre-trip training can be very useful in this respect and also serves to sort out possible problems with boots and other equipment.
Medical	Medical clearance is usually a requirement of the sponsoring authority for longer expeditions away from home. It is important to know of any medical condition which may affect a young person's performance in taking part in strenuous physical activity, e.g. asthma, epilepsy, heart weakness, recent illness, etc.
Skills	It may be possible to teach certain skills in advance so that the maximum enjoyment and interest can be obtained from the trip, e.g. navigation, lighting a primus stove, pitching a tent, the geology of the area, and so on.
Safety and emergency procedures	It is important that every one should be aware of the possible hazards and of the need for a disciplined approach where matters of safety are concerned.
Budget	An accurate estimate of costs should be made as soon as possible and submitted to parents. It is better to overestimate if in doubt. Under certain circumstances a deposit may be appropriate. Firm advice should be given on pocket money since it is invidious if there are large differences between members of the group.
Insurance	It is prudent to be aware of the situation regarding liability and insurance. In most circumstances the leader of a party is deemed to be 'in loco parentis' and is

required, 'to take such reasonable care of his party as a careful father would take of his children, having regard to all the circumstances'. Check the insurance cover provided by the sponsoring organisation. Does it extend to mountain activities? Do you require to take out additional cover for baggage, travel, etc.?

Clothing and equipment

A list of what is required should be given to parents in plenty of time. Insist on critical items, such as boots and anorak, but be as flexible as you can on non-essential items. Make a thorough personal inspection of the main items a week before you are due to leave to allow time for last-minute changes and adjustments.

Food

Menus should be prepared in advance and the appropriate quantities of food purchased or ordered. You will have to decide how you are going to organise the catering, cooking as a single unit or in small groups. Also, the type of fuel and stoves to be used, bearing in mind considerations of safety and the experience, or more likely lack of it, of the party. Pre-trip practice can be a great help in this respect. Resist the temptation to live entirely out of cans which, although they can provide a quick meal, are heavy to carry and tend to be left behind after the contents are eaten. Remember that the quality of catering can make or mar an expedition.

Helpers

If your party is a large one you may need to have additional help. The role of assistants should be clearly defined at the outset, and if they are to be involved in leading groups on the hill they must have appropriate experience.

Programme

Careful planning pays dividends. This does not mean that you have to prepare a rigid plan and stick to it come what may, but rather that you assess thoroughly the potential of the area and identify specific objectives, features, places of interest, summits, and so on, which can be included in the programme at the appropriate time. Give a lot of thought to what you can do in bad weather. Discuss the programme with the members of your party and as far as possible get them involved and contributing to the detailed planning.

Access

Find out well in advance whether there are likely to be any problems of access to the countryside and hills at the time of your visit, and if necessary obtain clearance from the landowner. The appearance of a large party can be very disturbing to activities such as deer stalking and grouse shooting. It is only reasonable that you should discuss your plans with those concerned with the management of the land, preferably in advance, but if not, on the spot.

Travelling arrangements   All too often the first and last experience of an expedition is the trauma of travelling; discomfort, travel sickness, hunger, boredom, all take their toll. With some forethought a great deal of this can be eliminated. Safety should be a prime consideration and this applies to travelling by public transport as well as by private mini-bus. If the latter, make sure that you are familiar with the Mini Bus Act, 1977, and other legal requirements.

Consent   It goes without saying that for all officially sponsored expeditions into the hills involving minors, written parental consent is required. A document should be prepared for signature which gives a clear statement of the nature of the expedition and the activities to be undertaken. It may be convenient to include a certificate of fitness to be signed by the family doctor. It is important that parents be given an address or telephone number to contact in case of emergency.

Number in Party

Without a doubt this is one of the most important, and yet at the same time one of the most neglected, of all the factors concerned with mountain safety. Perhaps this is because it can never be formulated as an inflexible rule. There are too many other factors which have a bearing on the number of people who can safely be taken on a mountain walk: the length of the route, the type of ground, and special difficulties of the terrain such as rock ridges and so on, the conditions to be expected overhead and underfoot, for example, wind, rain and snow, and the fitness, age and sex of the members of the party. Not only are large parties of 15, 20 and sometimes even 30 highly dangerous on the hill, but they stifle interest and make good instruction impossible.

One person cannot possibly look after such large groups even in the easiest of terrain, and when things go wrong troubles tend to multiply in proportion to the number of people in the party. As a general rule hillwalking groups should number between three and ten, the ideal being about six; the sort of number the leader can be aware of without actually counting heads. If the route is a long one, or perhaps one which involves some scrambling or ridge walking, six should be taken as the maximum. Three is taken to be the minimum safe number since in the event of an accident one member of the party can stay with the injured person while the other goes to summon help. This minimum becomes the maximum if long sections of difficult ground are to be encountered. An experienced assistant in the party can be an invaluable asset, particularly in the event of an accident to the leader.

The leader should never allow those in his care to go off alone in potentially dangerous country. This should not be taken to mean that a group must always be accompanied by a 'qualified' person. Programmes should be planned to encourage initiative and independence, but within a carefully chosen framework, which is judged by the leader to be well within the capabilities and experience of the group. For example, at an appropriate stage in their training, it may be more profitable for a party of young mountaineers to plan and execute a journey on their own through easy hill country, than to follow a more difficult route in the wake of an experienced leader. There is a time and a place for both in the scheme of things, but the opportunities which exist in the more gentle hills, usually closer to home, should not be ignored.

Going solo in the hills is almost universally condemned by those who are not themselves hillwalkers, usually on the grounds that if something goes wrong there is no one to raise the alarm, and as a consequence a great deal of unnecessary time and effort may have to be put in by the search and rescue services. This is a narrow view. The desire to be alone from time to time is a powerful and basic human need, and where better to fulfil this than in the mountains? There are few, if any, experienced mountaineers who have not, at some time in their lives, deliberately sought the solitude of the hills. Solo hillwalking can be a profound and rewarding experience, but it demands judgement and experience of a high order. In particular it brings a responsibility to make doubly sure that nothing does go wrong, and that as a result of foolhardiness or thoughtlessness others are not put to unnecessary inconvenience and risk.

Clothing

If you go walking in Antarctica you can be reasonably confident that your double-thickness Ventile anorak with fur-lined hood will protect you from the worst of the weather. No such certainty exists in the British hills where within the span of a single day you can experience conditions which range from the subtropical to the subarctic. It is the variety of our weather as much as its ferocity which makes it difficult to find the ideal clothing assemblage.

The most vital component in this assemblage is the anorak which has 3 primary functions:

to keep water out,
to keep heat in, and
to allow water vapour to escape.

It is useful to know why these functions are so important and how they are achieved in the garments. If water is allowed to penetrate the outer garment it is quickly absorbed by the inner clothing which, as a direct consequence of this, loses most of its heat insulating qualities. Body heat is conducted outwards through the layers of wet clothing to the surface where evaporation leads to still further heat loss. Cotton clothing is particularly prone to give rise to this refrigerating effect. It is vital, therefore, to have a fully waterproof outer shell and this is usually achieved by 'proofing' a basic nylon fabric with a coating of neoprene or other proofing agent. Unfortunately, having an airtight shell creates other problems since it prevents water vapour produced as a result of exertion from escaping into the atmosphere. Instead, this water vapour condenses on the inside surface of the anorak which can quickly lead to a situation where the inner clothing is as wet as if there was no anorak at all. But there is a difference. Clothing wet from within remains warm; in fact it acts as a primitive kind of wet suit. This is an infinitely preferable situation than being wet through to the surface where evaporation can lead to serious loss of body heat. New materials, such as Gore-Tex, provides the answer to this problem by allowing the passage of water vapour, but not liquid water. Condensation is thereby reduced to a tolerable level. It goes without saying that a garment which is waterproof will also be windproof although clearly the converse is not necessarily true. The prevention of loss of body heat is more a function of the inner clothing, but the anorak does contribute to this especially by reducing radiative heat loss, and by containing the circulation of warm air within the garment.

The function of inner clothing, sweaters, shirts, vests, long johns and so on, is to provide insulation, and it does this by trapping a relatively large volume of air within the fibres which go to make up the clothing. By and large the degree of insulation is proportional to the thickness of the inner clothing. If the air temperature is at freezing point a walker requires about a 2-cm thickness of inner clothing to insulate himself effectively against heat loss. Clearly the rate of heat loss is determined by the work-load as well as by the environmental temperature. The greater the work-load the less insulation is required to keep the body warm. Since this is a factor which varies even more sharply than the air temperature it is sensible to be able to adjust the insulative properties of the inner clothing. This is best achieved by wearing multi-layers of clothing which can be taken off or put on as circumstances require. Wool is undoubtedly the best of the natural materials since it retains much of its insulation qualities when wet. Nylon pile and modern spun synthetics have the advantage of retaining their structure when wet and drying out more quickly. Polypropylene underwear acts like a wick and transfers moisture from the skin surface into the outer layers leaving a dryer layer next to the skin. This minimises the refrigerator effect previously referred to. Cotton is not satisfactory for winter use. In general then, many layers of inner clothing are better than one or two, and you must be prepared to ring the changes as dictated by the prevailing conditions, and the amount of energy you are expending at the time. To give a practical example, it makes no sense at all to work flat out and fully clothed to construct a bivouac shelter, only to settle down in it to be frozen by the evaporation of all the sweat you have produced.

The same general principles apply to clothing below the waist although it is rather more difficult to achieve the right balance between water proofing and adequate ventilation. In cold wet conditions many walkers rely on good quality tweed breeches or heavy-weight stretch fabric trousers, which dry out quickly, overlapped by a long anorak or cagoule. Overtrousers should be carried. The most effective have zips which enable them to be put on and taken off quickly without removing your boots.

It is not widely appreciated that up to one third of the body's heat loss can take place from the head. A balaclava or ski hat that pulls down over the ears can make a substantial contribution to heat conservation. In hot weather the converse is equally true and it is sometimes necessary to wear a white sun hat or improvise one by tying a knot in each corner of a white handkerchief. In cold weather, mitts or gloves complete the protective shell, the former providing a greater degree of warmth. It is very difficult to keep gloves dry, especially if you are constantly taking them off and on. It is important, therefore, that they should remain functional when wet, and that brings us back to wool or synthetic pile or fibre. Proofed nylon or waxed cotton overmitts are useful. Leather gloves must be treated with candle wax or other proofing, but in spite of this it is next to impossible to keep them dry. Leather does, however, furnish a firm grip on the shaft of an ice axe.

Footwear

The first thing to realise is that there is no such thing as the ideal boot. Ideal for what and for whom? The average hillwalker can only afford to invest in one pair of boots, and he will use them in winter and in summer, for squelching through bogs, and for tip-toeing delicately across slabs. In other words, he wants a boot that will perform well in a whole range of conditions and circumstances. Unfortunately, such a boot does not exist. The characteristics which are required to perform well in one situation are the very ones which make it less suitable in another. So, one is obliged to compromise and select, from a bewildering array of models, a boot that will be comfortable to walk in, and yet sufficiently robust to offer the support and protection that is required, together with a measure of rigidity for walking on hard snow or steep grass. The alternative, of course, is to buy a light-weight boot for summer use, and a more robust stiffer soled boot for winter.

On the whole, you get what you pay for as far as the quality and durability of the leather is concerned. The boot should be high enough to provide support for the ankle, with firm toe and heel counters to provide additional protection in these areas. A bellows tongue is essential in this country to keep out surface water. The attachment of the upper to the sole is critical in boot construction, and may be welded, screwed, sewn, glued or any combination of these. Ask the retailer to explain the method of construction. A narrow welt is to be preferred, and the boot should have good adhesive qualities, and be of sufficient thickness to protect the feet from sharp rocks. A rubber-cleated lug sole is best. PVC is not a suitable material since it is extremely slippery on wet rock. The degree of stiffness of the sole is an important consideration, and the final choice will depend partly on personal taste, and partly on technical requirements. A boot for the high mountains, for the Alps or for winter mountaineering in this country requires a stiffish sole to give the boot an edge, to take crampons, and to stand up to the pounding of kicking steps on hard snow. The stiffness is usually provided by a steel shank set into the sole. A boot for general hillwalking can afford to be more flexible in the sole, and altogether lighter in weight. Nevertheless, some torsional rigidity is required to eliminate the sudden twist which would inevitably result from a bendy sole. A simple test of this is to take hold of the boot by toe and heel and twist. It is a common failing in the cheaper range of boots with moulded soles. It is not easy to give advice on fitting boots because it is such a personal thing. Ideally, one should wear the boots around the house for a day or two before clinching the deal, but this requires a very understanding retailer. When you try them on in the shop make sure that you wear the type of socks or stockings which you would normally be using. You should be able to wiggle your toes, and they must not be touching the toe of the boot. A useful test is to see if you can get a finger down inside the boot, just at the back of your heel, with your toe just touching the front of the boot.

A lot of foot problems can be traced to a lack of care and maintenance of the boots. The cardinal sin is to dry out the boot too quickly, in front of a fire or on top of a radiator. The result of such maltreatment is a hardening and buckling of the leather, which in extreme cases may even crack right

C

open. Boots must be dried gently, preferably stuffed with newspaper, and placed in a moderately warm room. Boot leather normally contains natural vegetable oils as a result of the tanning process which must be topped up from time to time, particularly after drying out. Several suitable preparations are available for this purpose.

One type of boot which has few of these problems is the plastic boot, which is a development from the sport of skiing. There is no doubt that this type of boot will become more popular as design problems are overcome. They are robust, light in weight and absolutely waterproof, an attribute not to be lightly ignored in a land which contains so much bog.

Blisters

Although a relatively minor injury, the blister can cause discomfort and disability out of all proportion to its medical significance. It is by far the commonest of all mountain ailments, and as such deserves serious consideration by party leaders. The cause is invariably due to rubbing of the foot against some part of the boot. This can be caused by ill-fitting boots, inadequate socks/stockings, loose lacing, or simply by the fact that the feet are unaccustomed to boots. The first question to ask is, 'are boots really necessary for the activity planned?' For many low level summer outings training shoes or similar footwear is more appropriate, but make sure that the tread on the sole is deep enough to give a good grip on wet grass or rock. If boots are necessary, they should have been well broken-in before being used on more demanding terrain. Unfortunately, hired boots rarely provide the degree of personal fit and comfort that is required, and special care is needed to both guard against and treat the blisters which will almost certainly result from their use.

The first rule is to keep your feet in good order and insist that those in your charge do the same: wash regularly, use clean, snugly-fitting socks or stockings (a single pair of loop-stitched stockings is probably best), cut toenails straight and short, and periodically apply surgical spirit to harden the feet.

At the first sign or sensation of discomfort, stop and treat the problem. Smear the sore area with an antiseptic cream and cover it with a broad plaster, cutting it as necessary to avoid making any creases. Self-adhesive 'chiropody felt' makes light work of plastering a blister. The toes can be taped with 'micro-pore'. If a blister is already present, improvise a ring plaster which serves to keep the pressure off the blister. Given time, the fluid will be reabsorbed into the blood stream.

In a severe case, it may be necessary to prick the blister with a sterilised needle, having first washed the feet thoroughly. The fluid is then expressed, taking care not to touch the pricked holes. Cover with a sterile dressing and change daily.

(i) Sterilising the needle

(ii) Pricking the blister:

(iii) Plastering

(iv) A ring plaster

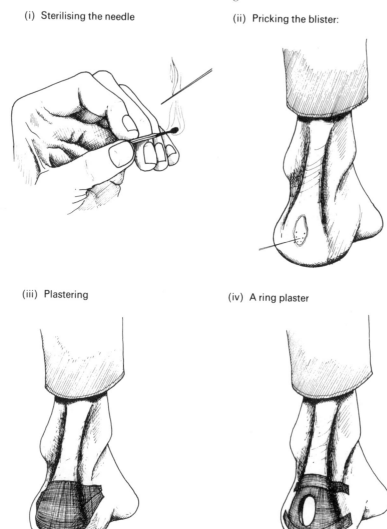

Fig. 40. *Treating a severe blister.*

Walking

On roads or flat ground, journeys are usually measured in kilometres or miles, but on the hills it is more expedient to measure in hours. A rough guide when estimating the time of a walk for an average lightly equipped party, is to allow five kilometres per hour, plus half-an-hour for every 300 m of climbing (see pages 34–39 for further discussion of this subject).

One of the golden rules of party leadership is that you must leave details of your intended route with someone who can raise the alarm should you not return before the deadline given. While this is the main purpose of filling in a route card, there are other more positive benefits in so doing. It is a discipline which forces you to consider in some detail the demands which a particular route is going to make on your party. It involves the measurement of distances and compass bearings in the comfort of base-camp which, on the day, might be difficult and time-consuming to take because of bad weather or darkness. Finally, it reminds you to consider ways of cutting short your chosen route should circumstances necessitate a retreat. The route card illustrated in Table 6 is a suggested format for an organisation which requires a standard procedure. For the smaller independent party it is usually sufficient to leave a brief description of your intended route and expected time of return, and take with you a note of any compass bearings which you think may be of use.

Speed is of less importance than economy of effort. To hurry, except in extenuating circumstances, is foolish. 'Tail-end Charlies' must be encouraged, and not left to struggle on their own to become exhausted and depressed. When you notice that someone is having difficulty, bring them up alongside where you can keep an eye on them, and provide a bit of encouragement. Keep together, and on no account send any member of the party back on his own. Except in emergency the party should act as a single unit.

There is no 'best position' for the leader of a party. He may be at the front, at the back, or in the middle. The position he adopts will depend on the circumstances prevailing at the time. Normally, of course, he will be in front, having appointed the next most experienced member of the party to bring up the rear.

Rhythm is essential to good hillwalking: jerky movements, springing and flexing the knees by taking too high a step, tire the muscles, and should be avoided. The leg should be allowed to swing forward like a pendulum; the natural swing of the body assists this movement. There should be no conscious use of the leg muscles. To assist rhythm and balance, the hands should be kept free, particularly in descent. Spare clothes, etc., should be carried in the rucksack or tied round the waist.

To maintain rhythm, the same speed of pace should be used on all types of ground, the length of the pace being shortened for steep or difficult ground, and lengthened for easy ground.

The feet should be placed down flat with a deliberate step, resting the heels on any available projections such as stones or tufts of grass. Where the slope is very steep, zig-zagging will assist the walker. Good rhythm and setting the feet is the sign of the experienced hillwalker.

When descending, overstriding and putting the foot down heavily should be avoided, as these jar the body and cause fatigue. A controlled descent can be assisted by placing the toes against projections. Running downhill, though good fun, can be tiring. A good walker uses downhill periods to rest the muscles.

Scree running is also fun, but it is bad for boots, and, unless closely supervised, can be dangerous. If you have to negotiate a scree, make absolutely sure that your party is deployed in such a way that loose stones do not fall onto those below (see page 136). Remember too, that screes are a limited resource and a habitat for hardy rock plants. Indiscriminate scree running will destroy the plants and eventually transfer the habitat to the bottom of the slope.

Constant stopping and starting breaks up walking rhythm and should be avoided. Halts should only be made at fixed intervals based on time and ground; these halts should be of a short duration, on average 5–10 minutes every hour. Large meals should be avoided— 'little and often' being the better approach during a day on the hills. It is a good plan to retain a portion of the day's food, and so maintain a reserve of food in case of emergency. Alternatively, an emergency ration should be carried.

Most mountain streams in the British Isles are fit to drink from. The body needs to replace fluid lost in sweat, in breathing, etc., and contrary to popular belief, drinking is to be encouraged, 'little and often' again being the safest maxim to follow.

Constant vigilance should be exercised, as weather conditions can deteriorate with extreme rapidity in hill country. Check the weather forecast before leaving.

Changes of weather can produce serious problems for the walker, and great care should be taken not to over-reach one's ability. Most accidents due to weather occur through rashness. Act before the weather dictates its own terms.

Exposure is an ever-present danger with young people in the mountains, and all leaders must be familiar with its recognition and treatment. If your party is fit, dry, well-fed and watered, and in good spirit, you have little to fear. If they are not, then you must modify your route to suit their condition and capabilities.

No attempt must be made to cross mountain streams in spate where there is possible danger to life unless each member of the party can be adequately safeguarded. Youngsters should not be given routes to follow independently which might involve the crossing of such streams.

Severe electrical storms are unusual in British mountains. In the event of one, do not seek shelter under overhangs or in cracks in the cliff face, or against large prominent boulders. Avoid being the prominent object in the neighbourhood. Get off peaks and ridges, and sit it out on open coarse-blocked scree. There is no need to throw away your axe, camera or other ironmongery—you may need them later, and they do not 'attract' lightning any more than you do yourself.

Consider roping the party together when visibility is very poor, and when there is the likelihood that a slip might develop into a dangerous slide. Remember, too, that a small error in navigation can lead you to the edge of a cliff or onto a cornice.

In addition to its chilling effect, the wind can exert sufficient force to sweep a party off its feet. In round terms a wind of 80 k.p.h. (50 m.p.h.) exerts a force of 23 kg (50 lbs) on a standing adult. The lesson is obvious: do not stand. Crouch down or crawl. Get out of the wind into the lee of a ridge. Keep your party close together and if necessary rope up. Be particularly careful round the tops of corries or on exposed ridges where a fall could be disastrous.

Good technique and safety measures can be learned. Good leadership and instruction is an art which embraces more than mere technical skill. Your job as a leader of a party is to stimulate interest and safe enjoyment in everything which the mountains have to offer.

Table 6. Sample route card

ROUTE CARD

Main Objective: _____   Date: _____

_____

From	To	Magnetic bearing	Distance	Height Gained	Lost	Description of ground	Time

Total

Add ten minutes per hour

Time Out: _____Time Back: _____

It is dark at: _____

ESCAPE ROUTES

1.   2.   3.

Table 6.   Sample route card, reverse side

NAMES OF PARTY	EQUIPMENT IN PARTY		
LEADER	IN SUMMER		
ASSISTANT	Anorak	Map	Whistle
	Boots	Compass	Rations
	Safety rope	Watch	First aid
	Survival bag/ Tent	Flares	
	EXTRA IN WINTER CONDITIONS		
	Ice axe	Crampons	Torch
	Balaclava	Over-trousers	Sleeping bag Duvet
	Gloves/Mitts	Goggles	Gaiters
	WEATHER FORECAST		
	WIND		
	Speed/Force		Becoming
	Estimated at altitude		Becoming
	Direction		Becoming
	TEMPERATURE		
	Sea Level		Becoming
	Estimated at altitude		Becoming
	Cloud base		Becoming
	Freezing level		Becoming
	Outlook:		

3 Campcraft and Expeditions

The use of a tent to provide shelter from the elements may not be as old as the hills, but it certainly has its origins far back in prehistory when man first learned to fashion the skins of animals to improve his own living conditions. It is surely one of the greatest attractions of lightweight camping, that in essence it remains a primitive technique which depends for its success on the skill and fortitude of the practitioner. To many people the perfecting of that technique and the satisfaction and enjoyment which that brings is a sufficient goal. To others, camping is seen as a means towards the achievement of some other goal; a peak perhaps or a scientific study in a remote corner of the globe. Of course the two goals are not mutually exclusive, and in reality it is very much a question of emphasis. The plain truth is that the more demanding the primary objective is, the more efficient the campcraft has to be to increase the chances of achieving it.

There are several different types of camping each designed for the attainment of specific objectives, and requiring quite different equipment and organisation. We are concerned in this chapter with mobile camping, which may be defined as 'living under canvas and moving through remote country carrying all that is required on your back'. It is generally regarded as the most advanced form of campcraft requiring considerable stamina, skill and experience. Perhaps, because of this, it can be one of the most rewarding of mountain experiences, but it is not one to be entered into without due thought and preparation, indeed it is hard to think of any aspect of mountaincraft which demands more comprehensive planning and application to detail. Without a doubt it is the most 'educational' of outdoor activities, and its potential in this area has been eagerly exploited by almost every youth organisation from the Scouts to the local education authorities. Done properly, it is a good way to introduce young people to outdoor life, and for many it may provide a key which will unlock the door to a marvellous world of untamed places. Many aspects of camping and expedition activity can be rehearsed beforehand, and this is essential both for personal assurance, and for the safety of young people who cannot be watched all the time. Much of this training can take place in and around the city, perhaps culminating in a trial overnight camp not too far from home. Pitching and striking tents, packing a rucksack, filling and lighting stoves, cooking a meal, working out a menu and shopping list, drawing up a budget, all these things, and a lot more, should be familiar to the youngsters before they set out on a mobile camping expedition.

One of the problems about camping is that it is potentially very damaging to the environment. Inconsiderate and incompetent campers can do irreparable harm to sensitive sites. The higher you go, the thinner the soil and vegetation cover, and the more fragile it is to structural damage. Rubbish pits, drainage channels, turfs removed, fires, all leave scars which may take tens of years to be erased, if at all. Pollution from a badly managed camp site may destroy 80% of the aquatic life in a mountain lochan. Those who go camping on the hills have an obligation to ensure that they and their charges do nothing which would result in change or harm to the environment. This is the first law of the mountain camper.

The Party

The party should be reasonably fit before starting. Care should be taken not to over-burden. Check for anyone with disabilities or special medical requirements.

The Timetable

The timetable should be flexible, and there should be some progression from easy to more difficult undertakings. If the weather is severe, stay put if possible; do not move merely to stick to an armchair plan. Mountain weather is unpredictable. Allow for this when planning. Do not attempt too long marches. Very hot weather can also be exhausting: if necessary be up at five and finish the day's walk by noon. Use local knowledge as well as maps, guides, etc.

Daily Routine

An early start always pays off. Work out a system that can be used by the party each day. Everyone should be employed. From waking to departure should not take longer than two hours for an efficient team. Try to be settled in a new site before evening. Tents should, as far as possible, operate as independent units, though, if the weather is set fair, it may be quicker for each tent to deal with one part of a meal. Two tents, pitched door-to-door, can also operate as a unit. Do not hesitate to stop for a 'brew-up' or a swim during the day. These are valuable mentally and physically. Check at the end of a trip to see what was carried and never used—question whether to take it again.

Food and Cooking

Adequate and appetising food is a vital part of any well-run expedition. See to it that your party takes a hot breakfast and evening meal each day. A communal brew of hot, sweet tea immediately on arrival at the camp site is an excellent morale booster and paves the way to a good meal. Light-weight expeditions can make use of the wide range of dehydrated foods now available on the market. Be careful to select those which have a reasonably short cooking time, and which can be cooked in a single pot. Dehydrated foods are of course expensive, but allow a great saving in weight and therefore of energy.

Before preparing a meal, make sure that everything you are likely to need is within reach. Work out a cooking plan so that food which takes longer to cook is put on first. Ring the changes on the stove—some things cook away quite happily in hot water and just need the occasional boost on the stove. Rice, for instance, can be brought to the boil for three minutes and then put aside for fifteen. Use pans with well fitting lids. This builds up a level of steam which will help to keep food hot and cooking when taken off the stove. Resist the temptation to lift the lid to see how it is getting on. This lets the steam escape and reduces the pressure. A towel or sweater makes a convenient cosy to conserve heat. By judicious rotation of the pots on the stove the various components of the meal can be timed to arrive on the 'table' cooked to perfection.

For a more detailed discussion of energy requirements and mountain diet refer to Chapter 8, 'Mountain Hypothermia', pages 191–192.

Personal Clothing and Equipment

Essential items of personal clothing, anorak, boots, etc., have been dealt with in the previous chapter on Hillwalking (see pages 56–60). Additional equipment required for lightweight camping is covered in this chapter and includes a discussion of tents, sleeping bags, stoves, etc. A comprehensive list of recommended clothing and equipment is given in Appendix III, page 354.

As far as clothing is concerned it is important to note at this stage that a dry set of clothes should always be kept for night wear or emergency. Wet clothes can often be dried out overnight, and in any case it is normally better to put on damp clothes in the morning than risk wetting your dry ones.

Never assume that the members of your party are properly kitted out. Before leaving, inspect all equipment and personal clothing.

Load Packing and Carrying

One of the most difficult of camping skills to acquire is that of being able to separate essential from non-essential items of equipment. Nothing is more calculated to kill enjoyment than to be labouring under an enormous pack, bursting with extras taken along 'just in case'. All this does is to increase the likelihood of the anticipated emergency actually taking place. Your total load should never exceed one third of your body weight, and for a party of young people 15 kg (33 lbs) should be regarded as the absolute maximum. Beware the effect of rain on the weight of gear which was previously within the limits.

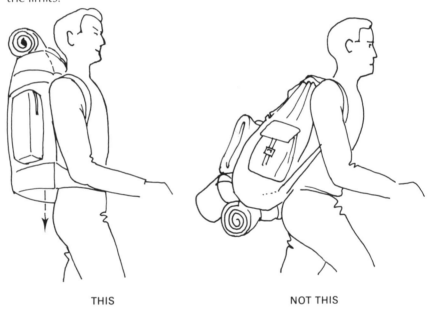

THIS   NOT THIS

Fig. 41.   *Carrying a rucksack.*

Rucksacks are made in every conceivable size and shape, but whether you prefer a framed or frameless sack there are certain basic requirements. First of all the sack should be made from waterproof fabric, and this means its closures as well as the material it is made from. However, no sack is completely waterproof, so use a polythene liner. It should have a capacity appropriate to its intended use. Some sacks are adjustable in this respect using extensions and/or compression straps. It should sit comfortably, carrying the load high and close to the back. Sacks come in various sizes , or are adjustable within limits to fit different sizes of people. Make sure yours fits. The straps themselves should be well-padded and easily adjustable for length. A hip belt, again quick to tighten or release, is an essential feature, and in the framed sack it can be used to distribute more of the load onto the hips. The addition of pockets and separate compartments is mostly a matter of personal taste, the main advantages being that they enable you to have access to certain items without opening the main sack, and that you can separate the stove and fuel from clothing, food, etc. A reinforced bottom (or corners) is useful and assorted straps may be used to carry such items as ice axe, crampons, etc. You want to avoid having too many things dangling or projecting from your pack. Apart from the discomfort and uneven weight distribution they can be dangerous to your companions as well as yourself.

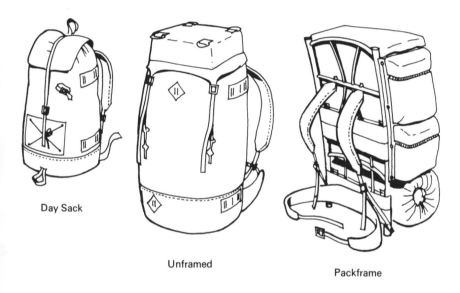

Day Sack

Unframed

Packframe

Fig. 42. *Different sacks for different purposes.*

The pack frame really comes into its own where heavy or awkward-shaped loads have to be carried. Its main advantages are, that it enables the load to be carried higher (though at the cost of some stability); it distributes the load evenly across shoulders, back and hips; and it allows air to ventilate the space between the pack and your back. The adjustment of the hip belt and shoulder straps is critical for comfort and stability. Its only real disadvantage is that it is an awkward shape, difficult to tuck away inside a tent, and liable to snag on branches and rocky projections while on the move.

Fig. 43.   *Packing your rucksack.*

How a rucksack is packed can make a surprising difference to the ease and comfort of carrying it.

Articles needed during the journey or immediately on reaching the camp site, should be on top or in side pockets, i.e. food for the day, first-aid kit, tent, and so on. Do not have articles dangling from the outside of the sack. Heavy items should be kept as high as possible. Balance the weight, and avoid sharp edges and corners against the back. Stove and fuel should be kept in a well-sealed polythene bag and stored in a separate pocket, well away from food. All clothing and sleeping bag should be kept in polythene bags, and the sack itself will benefit from a 500-gauge polythene bag liner.

Tents

In many respects a mountain tent is required to perform a similar function to the outer layer of clothing. It is expected to protect the occupant from the wind, it is expected to be hard-wearing yet reasonably light in weight, and it is expected to keep out the rain, but at the same time discourage excessive condensation on the internal surfaces. As with clothing, all these attributes are obtainable, but at a price; and as with clothing, there is a premium on keeping out the rain. The traditional solution to the water-proofing versus condensation problem is to provide two layers, an outer waterproof fly sheet and a lightweight inner tent, which 'breathes' and provides a dry inner haven. For the wet and windy conditions so common in the British Isles, it is advisable to have a sewn-in ground sheet and a down-to-earth all-round fly sheet.

The actual design of tent varies enormously, and within the constraints previously mentioned it is very much a matter of personal taste and what you can afford.

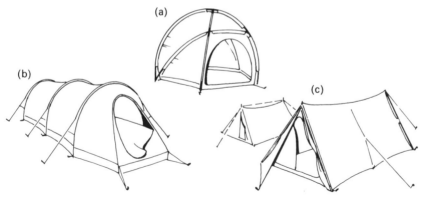

Fig. 44. *Lightweight mountain tents:*
  (a) *Dome tent*
  (b) *Hoop tent*
  (c) *Ridge tent with fly sheet and bell-end.*

Hoop and dome designs are supported from a framework of flexible fibreglass or aluminium wands. They have the advantage of providing the maximum amount of space for a given floor area, and they use the minimum number of pegs and guys. In fact, a dome tent can be moved short distances by the simple expedient of picking it up like an unfolded umbrella. Both designs can be recommended for experienced campers, but do require careful handling. The more traditional 'ridge' design still has much to recommend it. Ridge tents are generally tough and durable, and are still available in cotton fabric.

Other secondary, but nonetheless important considerations are:

Ventilation—especially important in completely sealed waterproof tents.

Storage space—for rucksacks, wet boots, anorak, etc. This is one of the advantages of the double bell-end.

Cooking area—A well-ventilated porch or bell-end is useful for cooking when weather conditions make it impossible outside.

Entrance—Rain and snow can get into the tent if the entrance is poorly designed.

Colour—There may be some justification for brightly-coloured tents in the Himalaya, but certainly not in the mountains of the British Isles.

With a group it is good practice for each tent to act as a self-contained unit making its own arrangements for cooking, sleeping, etc. Quite apart from the benefits of experience, mountain tents are not intended to hold more than two or three people. Any more than this and accidents are likely to happen.

Choosing a Camp Site

A good site should provide shelter from the prevailing wind. The ground should be as flat as possible and relatively free from lumps, tussocks and boulders. It should be well-drained, and safe from potential flooding. A handy water supply is almost essential, though do not pitch too near a noisy mountain stream if you want an undisturbed night's rest. Trees may provide some protection from the wind, but do not pitch directly under- neath them. Although they offer some immediate shelter from the rain, eventually large drops form, and these are much more effective in pene- trating the fly sheet.

If frost is expected, avoid hollows into which the cold air sinks at night. Try and find out if the site is accessible to domestic animals which can wreak havoc with tents, guy lines and food supplies. One of your first tasks will be to investigate the immediate surroundings for possible safety hazards such as old mine workings, nearby crags, fast-flowing streams, etc. Your party may have to be warned about them, and if youngsters are involved they may have to be placed out-of-bounds.

Pitching Tents

Even if the weather seems set fair, allow for the worst when pitching your tent. Put the back-end into the wind and peg out the groundsheet first, to ensure tent shaping. Erect the windward-end first and peg out all main guys, making sure that the ridge is taught. Other guys are pegged out in line with the tent seams. Rubber guys should be stretched before pegging. The pegs may be weighted with stones, but do not place stones on top of guy lines. In a wind the sawing action frays them through in no time. There should be no wrinkles in the canvas, and any unnatural strains should be corrected by adjusting guys. Door tabs should be tied in bows, not knots.

Striking Camp

As far as the tents are concerned, this is largely a matter of reversing the procedure for pitching. In bad weather, it is usually possible to fold up the inner tent first under the protection of the fly sheet. All pegs should be cleaned, and all the parts stowed away in their bags. Check the site before leaving to see that nothing is forgotten, and no litter is left. After a few days it should be hard to tell that the site has been used. On returning to base, tents should be hung to dry out thoroughly, and examined carefully for any damage before storing. Tents stored wet for any length of time will become mildewed and eventually rotten.

Sleeping Bags

The first thing to realise is that a sleeping bag can never provide complete insulation against loss of body heat by conduction to the ground. A separate mattress, air bed or mat, depending on taste, is necessary to do this, and at the same time to give that little bit of extra comfort. The trouble is that sleeping bag fillings, whether they be down or synthetic fibre, rely on their ability to trap air for their insulative qualities. Under compression the air is expelled, and one is left with a fairly compact layer of the material itself, which is a much less effective insulator. In some respects compressibility is a very useful characteristic, since it means that the sleeping bag can be packed into a small space for carrying. What matters is its ability to regain its loft, and its natural thickness, when it is unpacked. Good quality down, which is outrageously expensive, has this quality par excellence. It is also extremely effective in trapping air, and this provides an almost ideal filling for a sleeping bag. Alas, it behaves very badly when wet, and is well nigh impossible to dry out in the field. This criticism does not apply to polyester sleeping bags which, with the advances made in the manufacture of synthetic fibre, can provide comparable insulation. Polyester bags are moisture resistant, and retain most of their loft when wet. For these reasons they are becoming increasingly popular as a less expensive alternative to down. The actual design of the bag is not a critical matter, although for a really warm bag the 'mummy' design is probably the most effective.

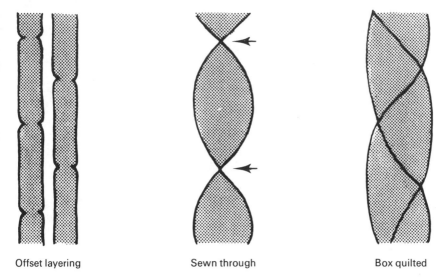

Offset layering   Sewn through   Box quilted

Fig. 45. *Construction of sleeping bags.*

In the case of loose fillings, such as feathers or down, the bag must be constructed in a way which eliminates the formation of cold spots along seams and zips, and also prevents the filling from migrating from one part of the bag to another. This can be achieved, first of all, by compartmentalising the filling and, secondly, by ensuring that at no place does the stitching pass through both surfaces of the bag. The technique used is generally known as 'box quilting', although in practice the filling is contained within a series of overlapping tubes.

In the case of polyester sleeping bags, the migration of the filling is not a problem, but the layers or batts of material do have to be stitched together, so that the same criticism applies to the 'sewn through' method of construction.

A great deal of body heat can be lost from the exposed head, so, if the bag does not cover it, wear a hat. Zips do make getting in and out a lot easier, but they also give rise to cold spots, unless the zip has a draught baffle behind it. Another advantage is that to a certain extent they allow you to adjust your heat loss according to the environmental temperature.

Some Further Tips for Warmth and Comfort

1. In winter, insulation from ground cold is essential. It is sometimes possible to pack the underside of the groundsheet with bracken, heather or grass to improve comfort and insulation. If you do not have a closed cell mat of the 'Karrimat' type, then improvise by making a mattress from your rucksack, spare clothing, rope, etc. If you do use a second sleeping bag, try to ensure that it provides a fairly loose fit with the first. Always do something about cold. Don't just lie there shivering!
2. It is more comfortable to sleep head uphill if on a slope, and on your stomach if the ground is rough and stony.
3. Polythene bags are useful for storing unwanted or wet clothes, personal belongings, sugar, salt, potato powder, or anything else in breakable packets. They can also be used as emergency bags for travel sickness.
4. Boots should not be worn inside tents. Wet clothes should be taken off before entry if possible. If soaked to the skin, remove all clothing, put on dry underclothes, get into your sleeping bag and prepare hot, sweet drinks.
5. Store tins, wet clothes, ropes and anything animals will not eat, under the flysheets. Pans, stoves and water carriers should be easily within reach.
6. Resist the temptation to wrap the sleeping bag tightly around you. This expels the warm insulating air which is trapped within the filling.
7. It is not a good idea to attempt to dry wet clothing either by wearing it or by taking it inside your sleeping bag. You will only end up with a wet

bag as well as wet clothing. When the weather improves, improvise a clothes line or, if on the move, tie some of the wet garments to the outside of your pack. In really cold conditions, it may be necessary to bring your boots and gloves into your sleeping bag at night to prevent them freezing up. If you do this make sure you wrap them up well in a polythene bag.

8. Newspapers can be used for a variety of purposes: for insulation under bedding, for cleaning material, to keep under supplies, cutlery or pans, to prevent dirt or grease spreading, to put under a pullover for body insulation, for drying boots and starting fires.

9. The following are some useful additional items: torch (reverse battery to avoid accidental switch-on in travel); alloy 'Sigg' bottle or equivalent for fuel; tin opener (small ones, 'Jiffy-type', can fold into a wallet); matches in waterproof container; toilet/kitchen paper; sponge for mopping up leaks and spills, and for using as a wet cold cover for perishable foodstuffs in hot weather; 5 m of boot-lace nylon; multi-bladed knife; one or two cooking pans with lids, non-stick if you can afford them, and if you can persuade your friends not to stir the food with metal spoons or clean them out with brillo pads; nylon pot scrubber; cutlery; deep plate and mug (not china); training shoes (wear on bare feet if wet, avoiding wet socks); a band saw can cut firewood easily; a small-size fish slice is valuable; as is an egg whisk for mixing milk powder; dubbin, etc., for boots; writing materials; transistor (for weather forecasts); anti-midge cream and/or spray (May to October); alarm watch or clock; first-aid kit including burn dressing and treatment for stomach upsets; repair-spares kit for tent and stove; water purifying tablets. For some types of expedition a pressure cooker may be worth the extra bulk and weight.

Rubbish Disposal

The burning and burying of rubbish can no longer be recommended. The accumulation of buried waste, and sometimes not even that, in some mountain camp sites has reached such proportions as to seriously affect their continued use. Unearthed rubbish pits are unsightly, unhealthy and a danger to both domestic and wild animals. In future the guiding principle must be:

RESPECT THE MOUNTAINS,
TAKE YOUR RUBBISH HOME.

A certain amount of rubbish can be burned, and liquid waste may be disposed of in a pit dug well away from the camp site and its water supply. Tins should be opened at both ends, burned, then flattened between stones, tied in a polythene bag and taken home.

Glass is unnecessary. Use plastic bags or containers, or light tins and transfer the contents into these. On no account must glass be smashed. Take your empties home! Polythene bags are particularly lethal to animals.

Hygiene

A safe and adequate water supply is the first prerequisite of any camp site. An adequate supply is not usually difficult to find in the mountains, but whether it is safe or not it is a matter for conjecture. Unless you are completely satisfied that the supply is unpolluted, precautions will have to be taken to render it safe for consumption, either by using sterilising tablets or by boiling (ten minutes is sufficient). Water should be collected above the site, and personal ablutions carried out below.

Personal cleanliness is essential, and with young people this must be insisted upon and checked. Hands must be washed thoroughly with soap after using lavatories, filling stoves, etc., and at all times before handling food. Cooking utensils, plates, cutlery, etc., should be washed thoroughly in hot water immediately after meals.

Toilet facilities depend on length of stay. Where at all permanent, a latrine trench is advisable. Excrement must be buried 15–20 cm (6–8 inches) below the surface, and at least 60 m from any open water. When filled-in there should be absolutely no trace left.

With a mixed party, separate arrangements may have to be made for male and female toilet and washing facilities, although how elaborate they are will depend very much on the situation and the length of stay.

Stoves

Gas: This is clean, requires no priming, but is expensive and, for half-an-hour before a cartridge runs out, burns at an infuriatingly low pressure. They are less suitable for winter use because of the reduction of gas pressure at low temperatures (below 0°C).

Pressure Stoves: Paraffin stoves require priming with solid 'Meta' fuel or meths, but give a wide variety of pressure. They are very cheap to run. Petrol stoves are not recommended for inexperienced young people.

Meths burners: The most popular system is the 'Trangia', which consists of a lightweight aluminium body housing a methylated spirit burner. The fuel is allowed to burn naturally, and not under pressure, and this heats the various utensils which are included in the kit. It is light in weight, compact and very simple to operate, but do remember that meths burns silently, and with a flame which is almost invisible in direct sunlight. Meths stoves are cheaper to buy, but more expensive to run than paraffin pressure stoves, and they are less efficient under normal operating conditions. On the other hand, unlike the pressure stoves, there is very little that can go wrong with them and they burn well in windy conditions.

Safety Factors

Changing gas cartridges or filling stoves must be done in the open, and away from candles or any naked flame. Used cylinders may contain some residual gas, and there is often a leak of gas under pressure as the new cylinder is tightened up.

Experience in using stoves is essential before going off on expeditions, when they may have to be used within tents or shelter.

With all stoves there is considerable danger of setting the tent alight when cooking is done inside the tent. If cooking outside is not possible because of weather conditions, adequate ventilation must be ensured. In addition to burning oxygen, incomplete combustion produces carbon monoxide gas, which may be highly dangerous in a sealed atmosphere.

Gas is heavier than air. During sleep, gas from leaking appliances could accumulate in a layer on the groundsheet (particularly if sewn in). Quite apart from the obvious danger of explosion, this layer could rise to nose level, with fatal results. Store gas stoves and cylinders outside.

Paraffin pressure stoves in fact burn paraffin vapour, and pumping too soon will result in flooding. This causes dangerous flaring, and soot is deposited which will ultimately choke the nipple. Pricking (only when needed) to clear stoves, as well as priming, should be done outside, if possible.

Make sure you have the correct fuel. Parties of young people are advised to use paraffin stoves only. Petrol stoves always have additional risks.

Do not overfill a stove. When doing anything to a stove, always remove pans. When stirring pans, always hold on to the handle. Scalding accidents are common. Make sure handles are up or extended properly, so that they do not hang down near the flame to become dangerously hot.

When cooking outside, a great deal of heat can be lost in combating the wind. In the first place the stove must be kept going at full blast or it will go out, and in the second place heat is constantly removed from the sides of the pan. Under these circumstances, an effective wind shield made from stones or turfs will greatly increase the efficiency of the stove.

Patience is the most important point in stove control.

Fire in Tents

The main causes are: mis-use of stoves/cigarettes/candles or other naked flame.

Precautions

See above, but also, do not fall asleep smoking, or with a candle or stove left burning. (Elementary—but it happens constantly!) Long candles should be snapped in half to make them less unstable. Even placing them on top of a tin usually ensures that if they topple they land end on, and so extinguish the flame. Some safety holder is easily created. With other forms of lighting—wick or pressure lamps, etc., care must be taken to ensure adequate ventilation.

A small internal fire can quickly be smothered with a sleeping bag, with little damage to the bag but, if the roof or walls go up, it is vital to get out fast. Poles and, if necessary, main guys, should be collapsed to smother the fire. Any other method is too slow and ineffective. A stove giving real trouble should be thrown outside at once. Work stoves near the entrance—if you must have them inside at all.

Outside fires may be pleasant, but great care must be taken to ensure that there is no fire risk to tents and to forests, or dry hillsides from falling sparks. Turf must be removed and replaced over the dead ashes. On no account should a smouldering fire be left unattended.

Conclusion

Camping makes a great impact on young people. It is after all concerned with survival in a potentially hostile environment using only the material which can be carried on your back. To be able to be comfortable under such circumstances is no mean achievement, but it is one which requires determination, meticulous organisation and a willingness to cooperate with others to achieve a common goal. Camping has many lessons to teach about living as well as merely surviving, but perhaps the most important of all is that it should foster a sense of harmony with the mountain world.

4 Access and Conservation

The Multi-use Mountain Environment

It has been estimated that there are well over half a million people who enjoy walking in the hills, and over fifty thousand mountaineers—all actively seeking their recreation on the hills, moors, mountains and crags of the British Isles.

This level of activity represents a rapid and sustained increase in participation since the end of the Second World War. In 1944, when the British Mountaineering Council was first established, it had 29 member clubs. By 1983 this figure had grown to 249. Population growth; vastly improved mobility through increased car ownership and a much developed road network; an increase in leisure time; a higher standard of living, and a growth of outdoor activities within education have all been contributory factors.

Every walker or climber venturing into the hills is seeking an experience that may be based upon peace, solitude, natural beauty, the natural environment, excitement, adventure and risk. However, the mountain and hill land of Britain is much more than just a recreational playground; it is productive land on which some depend for a livelihood, and on which the entire population depends for some of the most basic amenities of twentieth century living. Agriculture, forestry, water gathering, power generation, mineral exploitation, landscape and nature conservation, military training, sporting activities, tourism, recreation and education all take place, yet clearly not all are compatible. In some areas, by careful management an area of hill land supports several land uses, but in others there are direct conflicts.

Into this complex scene the mountaineer fits with some difficulty. There are few, if any, areas managed with outdoor recreation as the priority use. Most landowners wish to secure a return from their holdings and there is no profit, apart from the provision of facilities such as campsites or bunkhouses, to be made from hillwalkers or rock climbers.

Despite a campaign for free access to uncultivated land dating back a full century, there are still today few legal rights of access to hill and mountain land. Thirty years ago the few hillwalkers seldom caused problems; the hordes of today are ill-concealed and frequently present a potential if not real conflict with other land uses. Instances of damage and disturbance occur; access difficulties result, and even the careful management by bodies such as the national park authorities or National Trust applies only to limited areas.

The freedoms of mountaineering—of access and of practice—and the quality of the environments in which it takes place are traditionally highly prized, yet there remains room for improvement in standards of behaviour and attitudes towards the playgrounds of mountaineering.

A degraded environment lessens the enjoyment for those who follow. Damage or misuse give those who own, control or manage land reason to restrict, or even prevent access. If the tolerant attitudes of landowners on which access depends are to be maintained or the new legal rights so long sought in Parliament and elsewhere are to be won then there is a need for a responsible attitude, a new philosophy of minimum impact, and a depth of understanding of the multi-use environment of upland Britain. A new philosophy will not come overnight. It can come about in the long term by fostering an appreciation and responsibility in those people who take up mountaineering activities. In this respect leaders, teachers and instructors have a key role to play.

Designation, Ownership and Management of Land for Conservation and Recreation

A sophisticated designation system for land of scenic, scientific and recreational value has evolved in Britain since the Second World War. Areas of high quality are designated by the relevant government agencies, resulting in stringent planning policies, special consultative procedures for development control, special management arrangements, the injection of central government finance and in some cases special administrative arrangements for the designated areas. In contrast with many other countries, designation and protection of scientifically valuable land is completely separate from land of scenic or recreational importance. The former follows one system throughout the UK whilst the latter differs beween England and Wales, and Scotland. In addition to governmental involvement, there are two closely related independent bodies—the National Trusts—whose primary aim is the ownership of land for the conservation of scenic quality and natural history.

The following notes provide brief descriptions of the systems of designation, management and of ownership as they affect the interests of mountaineers.

National Parks

National parks in England and Wales (see Fig. 47) have been designated for the purposes of: conserving and enhancing natural beauty and amenity; providing appropriate opportunities for outdoor recreation; and for promoting the social and economic well-being of the local communities. Each park is administered by a national park authority, funded jointly by central government and local government.

The concept of national parks originated in the United States as a means of protecting large areas of completely natural habitat from development and exploitation, and making them available in a controlled manner for public enjoyment. This was achieved in the USA through land purchase by government. The idea rapidly spread and pressure grew from conservation and recreation organisations in Britain for the establishment of specially protected areas of landscape. The national park concept, adapted to British circumstances of inhabited, man-made landscapes and private ownership, became part of British government thinking in the 1940s. A series of reports was commissioned during the late 1940s and culminated in the National Parks and Access to the Countryside Act 1949 which laid down the procedures for the establishment of national parks. The National Parks Commission (which became the Countryside Commission in 1968) was given the responsibility of recommending areas for designation, and the first park, the Peak District, was formally established in 1951. Nine further designations were made during the 1950s; six in England: Northumberland, Lake District, Yorkshire Dales, North York Moors, Dartmoor, Exmoor; and three in Wales: Snowdonia, Brecon Beacons and the Pembrokeshire Coast. The ten national parks cover 13,000 sq km, one-tenth of the land area of England and Wales. With the exception of Pembrokeshire, they are all major areas of upland or mountainous country.

In the majority of cases the national park authority is a committee or a joint committee of the local authority(ies) in which the national park falls. In two cases—the Lake and Peak Districts—the authorities are special Boards exercising functions in their own right. The Committees and Boards are made up of two-thirds county and district councillors and one-third ministerially-nominated members who are intended to represent the national interests in the park. Each authority has a National Park Officer and supporting staff.

National park designation does not change land ownership; the authorities implement the aims through the essentially negative process of planning control and the more positive approach of management by formal agreement, co-operation and financial support. A national park plan has been produced for each park, carefully defining policies for all aspects of land use and management, and it is against these that the authorities consider all planning applications for development within the parks. The authorities' more positive roles include: providing facilities for the public such as car parks, toilets, picnic areas and local transport services; information and interpretation services; a warden service to undertake practical works and reconcile local difficulties on the ground; and seeking access agreements to open country.

As opportunities arise some national park authorities seek to fulfil their functions through purchasing important areas of land, for example, the Roaches Estate and the Eastern Moors and Edges in the Peak District.

Areas of Outstanding Natural Beauty

AONBs are designated in England and Wales for the purpose of conserving and enhancing natural beauty—the first only of the national park purposes. There is no statutory aim of provision for recreation.

By early 1984 35 AONBs had been identified by the Countryside Commission, and their designation confirmed—accounting for a total land area of 14,500 sq km. A further 12 areas had been identified, with consultations in various stages of progress.

There are no major mountain areas designated as AONBs (these are mostly national parks) but the 35 areas do include a wide variety of landscape types—Hills (e.g. the Malverns, Mendips and (proposed) the Berwyns), Downs, Vales, Coasts and Peninsulas. All planning and management responsibilities are carried out by County and District Councils, although a few have established Joint Advisory Committees. Designation ensures a more stringent approach to planning policy and development control than elsewhere in order to conserve the high landscape quality. Although there is no statutory responsibility for recreation provision, increasing pressure has led to some provision and management, where this is consistent with conservation.

National Scenic Areas

National Scenic Areas (see Fig. 46) are areas of the Scottish countryside that have been identified for their outstanding scenic qualities and for which special consultative procedures have been established to consider proposals for developments which could have a significant effect on those qualities.

Forty National Scenic Areas have been identified by the Countryside Commission for Scotland (CCS)—the government agency responsible for conservation of natural beauty and recreation for the general public in the Scottish countryside.

The Scenic Areas cover a total of 10,000 sq km—about one-eighth of the land and inland water area of Scotland—and include many of the main mountain areas: The Cuillin Hills, Wester Ross, Knoydart, Kintail, Ben Nevis and Glencoe, the Cairngorms and Lochnagar. The planning authorities consult the CCS whenever planning applications are received for certain classes of development within the Scenic Areas. The classes are as follows: schemes of five or more houses; sites for five or more caravans; developments requiring more than $\frac{1}{2}$ hectare of land; building and structures over 12 m high; vehicle tracks above 300 m altitude; and certain road development.

If the planning authority and the CCS are not in agreement on whether permission should be granted, the matter is referred to the Secretary of State for Scotland for a decision.

Sites of Special Scientific Interest

SSSIs are areas of land identified as being of particular importance for nature conservation because of the flora, fauna, physiographic or geological features they contain.

The sites are surveyed and identified by the Nature Conservancy Council, one of the principal official bodies, financed by government, that is responsible for the conservation of the natural environment throughout Great Britain. SSSIs are selected to represent the best examples of the total range of ecological variety in Britain, the aim being to protect sufficient areas to support sustainable populations of all the natural wildlife in Britain.

There are just over 4,000 sites covering 13,000 sq km of land; some are of international, some of national, and some of regional importance. Many of the sites are in the upland and mountain areas including blanket bogs; rare plants on cliffs and screes; heaths and grasslands, including the Arctic-Alpine plants of the high plateaux; birch, oak and native pine woodlands. Some rivers and lakes are also SSSIs. Most SSSIs are in private ownership and management. However, consultation procedures exist for protection. Local planning authorities are notified of the existence of each site and the views of the NCC are sought on any planning application for development with potential to affect the site. In this way the implications for the nature conservation value of the site are taken into consideration in deciding whether development should be permitted.

The Wildlife and Countryside Act 1981 introduced new measures whereby the owner of each SSSI is notified by the NCC of operations or activities, such as agricultural improvement or afforestation, which could be harmful to the scientific value of the site. The owner is required to consult the NCC before any such operation can proceed. If the NCC wish the operation not to take place, a management agreement can be drawn up whereby the owner receives compensation.

National Nature Reserves

NNRs are nationally important SSSIs which are managed primarily for nature conservation. They may be owned or leased by the NCC, or a voluntary conservation organisation such as the RSPB, or managed jointly with a private landowner under a nature reserve agreement.

There are 189 NNRs in Great Britain, many in the mountain areas. Examples are: Cwm Idwal, the Rhinogs, Snowdon, Cader Idris, the Cairngorms, Ben Eighe, Rhum and Ben Lawers.

There are usually no restrictions on access to NNRs in mountain areas. Exceptions occur where certain research or management operations are being carried out and prior permission to visit the NNR should be sought (e.g. the Isle of Rhum).

Further information about NNRs can be obtained from the NCC's relevant Regional Office or from local staff.

The National Trusts for Places of Historic Interest or Natural Beauty

The National Trust (England, Wales and Northern Ireland) and the National Trust for Scotland are both charities established to promote the preservation of buildings and land of great historic or amenity value for the nation's benefit. The Trusts are independent of governments and rely for income on rents, admission income, membership subscriptions, donations, bequests and grants (this last source includes some government money via the Countryside Commissions). Both Trusts are of importance to the mountaineer in that they own many large and important tracts of mountain land, and through ownership manage these properties to conserve their high landscape qualities and to provide public access, subject to the needs of agriculture and nature conservation.

The Trusts have been given unique powers by Parliament. Firstly the National Trust is able to declare its property 'inalienable' i.e. it cannot be sold, mortgaged or given away voluntarily. This security has encouraged many donations of buildings and land to the Trust. The National Trust for Scotland does have the power to grant feus of land, although the consent of the Lord Advocate is required if the area exceeds 8 hectares in extent. Secondly, government and most public authorities have the power of compulsory acquisition of property; both Trusts nearly always have the right to appeal to a joint committee of both Houses of Parliament if a compulsory purchase of Trust property is proposed.

THE NATIONAL TRUST

The National Trust was established in 1895 and now has well over 1 million members.

The Trust owns very extensive areas of mountains and moorlands in many of the prime walking and climbing areas of England and Wales, as an examination of the relevant O.S. maps will reveal. Nearly one-quarter of the Lake District National Park, including much mountain land, has been brought into Trust ownership over the years by steady acquisition. In Snowdonia, the Carneddau, Tryfan and the northern side of the Glyders; in the Brecon Beacons the central massif including Pen y Fan, and in the 'Dark Peak' the Howden Moors, Bleaklow and Kinder Scout are all owned by the Trust.

The Trust has also bought or been given restrictive covenants over many areas of land, particularly in areas where it is already a major landowner, e.g. the Lake District. The land remains with the owner but the covenants help to preserve the land from damaging change. The existence of covenants does not imply any right of public access.

While the Trust's policy is to give access on foot to all its open spaces, it is nevertheless very concerned about the intense pressure some of these are under from high levels of visitor use.

It is concerned to protect the fabric of the landscape—to halt footpath erosion, for example, and to protect areas of high nature conservation value but also to preserve the quality of experience that the open spaces provide—their remoteness and tranquillity.

The Trust has always adhered to the principle that preservation is the first task which must take precedence over public access and that it is essential to preserve for the future the qualities that so attract people that they are at times in danger of destroying them.

Thus in order to reduce impacts, the Trust attempts to manage public pressure by careful provision of the facilities that promote public access to sensitive areas. This has meant matching the size and positioning of car parks and campsites, for example, to the capacity of the land they serve.

THE NATIONAL TRUST FOR SCOTLAND

The National Trust for Scotland was formed, well after the National Trust, in 1931, and now has about 120,000 members.

The Trust now owns 90 properties—castles, houses and gardens—and 365 sq km of land of high scenic quality. It also has Conservation Agreements with private landowners to protect a further 220 sq km. There is no public right of access to land protected by Conservation Agreements.

The Trust's aim is to promote the permanent preservation for the benefit of the nation of its mountain and other properties, so far as is practicable. The Trust believes that in the case of mountain properties this includes the preservation of their natural aspect and features, and animal and plant life; mountains and wild life are worthy of conservation for their own sakes, and not just for the enjoyment of man.

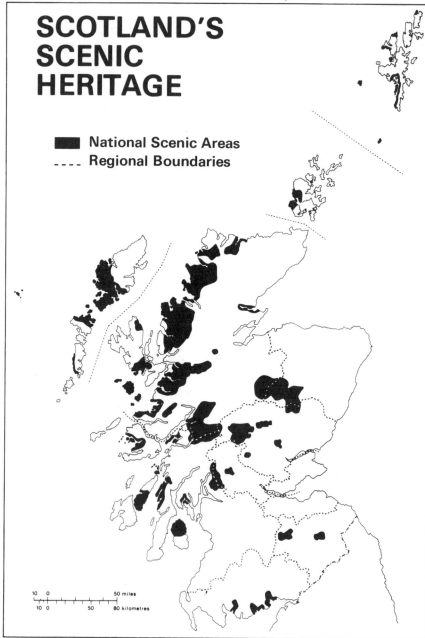

Fig. 46. *National Scenic Areas in Scotland.*

NATIONAL PARKS OF ENGLAND AND WALES

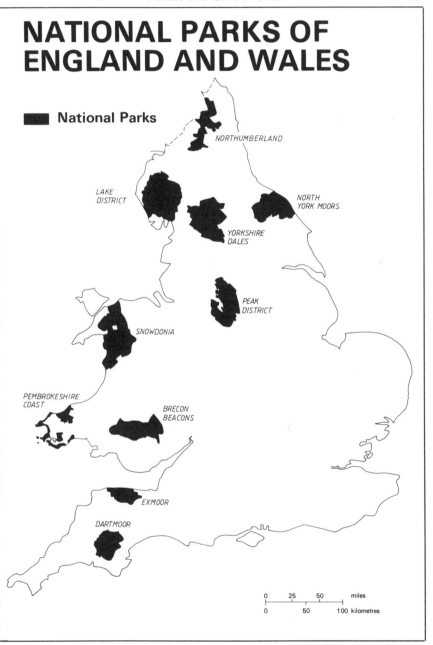

National Parks

NORTHUMBERLAND

LAKE
DISTRICT

NORTH
YORK MOORS

YORKSHIRE
DALES

PEAK
DISTRICT

SNOWDONIA

PEMBROKESHIRE
COAST

BRECON
BEACONS

EXMOOR

DARTMOOR

| 0 | 25 | 50 | miles |
| 0 | | 50 | 100 kilometres |

Fig. 47. *National Parks of England and Wales.*

Some of Scotland's finest mountain land is owned by the Trust. The history of the acquisition of this property is a very interesting and relevant one for mountaineers. In 1935, only 4 years after its formation, a large Glencoe Estate including Bidean nam Bian, was put up for sale. A Scottish climber, Percy Unna, was largely responsible for raising the necessary funds for the purchase. Two years later the adjacent Dalness Forest, including Buachaille Etive Mor, became available and Unna, by then President of the Scottish Mountaineering Club, organised a national appeal amongst climbing clubs which resulted in the money being raised and the land purchased. Unna made a large personal anonymous contribution to the appeal.

Following the purchase, Unna wrote to the Trust expressing the views of the subscribers to the appeal on how the land should be managed. These views have become known as the 'Unna Guidelines'. Summarised, they are that the land should be maintained in its 'primitive' condition for all time with unrestricted access to the public. 'Primitive' meant not less primitive than the existing state. Sheep farming and cattle grazing could continue but stalking, with the associated restrictions on access, should cease. Regulations should be kept to a very minimum. The hills should not be made easier or safer to climb and there should be no facilities for mechanised transport on the hills. There should be no new, improved or extended paths; no signs, waymarks, posts or cairns, nor any shelter built on the hills. Percy Unna also foresaw that new roadside developments might become necessary—such as hotels, hostels or caravan parks. Accepting this responsibility, except in Glencoe, he advised that the design of any buildings should be carefully considered by the Trust.

These guidelines were visionary for their time, for it would have been a farsighted person indeed who understood then the pressure this mountain land would be under 30 and 40 years later.

Unna was instrumental in the acquisition by the Trust of further mountain properties. In 1944 he purchased Kintail anonymously for the Trust. In 1950 he handed over an investment which became the Mountainous Country Fund. This fund then financed the purchase of Ben Lawers in 1951. The Trust also owns Goat Fell on Arran, the Torridon Estate, and Wester Alligin, immediately to the west of Torridon.

Access

Rights of Access and Access Permitted by Official Policy

In comparison with the large area of land regularly visited by hillwalkers and climbers, the extent of mountain and hill land subject to a legal right of access is very limited.

Although legal rights are very slowly increasing through purchases by public bodies or formal agreements, mountaineering has always been and will continue to be largely dependent on 'de facto' access—access as of practice, unhindered by the landowner. The rights of access are nevertheless important. They exist through a complex array of legislation, some representing the historical rights of local inhabitants, and some more modern in response to the needs of the urban-based, recreation-seeking population of the post-war years. The differences between access rights in England/Wales and in Scotland are considerable and the two will be dealt with separately.

Depending on the type of access right, information may be readily available or it may be difficult to establish if a public right exists or not. In many situations, although a right of access exists, there will be restrictions, often by byelaws, on other activities which are considered unsuited to the area or its agricultural productivity.

PUBLIC RIGHTS OF WAY

England and Wales

Public footpaths, bridleways and byways open to all traffic are all public rights of way (also called public highways)—linear routes along which members of the public have a right to pass and re-pass. All public rights of way from footpaths to main roads are subject to the same protection in law. On footpaths there is a right of way on foot only; on bridleways there is also a right of way on horseback and on pedal cycle. In legal theory most paths become rights of way because the owner 'dedicates' them to public use. In practice very few paths have been formally dedicated, but the law presumes that if the public uses a path without interruption or hindrance for upwards of 20 years then the owner intends dedication.

Public rights of way are shown on the Ordnance Survey Pathfinder and Outdoor Leisure maps (1:25,000), Landranger maps (1:50,000) and Tourist maps (1:63360). There may have been recent changes not indicated on the maps. For conclusive evidence that a particular path is a right of way one would need to turn to the definitive rights of way maps prepared for each county in England and Wales by the County Councils.

Appearance of a path on a definitive map is conclusive legal proof of its being a public right of way at the date of publication. However, a path may have been subsequently altered by a statutory diversion or extinguishment. A footpath not shown on a definitive map may still be a public right of way. Provisions for continuous amendment of definitive maps introduced in the Wildlife and Countryside Act 1981 should mean that the maps will provide a much more up-to-date source of information. The definitive

D

maps are available for public inspection at county and district council offices.

County councils are the authorities to which all duties for public rights of way are assigned. They are designated as highway authorities— responsible for maintaining and repairing public rights of way and keeping them free from obstruction. In some cases the actual work of carrying out rights of way duties has been delegated to the District Councils. Obstructions and other path problems should be reported to the highway authority or, where appropriate, the District Council. The authority or council has the duty and the powers to act but some are hesitant or short of cash to do so. If there is no progress towards solving the problem, it should be referred to a relevant councillor or the Ramblers' Association, the BMC or the Open Spaces Society.

A public right of way cannot be closed or diverted by the landowner, only by a local authority, central government, or a Magistrates' Court. Of course, a local authority may be persuaded to act by the landowner and a landowner may make an application for closure or diversion to a Magistrates' Court. A local authority may make an order to close a path if it considers that it is no longer needed for public use, or to allow certain new developments to take place. A notice of the order must appear in at least one, easily available, local newspaper and a notice must be displayed in a prominent position at either end of the path affected by the order. Members of the public may make objections to orders. Objections will usually lead to a public hearing and a decision by the Secretary of State.

Many rights of way have their origins deep in the past as cross country routes used by local inhabitants; footpaths being the routes between different dwellings or from dwellings to a church or graveyard; bridleways more usually being routes used for movement of livestock to market or elsewhere. However, because the responsibility for recording rights of way information on definitive maps was created in 1949, by which time routes in the countryside were well established for recreational use, the recreational routes too have been recorded as rights of way. Hence there are many rights of way in the mountain and upland areas which owe their existence to use by hillwalkers. There are, for example, public footpaths leading to the summits of many of the Lakeland fells.

For those particularly interested or concerned with rights of way issues, there is an extremely useful guide available to Rights of Way in England and Wales (see page 345).

Scotland

Footpaths, bridleways and highways exist in Scotland as public rights of way. However, a lack of any legal responsibility for any authorities to record comprehensively all public rights of way information means that the vast majority of public rights of way that exist in Scotland are not recorded on any register; there are usually no maps showing public rights of way; and it is, therefore, often difficult to determine whether a public right of way exists or not. Tracks and footpaths as shown on O.S. maps of Scotland give no indication of the existence or not of a public right of way.

For a public right of way to exist in common law the route has to have been in use by the public for a continuous period in excess of 20 years; have been used as a matter of right, not simply tolerated by the landowner: connect two public places or places to which the public habitually and legitimately resorts; follow a route more or less defined.

It is not clear from these requirements whether public rights of way may exist to mountain summits through established use by hillwalkers, but there is no legal precedent on the matter.

Local authorities do have a duty to protect public rights of way by keeping them open and free from obstruction, and they have powers to create, improve and maintain rights of way. Some local authorities are undertaking the work of preparing maps of rights of way. The only indication to a member of the public that a right of way exists in Scotland, is where the major cross country routes have been signposted by planning authorities or by the Scottish Rights of Way Society.

The public also enjoys a legal right to follow the Long Distance Ways that have been established in Scotland, sections of which are common law rights of way. The remainder of the Ways have been created by footpath agreements or access agreements. The Ways are signposted throughout their length.

The Scottish Rights of Way Society produces a useful guide to rights of way law in Scotland (see page 346).

PERMISSIVE PATHS

England and Wales, and Scotland
Permissive paths are linear routes that do not have the legal standing of public rights of way and do not appear on definitive maps. The landowner has simply agreed to permit the public to use the path, but usually with the intention that it does not become a public right of way.

Permissive paths are most common on land owned by statutory or public bodies—the National Trusts, the Forestry Commission, national park authorities, or water authorities—where the body will normally decide the alignment of permissive paths as part of a management plan for a particular area of land. Permissive paths may also occur where a local authority or national park authority has negotiated a route with a private landowner under a management agreement. The latter may occur if an access problem exists.

In mountain areas permissive paths will often be established in order to allow walkers to cross the lower enclosed land and so provide a convenient route to the open hill country which will cause the minimum of problems or disturbance.

Permissive footpaths may appear on Ordnance Survey maps, particularly Outdoor Leisure maps (1:25,000), and there will usually be information provided on the ground.

OPEN COUNTRY ACCESS LAND

England and Wales

Legal access exists to areas of land classified as 'open country' where an access agreement has been made under the National Parks and Access to the Countryside Act 1949 and/or the Countryside Act 1968. According to the 1949 Act, the definition of open country was land consisting wholly or predominantly of mountain, moorland, heath, down, cliff or foreshore. This definition was extended by the 1968 Act to include woodland and land alongside rivers, canals and other stretches of water.

A county authority may seek an access agreement with a landowner for an area of open country, or failing an agreement may declare an access order. In return for access, the landowner may receive compensation. Necessary practical works such as stile building will be undertaken by the authority, which will also provide a warden service.

Byelaws will probably exist governing certain activities, particularly control of dogs, damage to property, lighting fires, etc., and possibly also camping. A relatively small number of access agreements exist to areas of open country. The main areas are in the Peak District National Park, the Yorkshire Dales National Park, and the Forest of Bowland. Details of the areas covered by the agreements are available from county councils or the national park authorities. Access land is also shown on Ordnance Survey Outdoor Leisure maps (1:25,000).

Scotland

Access may be formally secured to 'open country' land by planning authorities in Scotland under the Countryside (Scotland) Act 1967. The powers of the local authority and the arrangements for access closely parallel those in England and Wales. Probably because of the widespread *de facto* access and rarity of access problems, the powers have been little used except to small areas of land under heavy recreational pressure and at the time of writing, there are few access agreements to land of interest to mountaineers. However, linear access agreements have been used to create sections of the West Highland Way.

COMMON LAND

England and Wales

Commons are a remnant from the manorial system which formed the basis of the country's social and economic system in the Middle Ages. Common land was the poor quality, unenclosed, 'waste' land to which the local inhabitants—the commoners—had rights for grazing animals, gathering fuel, etc.

Much of this common land was lost during the very extensive enclosures of the 18th and 19th centuries. However, over 6,000 sq km of common land still remains, and in many parts of the country common rights, especially of grazing, are of great agricultural importance; in others the traditional rights have fallen into disuse.

In the same way as any other land, common land is owned by some person or body, who holds it subject to the rights of commoners and to special Acts relating to common land. There is no general public right of access to common land, but some of these special Acts convey rights of access to specific kinds of common.

The Law of Property Act 1925 gives a public right of access on foot, for air and exercise, to all commons situated within pre-1974 local government reorganisation boroughs and urban districts. These areas are particularly important; many of the Lake District fells are commons that were within the old Lakes and Windermere Urban Districts.

The owner of any common may execute a Deed to bring a common under this same arrangement. Again this is of particular significance. The Crown Estate Commissioners, as owners of extensive commons in North Wales including many of the Snowdonia mountains, have made such a Deed.

In either case, there are three basic prohibitions: it is an offence to drive a vehicle, to camp, or to light a fire.

There may also be byelaws controlling public behaviour where access is of right.

There are other categories of common land to which a public right of access exists, but these are of lesser significance to mountaineering and it may also be far from easy to discover where such rights exist.

In theory, the owner of common land to which no public right of access exists may take an action for trespass. In practice, the prohibition of fencing common land prevents the owner from effectively taking any action to exclude trespassers.

Full details are found within a useful publication on commons (see page 345).

Scotland
Common land in Scotland is now virtually unknown. Local rights of pasturage do exist but these do not include any public access rights.

LAND OWNED BY THE NATIONAL TRUSTS

England and Wales
Although, strictly speaking, not a legal right, the National Trust's policy is to allow free access on foot at all times to its open spaces, subject only to the observance of the Trust's byelaws for commonsense behaviour which prohibit activities such as shooting, lighting fires or not keeping dogs under proper control.

There is not, however, unrestricted access to enclosed farmland, where walkers should keep to public or permissive paths in order to reach the open land; to young plantations and woods; or to certain nature reserve areas, particularly in the breeding season when the Trust is keen to protect rare flora and fauna. In certain areas the Trust also needs to restrict access either to make good damage such as erosion caused by access or to prevent it occurring.

National Trust property is indicated on Ordnance Survey maps, with, usually, differentiation shown between those areas of country where there is unrestricted access and those properties such as gardens or houses where access is restricted.

Scotland
The National Trust for Scotland permits unrestricted access to all its mountainous properties at all times of the year. These are Torridon, Glencoe and Dalness, Kintail and Morvich, Falls of Glomach, Grey Mare's Tail, Loch Skeen and White Comb, Ben Lawers, and Goat Fell.

Whilst the Trust has the right to make byelaws under its constitution, none has been adopted for any of its market properties because there has been no need to do so. As part of its management techniques, however, local directions may be given to encourage walkers to avoid areas where there is erosion, or where protection is desired for plant or wildlife habitats.

LAND OWNED BY THE FORESTRY COMMISSION

The Forestry Commission is responsible for 12,000 sq km of land in Great Britain, most of which is low grade agricultural land; much of it is located in the upland areas. A surprising proportion of Forestry Commission land is not in commercial timber production; areas are left unplanted for landscape reasons or if a Commission boundary extends above the tree line.

The Commission welcomes the public on foot to all its holdings provided that access does not conflict with the management or production of the land or forest. Access on foot is free of charge. The Commission also provides visitor centres, car parks, picnic places and camping sites and facilities and opportunities for specialist activities.

Trespass, de facto Access and Access Problems

TRESPASS

When in the hills or mountains, unless one is on land which is included in one of the categories described, or one has received the permission of the landowner, one is, legally speaking, trespassing. Trespass is commonly misunderstood, no thanks to the oft-seen signs in the countryside announcing that trespassers will be prosecuted.

It can be simply regarded as being where one has no right to be; a civil wrong against the personal right of property, not a criminal offence. However, trespass on land in the ownership of certain organisations, e.g. the Ministry of Defence or British Rail, is a criminal offence. Despite a commonly held belief, there is little difference in the law of trespass between England and Wales, and Scotland.

A landowner who objects to a person's presence on his property can only seek civil remedies against that person. The landowner or representative can tell the trespasser to leave the land and indicate the direction for leaving. If the trespasser refuses to leave, the landowner may use a reasonable amount of force to eject the trespasser.

In the case of a persistent trespasser, the landowner can apply to the courts for an Injunction (England and Wales) or an Interdict (Scotland) to prevent a particular person from continuing to trespass or from re-entering the property. That person would then be in contempt of court—a serious offence—if trespassing again. The courts would require to be convinced of serious expectation of continuing or re-occurring trespass for an Injunction or Interdict to be granted.

A landowner can proceed against a trespasser by bringing a civil action in the courts for damage. In England and Wales, in theory, the landowner can succeed in such an action and recover nominal damages for the 'loss' suffered due to the trespass itself. In practice, however, it would normally only be worthwhile bringing a civil action for damages if the trespasser had damaged or destroyed property. In Scotland there is no penalty for trespass itself, and so a civil action can only be brought in the case of damage to property.

The only exception to this situation exists in Scotland under the Trespass (Scotland) Act 1865. This Act makes it an offence to camp on private property or lodge in any premises without the permission of the landowner; or to camp or light a fire on or near any private road, enclosed land, or plantation without the landowner's consent, or on or near any public highway. This Act was brought in to deal with tinkers and gypsies, but is still in force and could be effective against recreational campers.

DE FACTO ACCESS AND ACCESS PROBLEMS

Despite the theoretical legal situation, there exists to most of the mountain and hill land in the UK a situation commonly described as de facto access: that is habitual access by the public, unhindered by the landowners. Where de facto access exists it is not common practice to seek the permission of a landowner prior to going on to land, but it may assist in establishing or maintaining good relations to do so, and is perhaps a good idea where access passes close to, or the most suitable parking place is prominent and close by the owner's house.

If challenged or asked to leave at any time whilst on private land the best course of action, especially in the long term, is to resist any temptation to argue or defy the request, to leave, and to seek another route to the chosen objective. Putting a reasoned case, if discussion is possible, will help to establish the responsible intentions of those seeking access, and any information gleaned will assist others in solving the difficulties that exist.

Any such incidents or problems over access should be reported to the British Mountaineering Council (BMC) or Mountaineering Council of Scotland (MC of S). Both organisations represent the interests of all hillwalkers and mountaineers in seeking to ensure that freedom of access without any unnecessary restrictions exists to all mountain and hill land. They are able to pursue difficulties through direct approaches to land-owners, via the landowning or farming representative bodies, or via the local authorities or government agencies with responsibility for public access and the powers, if necessary, to secure legal access rights.

It is unusual for difficulties to persist for long periods and any that are anything but local and short term will usually be reported in the specialist climbing and rambling magazines.

If in doubt about a particular access situation, and information is required in the planning of activities, the BMC or MC of S will endeavour to provide advice, as will the national park authorities for areas within the national parks.

Temporary or Periodic Restrictions on Access

In many situations of legal access or *de facto* access, temporary restrictions may exist. These may be for example, seasonal restrictions applying annually to allow shooting to take place; periodic closures for exercises on land used for military purposes; or emergency suspension of access agreements in the case of a high fire risk.

Additionally, there may be particularly sensitive seasons related to agricultural use of mountain land or a particular nature conservation interest, when access is not restricted but great care is needed to avoid causing any damage or disturbance.

GAME SHOOTING

Moorland country managed as grouse moor totals 4,000 sq km in England and Wales, and 12,000 sq km in Scotland. The birds breed during May and June and the shooting season extends from 12 August (the glorious 12th) until 10 December.

Research work has shown that public access to grouse moors has no harmful effect on either the grouse population or grouse bags, and public access exists as a right by access agreements to some grouse moors. *De facto* access exists to many areas but owners' concern over possible disturbance is one of the most common reasons for access being restricted. Shooting and walking are not simultaneously compatible and, where formal access agreements exist, the right of access to the moors is withdrawn under the terms of the agreements for a number of days each year during the grouse shooting season for the shoots to take place. Anyone entering the access land whilst the agreements are suspended is no longer exercising a legal right but committing a trespass.

The moorland access land in the Peak District is divided into more than a dozen separate areas. Access is withdrawn to each area for not more than 12 days per year, some for as few as 1 or 2 days. In the Yorkshire Dales the access may be withdrawn for a maximum of 30 days. These restrictions occur primarily during August, September and into October, but never on Sundays. If days are lost due to high fire hazard early in the season, shoots may extend into October and November.

Advance publicity is given to the restrictions. Notice boards in local villages and railway stations may carry information, as may the local press. The national park authorities can supply details and advice regarding the moors situated within the park boundaries. During shoots in the national parks, wardens may be present, particularly at access points, to warn people of the danger and to offer advice on other areas where access is not restricted.

Public rights of way across access land are not affected by these restrictions.

DEER STALKING

Many of the estates in the Scottish Highlands are managed as deer forests. Sportsmen, some visiting specially from abroad, are willing to pay large sums to stalk Red Deer, and consequently the estates derive a substantial income during the stalking season, and thus provide important employment.

The seasons for killing deer are laid down by law and are 1 July–20 October for stags and 21 October–15 February for hinds. It is the stags that provide the commercial stalking which usually commences when the stags are in prime condition and antler growth is complete and continues until the end of the season—mid-August until mid-October. Hinds are shot to control numbers, to prevent the deer population growing to exceed the capacity of the land to support it, and for venison production which provides the bulk of estate revenue. Public access to the estate land and stalking are not simultaneously compatible. There is an obvious danger to walkers whilst shooting is taking place, and there is the problem that the deer are disturbed by not only the sight, but also the scent, of humans.

In order to provide customer satisfaction, the estates put in a good deal of time and effort to the preparation for a successful stalk, which can be completely ruined by disturbance of the animals. Although there are differing views on how easily disturbance by walking occurs, even the threat of disturbance can cause great irritation and loss of sympathy.

It is standard practice, therefore, to contact the factor or stalker of an estate prior to going on to the hill during the stag stalking season to seek advice on which areas are restricted, and to which access will be permitted. There will almost always be parts of each estate to which access will be possible during the stag stalking season, and no single area is likely to be sensitive all the time.

As hind culling is a professional and economic operation, estates place fewer restrictions on access during the hind season. Since the professional stalkers efforts, often in bad weather, can be frustrated by disturbance of the deer, it may be wise and courteous to seek advice during this period.

The use of a public right of way is a legal right irrespective of shooting or stalking. However, in the interests of maintaining good relations, it may be helpful to make local inquiries before crossing a shooting estate via a public right of way during the stalking season.

No stalking for sport takes place on the estates owned by the National Trust for Scotland, namely Torridon, Ben Lawers, Goat Fell, Glencoe and Dalness, and Kintail.

The Trust's own staff do cull both stags and hinds to control populations. However, this is done without the need to restrict access to these estates at any time of year.

WOODLAND DEER

The control of populations of woodland deer is essential to ensure that forest damage is minimised. Stalking or culling is carried out by professional stalkers or rangers, day permit holders accompanied by rangers, or by others authorised by the owner or manager of the forest.

Most control is carried out at dawn and dusk throughout the summer months and in daylight throughout the winter. Enclosed woodland deer are exempt from close seasons.

To avoid accidents to the public, it may be wise for those wishing to camp or walk through forests to use recognised campsites if they are available and to check with the local forest office or forest manager if they intend to use other than normal access routes.

A very useful list of names, addresses and telephone numbers for most of the highland estates appears in a booklet published by the Scottish Landowners' Federation, prepared jointly with the Mountaineering Council of Scotland (see page 346).

MILITARY TRAINING AREAS

There are several Ministry of Defence military training areas in the moorland and upland areas, including some important and popular hillwalking country. The Dartmoor Ranges include much of northern Dartmoor and Warcop Range encompasses Mickle Fell, close to the Pennine Way above Upper Teesdale.

Most of the training areas are used as firing ranges, some are live ranges, others are dry (live ammunition is not used). There is access to many ranges, both dry and live, but mostly dry, on days when training is not taking place, but on some live ranges there is little or no access allowed. In most cases when access does exist, the ranges will be open more often than they are closed; usually at weekends, public holidays and during the high holiday season. Range areas are marked on O.S. maps 1:25,000, 1:50,000 and 1:63360, as 'Danger Area'. Special maps showing the exact boundaries and other details of those ranges where public access is most sought after are produced by the Ministry of Defence.

There are standard warning notices and procedures of providing on the ground information to prevent access when firing is taking place—red flags during the day, red lights at night. Other public information may be available in the form of advance notice of the dates and times when particular ranges are open. The emphasis on this depends upon the popularity of the area; hence for the Dartmoor Ranges the information is particularly comprehensive—firing times are advertised in the local press and displayed in local police stations, post offices and public houses; a map is available showing the different firing areas and there is a telephone information answering service. For other ranges the information available may not be so comprehensive; if not in the locality, it may simply be best to contact the relevant Range Liaison Officer.

There are byelaws for most of the firing ranges, which make it an offence to enter the range area during periods of closure.

FIRE RISK

The two vegetation types that are particularly susceptible to serious, long-term damage by fire are moorland and woodland.

There is a very obvious need for great care not to cause any risk of fire when walking in moorland areas. However, where rights of access exist to moorland through access agreements there are formal procedures for suspension of the agreements when the risk of fire reaches a critical level.

The suspensions result from consultations between farming, landowning and local authority interests and operate for one week periods. Notices usually appear in the press and signs are placed on all access points to the access land.

Public rights of way across access land are not affected by the access suspensions.

ANIMAL DISEASE

There is one, rarely occurring animal disease—Foot and Mouth Disease— which can result in restrictions on public access to the countryside. In order to prevent the spread of infection the Ministry of Agriculture has power under the Animal Health Act 1981 to close and restrict access to any area of land regardless of whether or not legal rights of access normally exist. Entry to a restricted area becomes an offence.

Since an epidemic in 1967–68 that resulted in widespread access restrictions, precautionary standards have improved significantly and only one outbreak has occurred, in 1981.

A Minimum Impact Approach

The mountains are a sensitive environment, under pressure from a whole host of activities and interests. Hillwalking and mountaineering contribute to that pressure and can themselves be damaging to the physical environment, can cause disruption to the interests of those who own and manage the land, and can mar the enjoyment of those who follow, expecting an unspoiled environment. The implications of continuing increases in the levels of participation in recreation are serious. There is a very real danger that the more popular areas in particular will become so degraded that either the potential for enjoyment will be severely reduced, or owners or authorities will seek to impose controls to reduce the impacts. If such situations are to be avoided and freedoms maintained, there is a need for a philosophy of responsibility and respect for the environment—a 'minimum impact' philosophy.

The following notes offer some advice on ways to minimise impacts associated with mountaineering without requiring any major limitation or curtailment of activity.

Travelling to the Hills

Mountaineers frequently approach the hills by private transport and there is a temptation to drive as close as possible to one's chosen objective. However, car parking space and especially mini-bus parking space is not always conveniently available. Farmyards, lanes and gateways are often in use, and bulky farm machinery needs considerable space for manoeuvring. For a farmer an inconsiderately parked vehicle can cause great inconvenience and annoyance.

—Vehicles should not be driven away from public roads on to bridleways, private roads or open country. (It is an offence to drive more than 15 yards from a highway without the landowner's permission.)
—Park with forethought and consideration.

On the Hills

PATHS AND EROSION

The most popular paths are suffering serious erosion. Heavy soled boots easily trample and break up the surface vegetation which dies to reveal a generally unstable soil. Heavy rainfall on steep slopes washes the material away and gullying results. The eroded section becomes unpleasant for walking and small detours result in path widening. Eroded sections on some popular hill paths have measured as much as 50 metres in width.

Expensive reinstatement schemes are underway in some areas but financial and practical constraints limit such work to the lower paths.

—Tread carefully, if possible walking on boulders or stony ground.
—Resist the temptation to cut corners on zig-zag descents.
—If alternatives are available, avoid running screes.
—Co-operate with diversions etc. where works are being done.

WALLS AND FENCES; GATES AND STILES

Dry stone walls and fences are extremely important boundaries for containing stock, and walls particularly are an essential element of the upland landscape. They can be easily damaged by climbing over and are extremely time-consuming and expensive to repair. Consequently, broken walls are often quickly and cheaply secured by unattractive fencing materials rather than rebuilding.

—Use gates or stiles even if it entails a short diversion. Close and fasten all gates.
—If it is absolutely necessary to climb a wall, do so carefully, and replace any dislodged stones.
—Keep to footpaths across enclosed land.

LITTER

The problem of litter is not unique to the hills, but there are many examples of severe litter problems that can only be attributed to hillwalkers or climbers. Vast quantities have been removed in 'clean-up jobs' from the worst spots. Litter looks unpleasant, it can be harmful to stock, and attracts scavenging animals and birds such as rats, sea gulls and crows which prey on and displace the natural species of the area.

—Plan to minimise rubbish, particularly on overnight trips, i.e. repackage food to avoid containers.
—Carry all litter down the hill; it is useful to carry a plastic bag for this.
—Don't bury it or throw behind rocks—animals will dig it up.
—Don't bury it in snow—it soon reappears in spring.

FIRES

Accidentally started fires can cause extensive, expensive and long-term damage to areas of moorland or woodland. Concern over fire is a significant reason for landowners not wishing to allow public access to areas of open country. It can take between 10 and 20 years for a burned heather moorland area to recolonise and more than 30 years for the full establishment of the original level of growth. Common causes of fires are (a) discarded cigarette ends and matches; (b) camp fires and stoves; (c) bottles and broken glass.

—Take special care not to risk starting a fire, particularly during dry periods.

CAIRNS

The proliferation of cairns on many paths is an unsightly 'urbanisation' of the hills; as a form of signposting they diminish the wilderness quality. Those venturing into the hills should aspire to self-reliance, navigating when necessary by map and compass. Cairns can give a false sense of security.

—Don't build or enlarge cairns.

PLANTS AND ANIMALS

Wild animals and birds can be disturbed by human presence. During the nesting season birds may desert a nest if disturbed, or may be frightened away for so long that the eggs will chill or the chicks die. Stock, particularly sheep, can be worried by dogs not kept under the strictest control. Sheep are particularly at risk during the lambing season and nothing should be done to disturb or frighten ewes in lamb. Dogs will also scent out ground nesting or sitting birds.

All wild plants are protected by law and it is illegal for anyone to uproot any wild plant without the permission of the landowner.

—Avoid hanging around close to bird's nests, particularly birds of prey.
—Keep dogs under close control at all times.
—Don't pick or uproot plants. If a record is required, take a photograph.

Staying Overnight in the Hills

Camping, bivouacking or staying in a primitive shelter can be one of the most rewarding experiences to be had from going into the hills. However, the use of additional equipment for shelter and cooking can result—unless great care is taken—in far greater impacts than single day activities.

CAMPING

Without attention to detail an idyllic campsite in the hills can easily degenerate into an unsightly and unhygienic mess.

—To avoid vegetation damage, tents should not be pitched on the same spot for more than 2 or 3 days. At pre-existing sites try to avoid pitch marks to allow vegetation recovery.
—Don't dig drainage ditches around tents. If the site is too wet, look for somewhere else.
—If boulders are used to hold down pegs or valances, replace them where they were found. Don't dig turfs for this job.

BIVOUACS

—If it is necessary to build a shelter wall, take it down in the morning.

BOTHIES

These rudimentary shelters provide excellent accommodation in remote areas. Most are not regularly maintained and it is the responsibility of visitors to leave a bothy as they would wish to find it.

—Leave the bothy clean, and secure doors to keep out sheep and deer.
—Avoid going to bothies with a party large enough to fill it; others may want to use it also.

FIRES

Fires can be very enjoyable, but they can also cause local damage. Although a good fuel source, dead wood is an important part of natural cycles.

—Keep fires small to conserve wood.
—Never cut live wood for fires.
—Select a non-inflammable, non-scarring site such as a dry streambed.
—Completely extinguish a fire before leaving the site. Tidy up by dismantling and replacing the rocks in natural locations.

POLLUTION

A certain amount of personal and equipment washing is necessary, so care should be taken to minimise water pollution.

—All washing should be done well away from any water source where foul water should be drained into an absorbent soil. It should not be returned to the water source.
—Toilet waste should be buried in a hole at least 15 cm (6 in) deep within the top soil layer, well away from a water source, and the soil and turf replaced and trodden in.

Obtaining Information and Advice

There exists, at times, a confusingly large number of bodies and organisations—both governmental and voluntary—responsible for or concerned with the management of mountain land, the conservation of its natural beauty or scientific value, and its use for recreation. Some have very useful information services and are able to provide both information and advice on issues directly related to mountaineering activities. For example, the national park authorities are a good source of access information and will give guidance on environmentally sensitive areas or seasons, and ways to avoid causing damage or disturbance. In contrast, looking to the voluntary sector, mountaineering organisations will always be the best source for the users' view of access to a particular area.

For those wishing to look at access and conservation issues in greater depth, there is a series of voluntary organisations with a primary concern for the environmental and recreational issues of the upland areas. These vary from those with a national viewpoint to those with a regional interest; some are quite definitely campaigning pressure groups. Most of the voluntary organisations produce magazines, newsletters or other material examining the issues of the moment, and almost without exception, they welcome interest in the relevant issues. Indeed, for those organisations with the specific aims of exerting influence on access and conservation issues in the mountain areas, the support of mountaineers is a crucial factor in the success of their work.

Although some of the organisations have more than one main concern making categorisation difficult, for the sake of simplicity they can be grouped as follows. Addresses, telephone numbers and full details are listed in Appendix II.

The Mountaineering Organisations

The interests of hillwalkers, rock climbers and mountaineers are represented in the British Isles by three main organisations, with responsibilities divided on a geographical basis. The British Mountaineering Council (BMC) covers England and Wales; the Mountaineering Council of Scotland covers Scotland; and the Federation of Mountain Clubs of Ireland covers both Northern Ireland and Eire. All three bodies have closely parallel objectives, the most important of which are securing and maintaining unrestricted access to mountain land, and ensuring the conservation of the unspoiled qualities of the mountains and hills. They are often closely involved in access negotiations and are therefore well placed to provide advice from the mountaineers' viewpoint on the practical access situation in any given area. To function efficiently the bodies need briefing on any developments relating to access and are particularly keen to be told of any problems encountered.

The Ramblers' Association has a much broader brief in geographical terms, being concerned about access and conservation issues affecting all the British countryside. The Association is particularly interested in rights of way issues, and has a wealth of information and experience. The RA has campaigned actively in recent years for the establishment of a legal right of access to all unenclosed hill country.

National Park Authorities

The primary source of information and advice for areas within national park boundaries in England and Wales is the national park authorities. The authorities, in general, run a three-tiered service for the public. This operates, firstly, in response to written or telephone inquiries; secondly, at information centres within the Park; and thirdly, via the national park wardens who may be encountered out and about in the Park. Most of the authorities have a Youth and Schools' Liaison Officer whose task is to try and ensure that visits of all types by school and youth groups are enjoyable and beneficial for those taking part and are not in conflict with other national park purposes. The Officer can provide information on access, land ownership, footpaths, transport, accommodation and local services; environmentally sensitive areas due to high fire risk or erosion damage; and links with conservation projects taking place within the Park, that are often in need of support from volunteer workforces.

Published material ranges from a full information pack in some Parks to a basic advice sheet in others, where the officers prefer to deal with specific individual inquiries. Teaching packs or slide packs may be on sale or loan and some authorities have a reference or study room available.

Local Authorities

Outside the national parks in England and Wales, the County and District Councils, and in Scotland, the Regional and District Councils, have statutory responsibilities for access and conservation in the countryside. Few provide specific information services, but nevertheless inquiries may be made or advice sought. Most countryside matters are dealt with by the planning department which will usually have a Countryside Officer concerned with countryside management and informal recreation, and a Recreation Officer concerned with formal recreation and sporting activities. Rights of Way matters are the responsibility of the Highways Department, which may have a Footpath Officer.

National Conservation Organisations

There are several organisations concerned with land use, planning and conservation issues on a national basis. The Council for the Protection of Rural England (CPRE), the Council for the Protection of Rural Wales (CPRW) and the Association for the Protection of Rural Scotland (APRS) express views on issues such as agriculture, forestry, motorway developments, new reservoirs or power stations, attempting to influence views at a national level but also through an involvement with significant local proposals.

The Council for National Parks (CNP) fulfils a similar role but is concerned solely with issues within the boundaries of the 10 national parks of England and Wales. It fulfils an essential watchdog role, ensuring that the purposes for which national parks were designated—conservation and recreation—are upheld against the almost constant threats of commercial exploitation and inappropriate development. The Scottish Wildland Group is a small, recently formed body concerned with the protection of wild and wilderness areas in Scotland.

Local Conservation Organisations in Mountain Areas

There are local conservation organisations in many areas of the country and most of the upland areas are the concern of one group or another; however, three bodies are particularly worthy of mention here, since their aims are quite specific to the conservation of premier mountain areas.

The Friends of the Lake District (FLD) represents the CPRE in Cumbria and concentrates effort on ensuring that the purposes of the national park designation are upheld in the Lake District. As a watchdog organisation the FLD monitors developments and proposals, and led the opposition grouping of independent bodies at the public inquiry into proposals to abstract water from Wastwater and Ennerdale Water. The Snowdonia National Park Society fulfils a similar role in Snowdonia.

The North East Mountain Trust was formed in 1980, as a grouping of many of the mountaineering and rambling clubs in north-east Scotland, in response to the need for a collective voice on the many crucially important land use and land management issues in the Grampian Mountains, and the Cairngorms in particular.

5 Security on Steep Ground

Probably no other aspect of the training of the mountain leader has aroused more discussion and controversy than this no-man's-land between hillwalking and rock climbing. Opinions range from those who would have nothing to do with the climbing rope, who would restrict their activities to the less demanding summits and to whom a little knowledge is a dangerous thing, to those who believe that the mountain leader should be able to climb confidently to a moderately difficult standard on rock and to whom no summit in these islands is barred. The truth is that it is neither possible nor desirable to define the frontier between the two. What is important is that the leader should have an unclouded appreciation of his own abilities and limitations and the good sense to operate in an area and in such a manner that will enable him to remain in full control of the situation at all times. There will be mountain leaders who climb and mountain leaders who do not and each must cut his coat according to his cloth.

The techniques described in the chapter which follows are not intended to train leaders as rock climbers. The purpose is to describe elementary techniques which will enable them to appreciate the limits of what should be attempted by a party without rock climbing experience, to recognise difficulties and potential dangers of terrain and to give competent help in cases of emergency. It is one of the drawbacks of a handbook on any subject that it tends to give the impression that there is only one correct way of doing things. In the case of climbing this would be a wrong impression and it should be understood that there are usually several perfectly safe and satisfactory ways of achieving the same goal whether that be a belay or an abseil, or picking a safe route down a rock buttress. If it is safe and appropriate and if you are confident in doing it, do it. What is described here is considered to be the minimum that should be familiar to the mountain leader and, for the more experienced, it is no bad thing to put aside the paraphernalia of the rock climber for a while and return to the one fundamental and indispensable item of equipment—the climbing rope.

It is worth remembering that there are many situations, apart from graded rock climbs, when the rope is at least desirable and sometimes essential, e.g. to safeguard the party up or down some unforeseen difficulty, to go to the assistance of someone who has fallen, to secure an injured but otherwise mobile member of the party, to provide a safety rope in an exposed situation. Leaders should be aware of the technical difficulties as they appear to the novice and be sympathetic towards their mental condition under stress. Psychological or physical succour brought about by the timely and effective use of the rope can mean the difference between an orderly retreat and a disaster.

For discussion of more advanced climbing techniques and equipment refer to 'Security on Snow and Ice', Chapter 13.

The Rope

The purpose of the rope is to provide a measure of security to those who use it, whether they be climbers or hillwalkers. In the case of climbers the rope is deployed continuously, its primary function being to hold a fall, should one occur, although it may also be used to provide direct support, as in abseiling, or when a tight rope is called for. More often than not the mountain walker's rope never sees the light of day. It remains in the leader's pack only to be produced on those rare occasions when the situation demands additional security, or in an emergency which may be circumvented by the timely introduction of the rope.

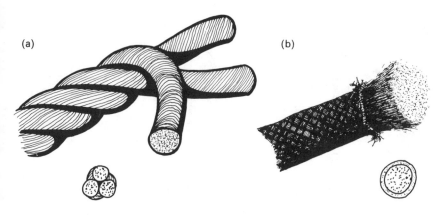

(a)   (b)

Fig. 48. *Types of climbing ropes: (a) hawser laid, (b) kernmantel.*

The size of rope is usually described by its diameter: 9 mm is the most suitable for mountain walking. There are many makes, but look for the U.I.A.A. label of approval.

Climbing ropes may be hawser laid or of kermantel construction. The former consists of three large bundles of fibres laid in a spiral manner. This traditional method of construction is perfectly satisfactory, but has largely been replaced by kernmantel ropes which consist of several bundles of nylon fibres enclosed in a woven outer sheath. The design and manufacture of ropes has come a long way since the days of Manilla hemp but the modern rope is still a compromise between sometimes conflicting requirements and so it is important to understand its limitations. One of the most important characteristics of a climbing rope is that it should be sufficiently

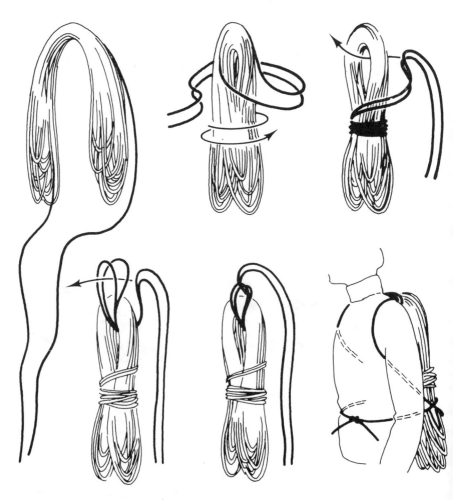

Fig. 49. *Butterfly coil—handy for carrying a large volume of rope.*

elastic to absorb the energy of the impact of a fall without imposing an unacceptable strain on the falling body or, for that matter, on the person belaying. Clearly, the rope must also be sufficiently strong to withstand the very considerable forces which are generated in a leader fall. This means that the rope must be of a minimum weight or thickness, all of which adds to the burden to be carried by the climber. The hillwalker, on the other hand, is extremely unlikely to find himself in the position of having to hold a falling leader, even in the most dire emergency, so it seems reasonable for him to sacrifice some of this extra strength in the interests of lightening his load. But one must not take this too far. The thinner the rope, the more difficult it is to handle and ropes of 7 mm diameter and under are extremely difficult to hold. It is unlikely, too, that the hillwalker will be contemplating even the remote possibility of long abseils, so that 30 m of 9 mm diameter rope should be sufficient for most purposes. Choosing between different brands is largely a matter of personal taste and the feel of the rope. Make sure that the rope has been properly tested and meets the requirements laid down by the Union International des Associations d'Alpinisme, (U.I.A.A.). Hawser laid ropes should conform to British Standard 3184.

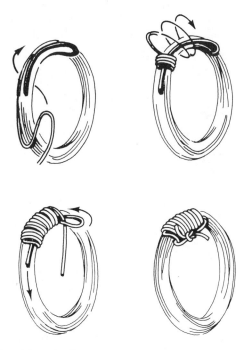

Fig. 50. *Mountaineers' coil.*

One serious disadvantage of nylon as a material for a climbing rope is its very low melting point. Considerable heat can be generated as a result of friction if, for example, a moving rope is pulled through a static loop. Under such circumstances enough heat may be generated to cause the static loop to fail. Another disadvantage is that it is relatively easy to cut, especially when the rope is under tension. Sharp rock edges and excessively abrasive surfaces can do a lot of damage. A rope is worse than useless if it is damaged because it induces a false sense of security. When you need a rope, you need to be able to depend upon it. It is important, therefore, to look after it. On no account stand on it or let anyone else stand on it. Do not use it for any other purpose such as a washing line or the ultimate sin, as a tow-rope. If it gets dirty give it a thorough wash to get rid of all the small particles of grit which can damage the fibres. A cool wash in a washing machine, without detergent, is as good a way as any of doing this. Make sure that the rope ends are fused and that the rope is properly coiled.

Inspect the rope thoroughly every so often and discard it if you find any serious damage, such as a cut sheath. Keep the rope away from hot objects and store in a cool place out of direct sunlight. It is difficult to give firm advice on when to retire a climbing rope. Much depends on the level of use—and abuse. Obviously, a rope used very occasionally by a hillwalker will last a lot longer than the same rope used constantly by a rock climber. The golden rule must be: if in doubt, discard.

Some Essential and Useful Knots

Fig. 51. *Overhand knot.*

Used to tie-off a loose end of rope after a bowline or other knot has been tied.

Fig. 52. *Overhand loop.*

An overhand tied in a doubled rope provides a loop for belaying or for a waist loop.

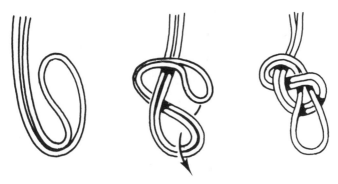

Fig. 53. *Figure-of-8 loop.*

A more effective knot than the overhand for forming a waist loop. A useful knot for novices to learn because any mistake in tying it results in an overhand, which is still a safe knot. It can be easily untied after loading.

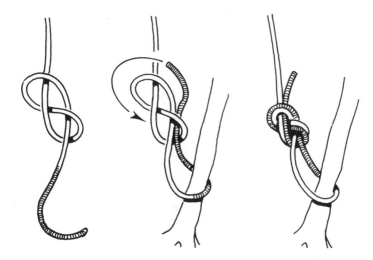

Fig. 54. *Figure-of-8, rewoven.*

Tie a figure-of-8 knot in the single rope, pass the end through or round the anchor point, then follow in reverse order the exact line of the rope in the original figure-of-8. A useful knot for attaching the rope to a waist loop, tree, thread belay, etc., where it is not possible simply to slip a loop over the top.

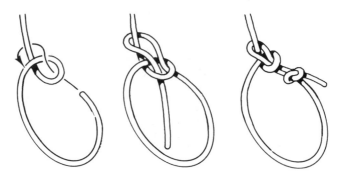

Fig. 55.   *Single bowline.*

Still the standard knot for tying on. Do not have the rope too tight round the waist; it should ride up round the lower rib-cage. Allow 12–18 inches of tail and secure it with an overhand knot tied on to the waist loop.

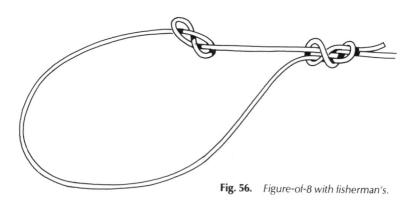

Fig. 56.   *Figure-of-8 with fisherman's.*

Useful when you need one knot that will fit several people, without re-tying. Use only as a safety rope. Not for use in rock climbing.

(a) Tie a single figure-of-8 about 4 ft from the end of the rope.
(b) Tie half a fisherman's knot back on to the main rope. The fisherman's knot must have at least three turns around the main rope. For clarity only two are shown.
(c) The figure-of-8 acts as a stopper knot. The size of the waist loop can be adjusted by changing the position of the figure-of-8 knot.

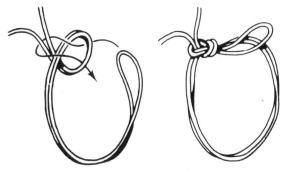

Fig. 57. *Triple bowline.*

A bowline tied in a doubled rope provides three loops which, with a bit of adjustment, can be fashioned into a rope chair. Used to lower an injured or incapacitated person.

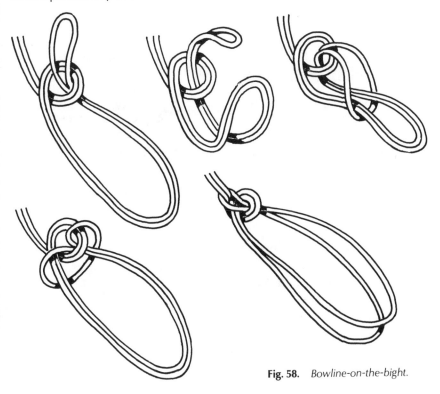

Fig. 58. *Bowline-on-the-bight.*

A simple knot to tie, once you get the hang of it, which provides two loops which can be used to make a chair.

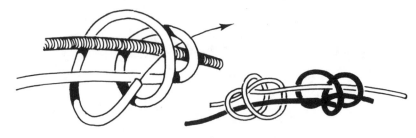

Fig. 59. *Double fisherman's.*

The best knot for tying two ends of rope together. Each end is passed twice round both ropes and back through the loops so formed. Leave about 6–9 inches of tail.

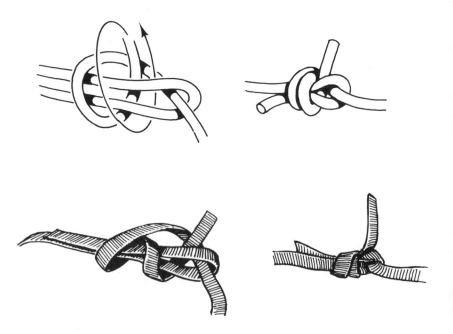

Fig. 60. *Double sheet bend.*

A useful knot for attaching a heavier rope to a lighter one. It has a tendency to work loose if not tightened properly.

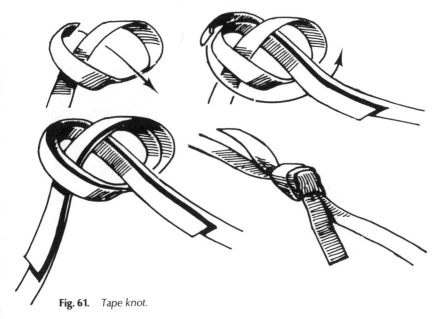

Fig. 61. *Tape knot.*

A rewoven overhand knot, commonly used for joining lengths of tape to make slings, etc.

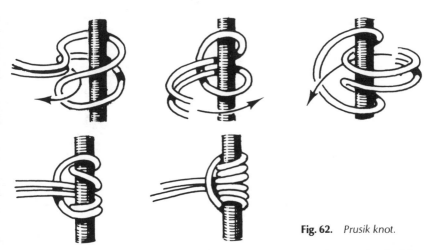

Fig. 62. *Prusik knot.*

This is one of the most useful knots for more advanced climbing techniques. The knot grips the climbing rope when it is tensioned, but can slide when the tension is released.

Belaying

The purpose of belaying is to provide mutual protection for the members of a climbing party by the use of the rope. The principle is that only one person is actually climbing at any one time and that person is secured by the rope which is held by the belayer who is himself secured by a loop of rope to the rock face. A climbing party will proceed up the face in a series of pitches each one starting from and finishing at a belay. In this way if any member of the party should fall he can be held by the person belaying him.

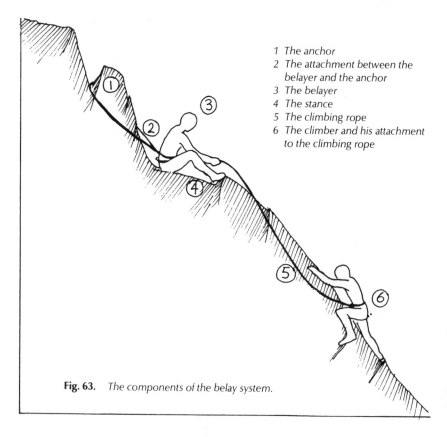

1 The anchor
2 The attachment between the belayer and the anchor
3 The belayer
4 The stance
5 The climbing rope
6 The climber and his attachment to the climbing rope

Fig. 63.　*The components of the belay system.*

In the mountain situation it is highly unlikely that the leader of a group would ever be in a position where he might be required to hold a fall from above. Nevertheless, it is as well to be prepared for the worst and you should have some experience of the very considerable forces which can be generated by a 'leader fall'. A more likely scenario is that he would be safeguarding his party down a short rock pitch or across an exposed section of ridge. In these circumstances he should be able to provide a tight rope even to the extent of taking the whole weight of an individual on the rope and lowering him to the bottom.

It will be appreciated that a belay system has several interdependent components and like all such systems it can only be as good as its weakest link. Poor equipment, a faulty knot, a moment's inattention, a weak anchor point, and the strongest rope is made worthless.

When to Rope-Up

There are no hard and fast rules about when to rope-up. This is a decision which is influenced by a number of interrelated factors:

—Exposure—would a slip result in serious injury?
—Difficulty—is the terrain difficult to a degree that makes a slip a possibility?
—Ability—how do individual members of the party react to exposure and how do they perform on rock?
—Security—can the situation be properly safeguarded by the use of the rope?
—The time factor—speed is often a safety factor in itself. Is the saving of time more important under the circumstances than the additional security which can be provided by roping-up?
—Margin of safety—other than in an emergency situation, the leader must be operating well within his experience and capabilities.

If, having weighed these factors, you decide to rope-up, you must see to it that the rope is used as effectively and efficiently as possible. 'Confidence roping' is not on and, indeed, such practice is only likely to ensure that the confident climber will not fall alone.

Sound belaying is the only key to safe practice in this area. This depends on the selection of a safe and suitable anchor for the rope and on a thorough appreciation both in theory and practice of the technique of belaying.

Among rock climbers it is almost universally accepted practice to wear a helmet. It is not expected that mountain walkers will wear them but there are likely to be occasions during training when it would be sensible to do so.

The illustrations in this chapter show helmets being worn in rock climbing situations.

Anchors

The selection of a really solid anchor is the first essential in setting up a belay system. It cannot be considered in isolation, although it is likely to be the determining factor in locating the belay. The best type of anchor is one which will take a pull from any direction, including an upward pull, such as a tree or a thread. More often than not you will have to settle for a spike and this is perfectly satisfactory in those circumstances when any pull on the rope attached to the anchor is in a downward direction. Ideally, the anchor should not be too far away from the stance and about head height above it.

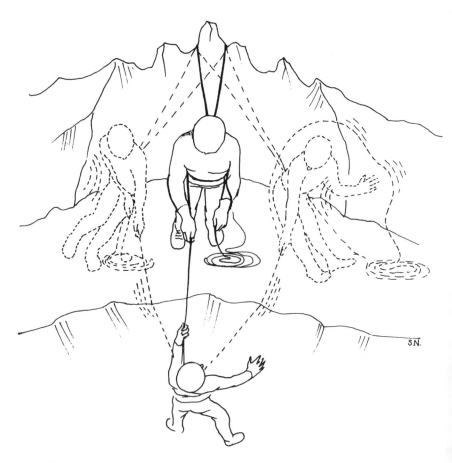

Fig. 64. *The relationship between anchor, stance and climber. The best situation is when all three are in the same vertical plane—centre above.*

The Stance

Sometimes only one stance is possible, at others you may have a limited choice. Choose the best position from which you can safeguard the person climbing, keeping in mind the following points:

—You should be able to follow the climber's progress on the pitch so that you can offer advice and encouragement.
—With beginners it is even more important to be able to keep an eye on the start of the pitch to observe tying-on, etc.
—The rope should be kept clear of loose debris.
—The rope should not run over any sharp edges.
—You should have sufficient room to adopt a good belaying position, sitting or standing with a firm brace for the feet and legs.
—The stance should, if possible, be in the same vertical plane as the climber and the anchor. Consider what will happen if he falls. The rope will tend to straighten between the climber and the anchor and if the stance is outside that straight line, the belayer will be pulled sideways.

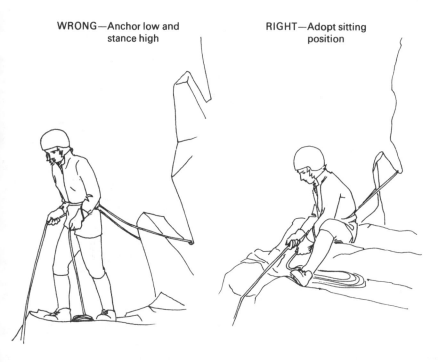

WRONG—Anchor low and stance high

RIGHT—Adopt sitting position

Fig. 65. *Bad and good body positions in relation to the anchor.*

E

Attachment of Belayer to Anchor

The rope from the waist is passed round the anchor and the belayer takes up his stance. A bight of the returning rope is taken through the waist loop and tied off in a figure-of-8. It is important that when the belayer is in position there is no slack in the rope connecting him to the anchor.

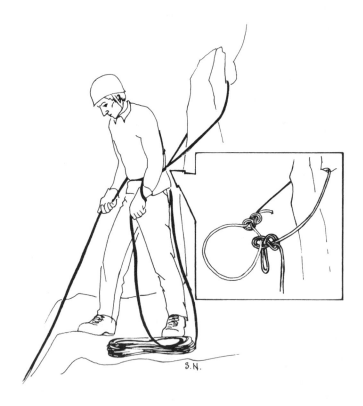

Fig. 66.   *The spike belay.*

Spike Belay Tied off at the Anchor

An alternative method to the above is to tie a figure-of-8 or an overhand knot in a bight of rope taken from the waist and place it over the spike. It is difficult to adjust the length of this belay, but it does have the advantage of allowing the belayer to untie himself from the rope if necessary, while still leaving the second man secured to the belay.

BAD
Belay slack—belayer can be
pulled off stance

GOOD
Belay tight and inline with
expected strain

Fig. 67. *The rope joining the belayer to the anchor must be kept taut.*

Fig. 68. *The spike belay tied off at the anchor.*

The Thread Belay

A 'thread' anchor is a natural hole or space in the rock through which the rope is passed to provide an attachment which can resist a pull in any direction. In practice most thread anchors are formed by stones or small boulders wedged in cracks and have to be inspected and tested to see that they are sound. A good thread is undoubtedly the most secure of all anchors. There is a number of perfectly acceptable ways in which the belayer can attach himself to it and these are listed below:

Fig. 69. *Thread belay with a single bight tied back to the waist loop.*

In this method a bight of rope taken from the belayer's waist is threaded through the anchor and tied off with a figure-of-8 through the waist loop, exactly as in the spike belay. The belayer takes the active rope round his hips in the usual way.

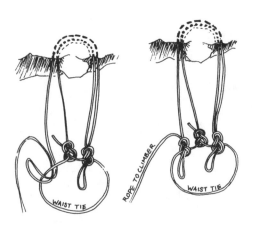

Fig. 70. *Thread belay with two bights tied back to the waist.*

For additional security a second bight may be taken from the active rope and tied off at the waist in the same manner as the first. This method is expensive on rope.

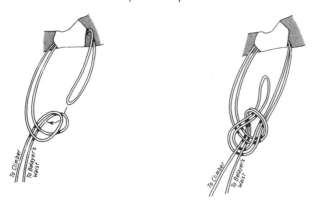

Fig. 71. *Thread belay tied off with a bowline at the anchor.*

A bight of rope is passed through the anchor and tied back on itself with a bowline. This method is perfectly sound and economical of rope but it is very difficult to adjust for length once the belayer has taken up his stance.

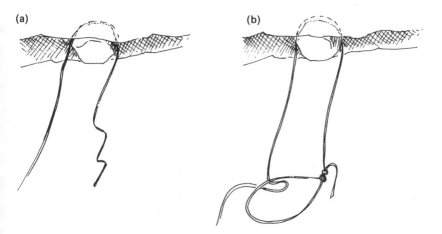

Fig. 72. *Thread belay by untying and threading the end through.*

(a) *untie and thread end through.*
(b) *tie on to end.*

On a single pitch climb the leader may be justified in untying from the rope and passing the end through the thread and retying on again. A belay can then be arranged in the normal way for a spike.

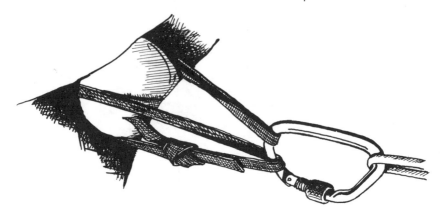

Fig. 73.   *Using a sling and karabiner to provide a thread belay.*

For those with rock climbing experience it is a simple matter to pass a sling through the thread, clip a karabiner on to the sling and belay to the karabiner in the normal way. Please note that you should always use a screw-gated karabiner and that it should be used with the gate underneath where it cannot be unscrewed by the rope running across it.

The Belayer

The final link in the chain of security is the belayer himself. It is his responsibility to ensure that the rope is taken in or paid out as required and to provide support if and when it is needed. Because of the energy absorbing qualities of the modern climbing rope it is no longer necessary to provide a dynamic brake in the event of a fall. The belayer's job is to hold on to the rope as tightly as possible and let the rope do the rest. The hip belay is undoubtedly the most reliable method available which does not involve the use of special equipment. It is simple and depends for its satisfactory operation in the event of a fall on achieving the maximum amount of friction between the rope and the back of the hips. It is important to use this part of the anatomy which has a bony framework rather than the waist which is soft and vulnerable. The hands, too, are vulnerable and should be protected by leather gloves.

Let us now assume a situation where the leader has climbed a pitch and taken up a stance and belay at the top. He brings the rope in quickly hand-over-hand until it tightens on the second man. He then passes the rope over his head and down to his hips. The inactive rope is twisted once round the forearm before being firmly held in the braking hand. The second can now be brought up the pitch using the technique shown in

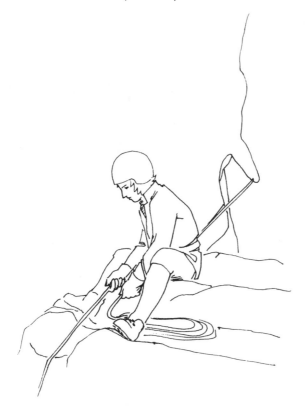

Fig. 74. *Sitting hip belay.*

Fig. 75. The active rope should be kept under just the right degree of tension so that at no time is there any slack rope between the belayer and the person climbing. In the event of a slip the rope is held tightly in the braking hand which is moved across the front of the body so as to provide the maximum contact and friction between the rope and the hips. Even a short fall can impose a tremendous load on the belayer that can severely test his strength and skill. It is a technique which is well worth practising so that you are better prepared for the real thing. If the fallen climber is unable to resume climbing he should be lowered to the bottom of the pitch. It is very important for the belayer to keep alert at all times and be aware of the various components of the belay chain and how they may be affected by the changing position of the person climbing. Constantly ask yourself the questions, 'What direction will the pull come from if the person climbing falls off?' and, 'Am I in the best position to resist this pull?'

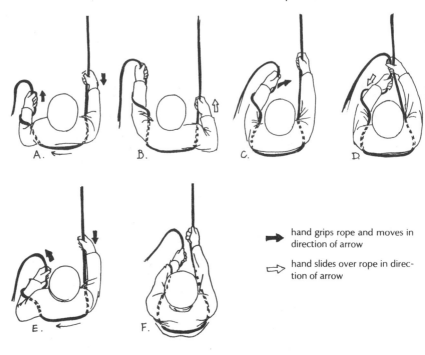

Fig. 75. *Taking in the rope. Left hand is braking hand; right hand is leading hand.*

A *Pull in rope with both hands on rope until braking hand is fully extended.*
B *Hold rope with braking hand and slide leading hand out.*
C *Bring hands together.*
D *Hold both parts of the rope with leading hand: slide braking hand toward body, keeping it ready in case of a fall.*
E *Repeat cycle.*
F *Holding a fall. Arrest position: braking hand wraps rope around body and tightens grip to hold fall.*

Communications

It is essential to have a well understood system of communication between the members of a climbing party and particularly between the belayer and the person climbing. Over the years certain standard calls have come into almost universal use and you should know what each means. Under some circumstances it will not be necessary to follow the complete sequence when, for example, the belayer and the belayed are in close visual contact. A common sense approach is required.

Table 7.   Communications between belayer and climber

Belayer	Climber	Meaning
Taking in'		I am belayed and about to take in the slack rope.
	'That's me'	All the slack rope has been taken up.
'Climb when you're ready'		I have taken up my stance and am ready to bring you up.
	'Climbing'	I have untied my belay and have started to climb.
'OK'		
Other calls which may be used	'Take in'	Take in slack rope.
	'Tight'	Give me a tight rope.
	'Slack'	Pay out some rope.

Fig. 76. *Direct belay.*

Direct Belaying

The decision to put the rope on and belay each individual member of a party on a section of rock is not always an easy one, especially if there are other pressing factors to consider, such as approaching darkness. It requires judgement and experience. There are situations, such as a short, relatively easy pitch on an otherwise straightforward descent, when the leader would be justified in arranging a direct belay for each member of the party. This involves the leader taking the rope from the climber directly round a convenient rock spike without attaching himself to an anchor. In the event of a slip the weight of the climber comes directly on to the rock spike. As the direction of pull on the leader is towards the spike he must adopt a stance facing the spike with the rope passed under both armpits for a high spike or round his hips for a lower spike, when it will also be necessary to find a good bracing stance so that the legs can resist a pull towards the anchor.

Descent

Finding a good safe route of descent down a rocky hillside is a skill that only comes with a great deal of practice and many a false cast. It can be a wearisome business, retracing your steps to find the right line, so learn to 'read' the terrain. A sight of the route from across the valley earlier in the day can save a lot of toil and trouble later on. Are there any lines of weakness which could be followed, perhaps a series of gently sloping terraces of grass or scree, separating bands of rock? Gullies should normally be avoided, unless they are known to be safe. They tend to consist of a series of vertical steps, often with huge boulders wedged between steep side walls forming overhanging pitches. Furthermore, on a rock face, they frequently follow lines of weakness where the rock is perhaps softer or more broken and this gives rise to an accumulation of debris which can be particularly hazardous to a large party.

Loose rock is probably the greatest hazard on any descent of steep rocky ground and the larger the party, the greater the risk. Good discipline is absolutely essential. Do not let the party get strung out and brief everyone forcefully on the dangers of standing about in the line of stonefall from those higher up.

As far as technique is concerned it is best to face outwards as long as possible, using downward pressure holds with the heel of the palms. Keep the upper body bent forward, partly to see where you are going to put your feet and partly to ensure that your weight is applied vertically downwards on to them. As the going becomes steeper it will first be necessary to turn sideways, using the inside hand, leaning out occasionally

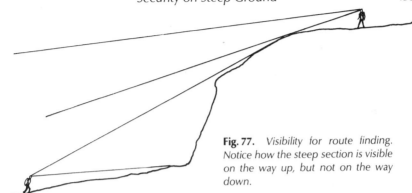

Fig. 77. *Visibility for route finding. Notice how the steep section is visible on the way up, but not on the way down.*

to get a better view of the next moves. On the steepest rock you are obliged to face the rock and go down as you would come up. Confident foot placement and balance is the key to success in mastering this difficult skill. When you are climbing up you can see the holds ahead of you. Climbing down, the holds you want to use are out of sight below your feet. This makes it peculiarly difficult to make these linked series of moves which one does almost without thinking on the way up.

Fig. 78. *Climbing down.*
(a) *easy—face out*
(b) *intermediate—face sideways*
(c) *difficult—face in*

Security on Descent

It is unrealistic to expect inexperienced hillwalkers to belay each other down steep rock. Indeed, such a practice would be extremely foolhardy. In the context of mountain walking one is talking about a relatively short section of steep rock where, because of the combination of exposure and difficulty, the leader deems it necessary to put on the rope. Under these circumstances he must come down last after he has belayed each member of the party safely down. How this is achieved depends on the circumstances, but whatever method is used, it should be used safely and swiftly—in that order.

If the party numbers less than five and is tied on to a single rope and the pitch is shorter than the length of rope separating each of them, the leader can take a belay and either lower them down in turn or secure them on a tight rope while they climb down. For a larger group, or a longer pitch, it will be necessary to tie a loop on the end of the rope and belay each person. When they get to the bottom they untie and stand well out of the way while the rope is retrieved to be attached to the next in line.

This is a time-consuming method, even when it is conducted by an experienced climber. If the pitch is short and not too difficult, a direct belay around a suitable projection can save a lot of time and effort.

Abseiling

There is a tendency in some quarters to treat abseiling as if it was a sport in its own right. It is worth remembering that every year experienced climbers are killed abseiling and often as a result of some careless elementary mistake. As a technique for descending difficult rock, it is of more practical value in the Alps and elsewhere than in the British Isles where it is normal to walk off from the top of a climb. Nevertheless, there are occasions when it may be necessary for the leader of a non-climbing party to abseil to the assistance of someone who has fallen into a position which might be difficult to reach by any other means. In a different situation it might be necessary for the leader to abseil down a pitch to get assistance to deal with an emergency. It must be stressed therefore, that in the context of hillwalking, abseiling is an emergency technique to be used by the leader of the party and not by the individual group members. It follows from this that on a real, as opposed to a training situation, a safety rope will not be available and some practice should be obtained without having the security of an extra rope from above.

Fig. 79. *Abseiling: the 'classic' method using the rope alone.*

The Classic Abseil

This is the basic method involving the use of the rope alone and all mountaineers should be familiar with it. Undoubtedly, the method has certain drawbacks, but it has the considerable merit of simplicity. Take great care in selecting a suitable anchor point for the doubled rope. It should, if possible, be above waist level and it must allow the rope to move freely when one end is pulled. This enables the rope to be retrieved from below when the abseil is completed. Test the anchor before you start by applying your full weight to the rope. One of the drawbacks of the method is that it can damage your clothing and your flesh if you are not careful. Wear your spare sweater over the top of your anorak and wrap some padding round the thigh that is going to take the rope. Wear gloves. Getting started is usually the most difficult manoeuvre and may involve climbing down a step or two until you are in a good launching position. The friction, not to mention the pain, will usually limit your speed of descent. Take it steady. Do not try to support your weight by clutching on to the rope with the upper hand. The lower hand is the one which controls your rate of descent; indeed, it may be necessary for you to feed the rope round your body to overcome the friction. Resist the temptation to try to climb down. This upsets your body position, which should be well out from the rock face with your feet pushing against the face and about 18 inches apart. Be constantly on the look out for rock loosened by the rope or by your feet and make sure that no one is standing at the bottom in the line of fire. When you get down, the rope is retrieved by pulling steadily on one end. Before doing so, separate out the two strands of the doubled rope and untie any knots.

For those who are familiar with climbing techniques and equipment, the use of sit sling and screw gated karabiner greatly facilitates the abseil. The method is identical to the classic method except that the rope passes through the karabiner instead of round the thigh.

Scree Slopes

This ubiquitous feature of mountain country can be something of a mixed blessing. Given the right size of stone in sufficient quantity it can provide an effort-free escalator ride to the bottom of the slope. Unfortunately, not all scree slopes conform to such high standards and many a sprained ankle and worse has resulted from an over-enthusiastic descent.

There are two dangers to be aware of: runaway boulders and hidden crags. The former can be avoided by keeping the party close together or by spacing individuals out horizontally. The important thing is to avoid releasing a shower of boulders on to those below. It is not unusual for a

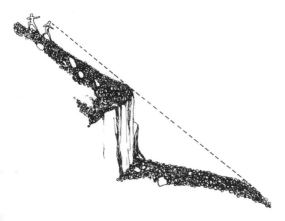

Fig. 80. *Beware! The cliff separating the scree slope is not visible from above.*

scree slope to end in a cliff which can be very difficult to pick out from above, particularly if there is a background of more scree further down.

Climbing Technique

It is one of the great joys of climbing that it is such a spontaneous and uncomplicated activity. Of course, there are techniques to learn and some modern climbing involves the use of a lot of highly specialised hardware,

Fig. 81. *Slab climbing in balance.*

but in spite of all this, down at its roots, it is very much a matter of doing what comes naturally. There are many excellent books which will explain the great variety of rock climbing techniques. That is not the purpose of this handbook. Nevertheless, there are some basic principles which, if applied to your own natural climbing style, will improve your performance and help to make you a more confident and secure leader on rock. These basic principles are:

—From the foot of the rock, work out the line you are going to follow.
—Climb in a series of continuous movements between one resting place and the next, having first worked out the sequence of moves.
—As far as possible climb in balance keeping your weight on your feet and not hanging from your arms.
—Maintain 3 points of contact with the rock, moving one hand or foot at a time.
—Keep your hands low and avoid getting spreadeagled.
—Keep your heels low with ankles flexed and watch where you are placing your feet.
—Test doubtful holds.
—Use your common sense in interpreting these principles.

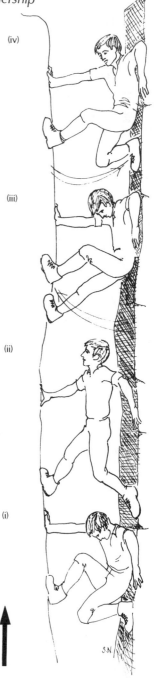

(iv)

(iii)

(ii)

(i)

Fig. 82. *Chimney climbing sequence.*
 (i) *Legs drawn up*
 (ii) *Legs straightened*
 (iii) *Left leg across*
 (iv) *Right leg back*
      Repeat sequence

Fig. 83. *Mantelshelf technique.*

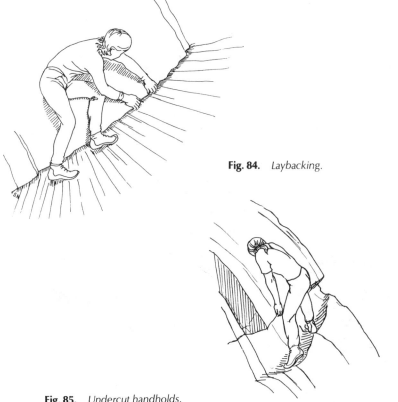

Fig. 84. *Laybacking.*

Fig. 85. *Undercut handholds.*

Negotiating a Rocky Ridge

This is without doubt one of the most testing situations for the leader; of his assessment of the surefootedness and individual competence of his party and of his judgement of the total situation, taking into account both the likelihood and the possible consequences of a slip. Remember that it is normally much more difficult to descend than to ascend a ridge, so make up your mind, before you become too committed and therefore influenced by the prospect of a difficult retreat, whether the route is within the capabilities of your party.

Fig. 86.   *The dangers of negotiating a narrow ridge.*

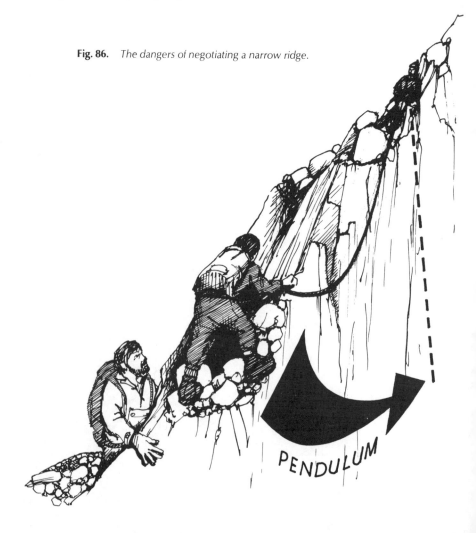

It is difficult and sometimes impossible, to provide security for a party on a ridge with precipitous flanks. If the rope is used it should be belayed by the leader who brings each member of his group in turn across the difficult section. If there are more than three or four, it will be necessary to throw the end loop back each time. Consider what would happen in the event of a fall. In the case of a horizontal ridge the victim could pendulum the full length of the rope into a position from which it could be difficult to escape. It is usually possible to flick the rope to either side of suitable projections on the ridge so that the radius of any possible pendulum is reduced to the length of rope between the climber and the projection. Take care that the projection is not too sharp and that your belay and stance will take a pull from the direction of the projection.

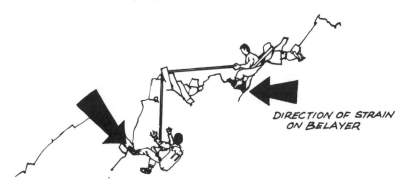

DIRECTION OF STRAIN ON BELAYER

Fig. 87. *Using intermediate projections to reduce the arc of the pendulum in the event of a fall.*

GOOD POSITION FOR LEADER

BAD POSITION FOR LEADER

Fig. 88. *Good and bad positions from which to safeguard a traverse.*

Traversing

Traversing poses a similar problem for the leader, although it is sometimes possible to climb up into a position above the traverse from where a more direct belay can be given.

Loose Rock

Handling loose rock requires a combination of personal discipline and alertness. Injuries resulting from rock fall are common and the larger the party the greater the risk. Although the leader can arrange things so as to minimise the danger, he can not eliminate it entirely. A rock does not have to be very big, or fall very far, to do a great deal of damage. Each member of the party must be responsible for exercising the greatest care in handling loose rock. Hand and footholds should be tested gently. A suspect hold must be used in a way that tends to bed it more firmly into place—downward pressure holds are generally best in this respect. Never pull outwards on a loose hold. Climb softly like a cat, but if you do knock something off and cannot stop it, give a warning shout of 'below', so that those in the line of fire can take avoiding action or get their rucksacks over their heads. If the rope is being used, be particularly careful that it does not dislodge stones lying on ledges. One of the worst places for this is often on the top of a rock pitch topped by scree.

Wet Rock

Provided the rock is clean, the fact that it is wet should not make very much difference. Rock made greasy by lichen or other vegetation is a different matter and care must be exercised, particularly on slabs, or when using sloping holds. If all else fails, climbing in stockinged feet may provide the answer although this technique is not to be recommended for all the party.

Wind

A strong wind can upset your balance and your confidence on rock. Furthermore, it can make communication difficult or even impossible. It is important, therefore, for all members of the party to be thoroughly familiar with the procedure to be followed and the system of calls and signals to be used.

6 River Crossing

Introduction

One glance at the rainfall map of the British Isles should be enough to convince anyone that mountains and rain go together and that in these islands we sometimes appear to get more than our fair share of the latter. One of the effects of this, of course, is that our mountain areas abound with streams which, in times of heavy rainfall, literally gush from the mountain sides. The evidence of the power of such streams is there for all to see, the deeply cut gorges, the waste of transported boulders and debris and yet how often do we take this into account when drawing up our expedition plans? There can be few mountain days when it is not necessary to cross a stream, however small, and even the smallest stream can become impassable when fed by torrential rain or melting snow. Almost every year someone is drowned while crossing a river which should never have been attempted. So, while the techniques of making a crossing safely are important, it is much more important to be able to make a proper assessment of the situation, including the alternatives to crossing, on which a sound judgement can be based.

Planning Ahead

There is, unfortunately, no simple relationship between the amount of rain that falls and the volume of water in the streams and the rate at which it increases. However, in the mountains, as a consequence of the relatively thin soil and vegetation cover, run-off is usually very rapid and streams can quickly become impassable. The converse is, of course, equally true, that when the rain stops the volume of water in the streams diminishes just as rapidly and this is a fact worth bearing in mind when considering alternatives. It is sensible, then, to anticipate these fluctuations in water volume and plan your route taking into account the weather forecasts, the time of year and the possibility of a spate caused by melting snow and even such events as the release of water from hydroelectric schemes. In general, the completion of your route should not require the fording of a stream which could be hazardous in conditions of high water.

To Cross or Not

Nevertheless even the most meticulous planning cannot provide for all unforeseen circumstances and eventualities. It is in the nature of mountaineering that the unexpected happens, the sudden emergency or forced change of plan which may lead you into a situation where you are faced with a difficult choice; to attempt a crossing or not? If the crossing is straightforward and there is no element of risk involved, select the most convenient place and get on with it. If, however, there is any doubt at all in your mind about the outcome, then you must carefully consider all the alternatives before committing yourself to the crossing.

As with most other aspects of mountaincraft sound judgements are based on experience and a good measure of common sense. Factors to take into account in making your assessment would include the width of the river, the depth of water, the colour or opacity of the water, the current and turbulence of the stream and the nature of the stream bed. Quite apart from these technical considerations you should reassess the physical condition of your party and ask yourself the question, 'How safe is this crossing for the most vulnerable member?' Let us assume that you have some doubts about the wisdom of attempting to ford the stream. What are the alternatives?

Alternatives

(a) First of all, a great deal will depend on the remoteness of the location. In the British Isles it is highly unlikely that the situation will make a fording imperative, and if it is then you are unlikely to have the resources necessary to make a safe crossing. You should be wary of the psychological pressures to which you will be subjected, usually in favour of crossing. After all, it is only human nature to want to get it over with, when you can see the bothy and the prospect of a hot meal just a stone's throw away. Do not be fooled!

(b) Examine the map very carefully both upstream and down. Where is the nearest bridge and what would be the implications of making a detour to it?

(c) Bearing in mind the weather forecast you could decide to wait until the water level dropped to a safe height. A long wait might mean a night out in the open. What would be the effect of a forced bivouac on your party? If you do decide to sit it out remember to mark the water level so that you have some idea of how much it has dropped during the night.

(d) If your party is fit and you have time on hand you might elect to follow the river upstream and ford the tributaries where the volume of water will be less. But how far will you have to walk and over what sort of terrain? How certain can you be of finding safe crossing points and have you the stamina to see it through? These are questions which you will have to attempt to answer.

It cannot be stressed too strongly that fording a river by whatever method, where there is some degree of risk, is an emergency procedure, only to be adopted when the alternatives to crossing are more hazardous than the crossing itself.

The 'Vee' of smooth water indicates the line of the main flow. Note the upstream eddies behind obstructions such as boulders or trees.

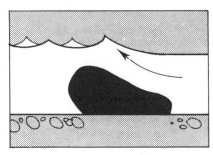

Standing waves produced by an uneven bottom.

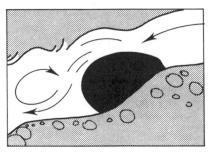

A stopper, commonly formed where there is a sharp fall in the river level, such as at a weir, waterfall, etc.

Fig. 89. *Reading moving water.*

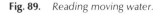

Inspection

If you decide that the river can be forded safely you will want to inspect as much of it as practicable to find the best crossing point. It is a great help to be able to interpret the surface movement of the river since this is largely determined by the nature of the bottom. The main flow of water is usually indicated by a large 'V' of smooth water pointing downstream. Large stationary 'standing waves' are the tell-tale signs of boulders on the river bed which deflect the water upwards towards the surface. They are not dangerous in themselves but they reflect an irregular bed which could make for a difficult crossing. Closer to the surface such boulders create eddies immediately downstream where the current runs counter to the main flow. Where the obstruction is large and the fall steep a vertical eddy can sometimes be formed causing a very strong back-flow towards the obstruction on the downstream side. These vertical eddies, or 'stoppers' as they are called, can be extremely dangerous since once caught in one, it can be almost impossible to escape. Submerged or partly submerged obstructions, such as tree branches, are particularly dangerous.

Provided you are moving down with the current the force of the water is not apparent. As soon as you lodge against some obstacle the full force and power of the river is brought to bear and can easily trap you.

Selection of Crossing Point

In selecting the best crossing point, these and many other factors must be carefully considered:

Look at the map again to see if it provides any helpful clues. Remember that streams wider than 8 m are shown with a double line on the Second Series, 1:50,000 maps. The 1:25,000 map may well show places where the stream is braided into a number of smaller streams which may be crossed more easily than the main stream.

It is often quite easy to ford a river near its mouth. Mountain burns running into lakes normally flatten out and consequently slow down in the last half mile or so. Generally, the water is quite deep but slow-flowing. However, great care must be taken in crossing, particularly with the non-swimmer.

The area selected should be free of obstructions, submerged or otherwise, such as large boulders or fallen trees, which could snag ropes or trap a swimmer. Avoid high banks, and make sure that the exit point is reasonable, with good access along both banks. Inspect the outflow: as far as possible it should also meet the above conditions.

Man-made obstructions such as collapsed bridges or broken down weirs provide additional and often unforeseen hazards.

The current is usually strongest on the outside of bends. Here you are likely to find undercut banks and deep, fast-flowing water which is not conducive to a safe crossing.

The river bed should be as even as possible, of uniform depth and free of boulders, rock outcrops or clinging mud. Shingle makes an ideal surface.

Do not rely on always being able to cross a river at a particular point. A rise in water level can change a safe ford into a dangerous one.

To some extent the selection of the best crossing point will be influenced by the limitations of the equipment carried by the party. If the crossing cannot be safeguarded by the use of a rope then it should be abandoned. The length of the rope itself limits the width of the river which can be crossed to one-third of the total length of the rope. Crossings wider than this can only be safeguarded by the use of some type of flotation or personal buoyancy.

Finally, you should run through in your mind what would happen if someone should fall in and be swept away. How can they be safeguarded, if at all?

Preparations

Once you have selected the crossing point you must choose the method best suited to the situation and the physical condition of the party. Do not rush. A little extra time spent on preparation at this stage is time well spent. Brief the party carefully on procedure, how to tie on to the rope if one is to be used, how to adjust clothing, how to stand against the water, what to do in the event of a fall and so on. Agree on the order of crossing and make sure that everyone knows exactly what their responsibilities are. It may be necessary to number the party or to arrange them in groups according to size and strength. Go through a dry run on the bank to make sure that the whole operation will go smoothly. A good simple system of visual communication is essential. Rivers can be noisy places, particularly if there is any white water around. If a rope is being used, clear signs are needed for taking in and letting out.

River Crossing Techniques

Many streams can be crossed without any more thought than that required to find the narrowest place to jump across. Just remember that even a $1\frac{1}{2}$ m leap may present a daunting prospect to some of your party especially if they are carrying heavy packs. In the same way, hopping from boulder to boulder may be a fine way of demonstrating your agility, but for the less able it may be the quickest way to a sprained ankle, or cracked

Fig. 90. *Crossing with the aid of a stick.*

elbow. Choose a method of crossing which is well within the compass of all the party and be particularly careful crossing on wet or greasy boulders and on cold winter days when the rocks may be glazed with ice. Better to take to the water and suffer wet feet than risk an accident trying to cross dry-shod.

If you decide to take to the water there is a basic technique for crossing which can be adapted to suit all the methods described whether roped or unroped. The first rule is to keep your boots on. They protect the feet from bruising and provide a much firmer placement than bare feet. By all means take off your stockings and keep them dry in your pack, but put your boots back on. If you have gaiters, keep them on too. They add to the protection and help to insulate the legs against the numbing cold, as well as stopping small stones from accumulating in your boots. Since remaining dry is no longer an issue, remove any overtrousers or roll them up above water level and tuck your anorak into your trousers. Baggy clothing is to flowing water what a sail is to the wind. As far as possible you want to reduce the surface area you present to the current. Keep your rucksack on, but do not secure the waist belt so that you can shed your sack in the event of a mishap. Your sack will almost certainly float. Indeed, you can ensure that it does by packing clothing, etc., in sealed polythene bags and by pulling out the bivouac extension and tying it off tightly so that it acts as an air bag. Now, if the worst should happen, you have a ready-made life raft.

In the water always face upstream with the feet half a metre apart. If you face the other way the force of the current acting on the back of the legs can cause the knees to give way. Avoid crossing your legs but rather proceed by a series of sideways shuffles making sure that one foot is firmly placed before moving the other.

Fig. 91. *'Ferry glide'.*

Try to maintain foot contact with the bed of the stream. It can sometimes help progress to stand at an angle to the current so that it pushes you in the direction you wish to go. Your back should be half turned towards the bank you are heading for to achieve this 'ferry-glide' effect (Fig. 91).

A stout stick, if available, placed upstream acts as a third leg and greatly improves stability. It can also be used to probe for depth.

Should you have the misfortune to lose your footing, shed your pack immediately, but hang on to it. It floats. Don't try to fight the current. Allow yourself to drift downstream feet first so that you can fend yourself off from rocks or obstructions using any eddies and slack water to work your way towards the bank. At all costs avoid getting caught up in submerged branches where you could easily become trapped by the force of the water.

Crossing with the Aid of a Rope

The Continuous Loop System

In this system the two ends of the rope are tied together to form a continuous loop. The length of the rope will dictate the width of stream which can be crossed. For example, a 40 m rope will enable you to cross a stream 12 m wide. Since only one rope is likely to be carried by the average party this is a limiting factor which ensures that only relatively small streams are attempted by this method. Nevertheless, a great deal of power can be concentrated into even a small mountain stream in spate. Figure 92 illustrates the method.

(a) B, who should be one of the larger and stronger members of the party, crosses first. He ties on to a slack loop keeping it high under his armpits and sets off across and slightly downstream supporting himself on the rope held by A. He should face upstream at all times. A and C should not be belayed but should pass the rope through their hands. In the event of B slipping in, he is pulled to the shore by C while A lets his rope run.

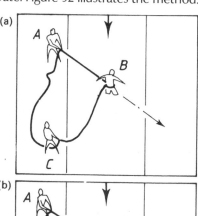

(b) On reaching the far bank B slips off his waist loop but leaves it tied to the rope for C to use. C ties on and sets off, supported by A, who should, if possible, take up a position on a suitable promontory. If C should fall in he is pulled to shore by B on the downstream side.

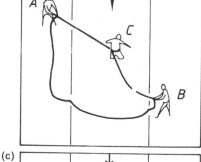

(c) Once two men are established on the far bank the method can be varied slightly to assist those who come after. B can now take up a position upstream of D who is crossing, and offer him considerably more support on the rope. Should D fall in he can still be fielded by C on the downstream side.

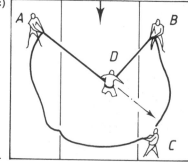

Fig. 92. *Continuous loop system.*

(d) The last man crosses in a similar manner to the first, supported by B and pulled to the bank by C should he fall in.

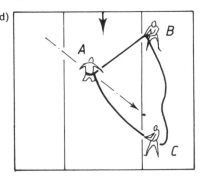

It is important that as far as possible the rope is kept clear of the water to avoid drag. To achieve this it may be necessary for other members of the party to assist those who are managing the rope.

Fig. 92. *(Continued.)*

If two ropes are available the leader and second man may cross as in Fig. 92 (a) and (b). The third, D and subsequent members of the party tie on to the middle of one rope and the end of the other as shown. D is supported by both A and B as he crosses diagonally downstream. In the event of a mishap he can be fielded by C. On reaching the far bank he unties and secures the rope from B and C to the 'tail' held by A. A then pulls all the ropes across for the next man.

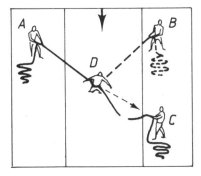

Fig. 93. *Variation of continuous loop method if two ropes are available.*

The Pendulum System

In the pendulum system, one end of the rope is held from a point upstream to provide support for those crossing. As in the continuous loop system, the first person across has the toughest job and should be the largest and strongest member of the party.

(a) B, ties into a slack loop about one-third of the total rope length from A. The tail-end of the rope is tied back into this loop to make a continuous loop. A takes up a position upstream from B, taking the rope in round any convenient anchor. If no anchor is available then other members may have to assist in holding the rope. B then crosses the stream, leaning back on the rope held by A. In the event of a slip B can be fielded on the doubled rope held by C. It is important to keep this rope clear of the water to prevent drag.

(b) Once safely across, B slips out of the loop and feeds it back to C who ties in and crosses, supported by A and belayed from both banks by B and D.

(c) At this point the pendulum rope can be transferred to the opposite bank to be held by C to assist the remaining members of the party. The pendulum effect now tends to take those crossing towards the bank they are heading for.

(d) The last man, D, crosses in the same way as the first except that the pendulum is now on the opposite bank rather than the same one.

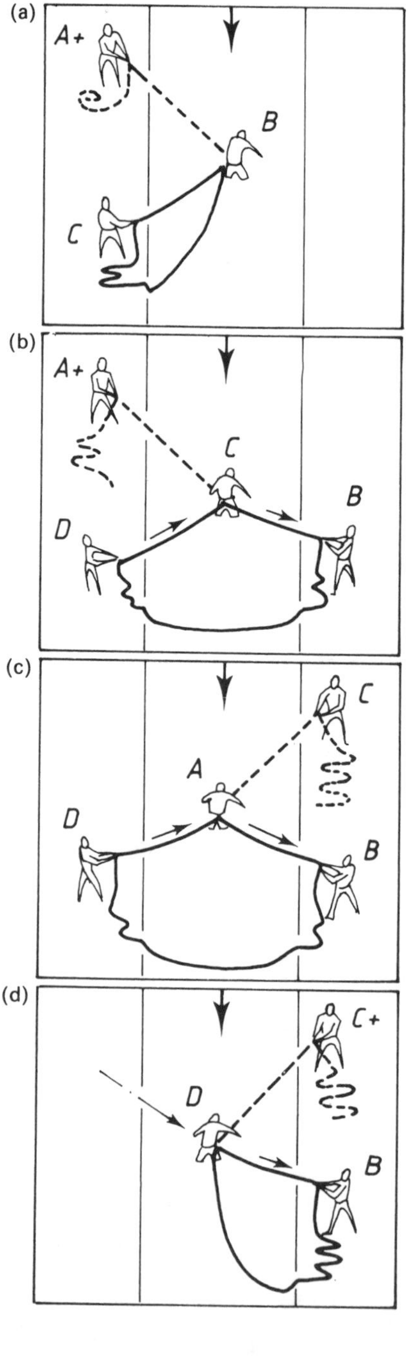

Fig. 94. *The pendulum system.*

Crossing on a Tensioned Rope

Fig. 95. *Crossing on a tensioned rope.*

Figure 95 illustrates an alternative method of getting the main body across when high banks or trees permit a single rope to be stretched taut across the river.

The leader, B, crosses in the manner previously described, tying on to two ropes instead of one.

On reaching the far bank he unties, and one of the ropes is stretched taut across the river diagonally downstream as shown and some 3 m to 4 m above the surface. Any solid anchor can be used, such as a tree or rock, provided it gives sufficient clearance. The rope can be tensioned by A and the remainder of the group using a simple pulley system.

It is vital that this rope should be tight enough not to sag into the water when holding the weight of a man at its mid point.

C then ties on to the middle of the second rope held by A and B on opposite banks. He attaches himself to the taut rope by means of a sling (or loop in his safety rope) and karabiner. For stability, he can hold on to the fixed rope and assisted by B makes his way diagonally downstream to join him. The remainder of the party cross in the same way with the exception of the last man who crosses in a similar manner to the first.

The method is effective and safe if properly rigged, but is dependent on finding suitable anchors in the right position and high enough above the river. The party must also be carrying two ropes, karabiners and slings.

Crossing without a Rope

No attempt should be made to cross a river without the security of a rope unless it is obvious that the crossing can be accomplished in complete safety. In other words the methods which are now described are appropriate for low water crossings when the consequences of a slip are likely to

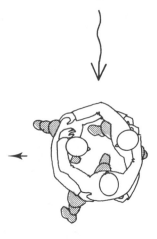

Fig. 96.   *'The huddle'.*

be no more than a wetting. The three methods all depend on the principle of mutual support and the additional stability afforded by a group configuration as compared with a single individual.

Three people, preferably of similar height, get into a huddle with their arms linked (as shown in Fig. 96). The strongest one of the three should face upstream. Holding firmly on to each other the group proceeds across the stream supporting each other when required. If the bottom is very uneven it may be necessary to move one at a time. Otherwise the group should move at the command of the leader. Take particular care when entering or leaving the stream because it is at these points that one of the team must release his grip to gain or leave the bank.

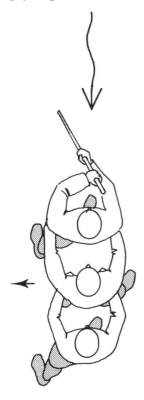

Fig. 97. *In line astern.*

A group of three or more takes up position as shown in Fig. 97, each member facing upstream and holding on to the waist of the person in front. The lead man should if possible, use a stick for support. The whole line should move sideways simultaneously, each shuffling step being co-ordinated by the leader.

F

Fig. 98. *In line abreast.*

In this method, three or more people cross in line abreast linking arms and holding on to a long branch. To present as small an area as possible to the force of the current the group faces across the stream with the branch held parallel to the banks.

Falling In

If the worst happens and you lose your footing and are swept away, remember that you are likely to remain buoyant for some time before your clothing becomes saturated. Don't panic. If you are on a rope you will either pendulum in to the bank or you will be pulled ashore on the downstream side. If you are not on a rope, take off your rucksack, but keep a firm hold on it and float feet first downstream avoiding any obstructions. Do not try to fight the current, but rather strike out across it to one bank or the other choosing a landing spot which is clear of submerged branches.

Once Across

A dry river crossing is a rare luxury. It is nearly always a cold and sometimes frightening experience. Once you and your party are safely across get your dry socks on and put on any spare clothing you may have. A hot brew at this point can be a great morale booster.

Conclusions

Streams and rivers are part of the mountain environment and learning to cross them safely is an essential element in the making of a mountaineer. Water on the move is a powerful and occasionally awe-inspiring force. Recognise this in your planning and avoid leading your party into a situation where you may be forced to consider a risky crossing as the least risky of several options. Sound judgement based on experience and a thorough knowledge of the various techniques and their limitations is the key to a safe passage. Better by far to make a lengthy detour than to risk a life in attempting a difficult river crossing.

7 Mountain Weather

Introduction

Weather is a constantly recurring theme in the conversation of the inhabitants of these islands and no more so than in the conversation and writings of those who walk and climb in the mountains. The reason is not hard to find. We are fortunate enough to live in a country which lies at a meeting place of great air masses of contrasting character which are constantly vying for supremacy in the atmosphere. The result is a constantly changing pattern of weather, softened by the more benign influence of the surrounding and relatively warm sea. The effect of mountains is to accentuate these changes and in some cases to introduce an entirely new local dimension into the general pattern. The mountaineer is immersed in weather; it is the medium within which he moves and is as much a part of his total environment as the more solid rock under his feet. At all times his comfort, and on occasion his safety, depend on it and on his ability to anticipate changes and to find an appropriate response. To equip yourself to do this you require:

(a) to be able to recognise the main pressure systems and the cloud and weather patterns associated with them;
(b) to be aware of the sources of information, including forecasts, and to be able to use and interpret them;
(c) to appreciate the effect of local conditions and altitude in modifying forecast conditions.

Finally, and most importantly, you must learn to blend your theoretical knowledge with the real-life situation on the mountain. If the wind is forecast to freshen in the afternoon, how will this affect you and your party and, as a consequence of this, do you need to modify your route? No doubt you will be asking yourself some questions such as: will it be a head-wind or a tail-wind, how strong will the wind be at 500 m, how tired is the party likely to be at this point in the day, is there likely to be any loose snow on the tops which could mean spin-drift or even white-out conditions, what will the wind chill be at 500 m? To answer these questions you need more than theory or a weather forecast. The most accurate forecast possible would not save you from benightment, unless you made that vital link between theory and practice. Fortunately, practice is not too difficult to obtain. Weather is there all the time. It can woo you with warmth and sunshine or it can be a killer. It is an ever present dimension of the outdoor scene without which our mountains would be a good deal less interesting. In more ways than one it can be said to be the icing on the ginger bread.

Fig. 99. *A satellite photograph dated March 1980 showing the general atmospheric circulation. Clouds are white, oceans dark and land surfaces grey. The Central and South American coastline is clearly visible. Notice the Great Lakes in the top centre of the photograph with the frozen surface of Hudson Bay to the north. Thick cloud associated with the depressions of the temperate latitude low pressure belt can clearly be seen.*

The Global Circulation

Every school child knows that the earth's atmosphere is constantly on the move. Photographs taken by weather satellites orbiting the earth are displayed daily on our television screens and show the swirling masses of clouds moving across the continents and seas of the world (Fig. 99). At first sight there seems to be little order in the general turbulence, but closer examination reveals a pattern which can be explained in terms of the global circulation.

The energy to drive the world's machine is derived from the sun which heats the earth's surface unevenly with the result that warm air rises at the equator and flows towards the poles at high levels, while cold air sinks at the poles and returns towards the equator at the surface. This basic vertical circulation is modified in a number of ways, and one should consider the situation in the northern hemisphere, remembering that a similar situation exists in the southern hemisphere. As the warm equatorial air moves northwards it becomes crowded because there is less room towards the pole and some of it descends where it gives rise to the subtropical high pressure belt which encircles the globe. This sinking air spreads out at the surface where it is influenced by the spinning motion of the earth which, in

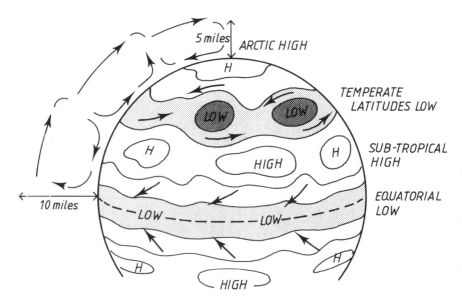

Fig. 100. *A diagrammatic interpretation of the general circulation showing the four main pressure belts in the northern hemisphere. Compare this diagram with the satellite photograph.*

the northern hemisphere, has the effect of deflecting the air to the right. Thus, air moving towards the equator is deflected to form the north-east trade winds while the air moving towards the pole is deflected to form the westerly and south-westerly winds of temperate latitudes. Air flowing outwards from the Polar high is similarly deflected to give generally north-east winds, and the boundary where these meet the warmer tropical air is known as the polar front. The fact that the British Isles lies close to the polar front accounts for many of the main characteristics of our weather. The pattern is still further modified by the effect of the great land masses which heat up and cool off much more quickly than the oceans and which, in the course of a season, can establish pressure systems which distort the general circulation. In winter the intense cooling of the atmosphere over the cold areas of Canada and Siberia causes high pressure systems to develop in these areas within the temperate low pressure belt.

Air Masses

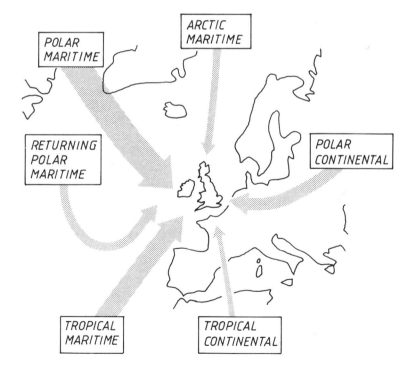

Fig. 101. *The main air streams which affect the British Isles. The width of the arrows is proportional to the frequency of occurrence.*

Air that remains in contact with a part of the earth's surface for a prolonged period of time gradually acquires the properties of that surface, notably temperature and humidity. Such stagnant oceans of air or air masses are usually to be found in the polar and sub-tropical high pressure belts. From these source regions the air flows out gently as air streams which themselves are modified by contact with the land or sea. A Maritime airstream will tend to become saturated, especially in its lower layers in contact with the ocean surface. A continental airstream on the other hand is likely to be dry. Polar or arctic air moving south is warmed from below and therefore tends towards instability. Tropical air moving north is cooled from below and tends to become more stable. It is clear then that airstreams from particular source regions have fairly distinct characteristics and it is possible to deduce the general weather pattern associated with each of them by considering the properties of the original air mass and how it is modified during its migration from the source region. But take care. Few airstreams follow such an idealised pattern and many therefore have characteristics which fall somewhere between the standard types.

Weather Associated with the Main Airstreams which Affect the British Isles

In the following diagrams the synoptic situations associated with each of the six main airstreams which affect the British Isles is illustrated, together with a brief resume of the type of weather to be expected in winter and summer in Britain.

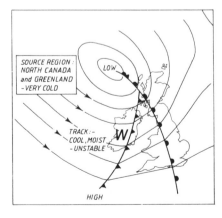

POLAR MARITIME

SUMMER: *Heavy showers, thunder storms in mountains.*

WINTER: *Heavy showers in west, snow in mountains in north-west. Clear skies in east at night giving frost. Dry in lee of mountains.*

Fig. 102. *Polar maritime, Pm.*

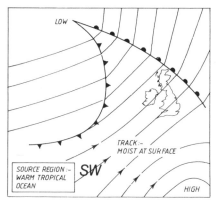

TROPICAL MARITIME

SUMMER: South-west winds. Warm and sunny inland. Low stratus clouds round west coast.

WINTER: Stratus clouds/hill fog/drizzle clearing in north-east. Warm, muggy with prolonged rainfall in westerly mountains.

Fig. 103. Tropical maritime, Tm.

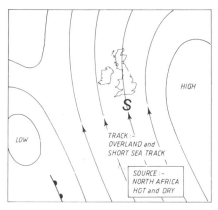

TROPICAL CONTINENTAL

SUMMER ONLY: Heat-wave weather, hazy with occasional thunder.

Fig. 104. Tropical continental, Tc.

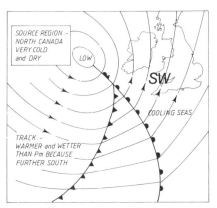

RETURNING POLAR MARITIME

SUMMER: Very warm, stratus cloud in south-west. Squally showers and storms inland.

WINTER: Stratus cloud. Showers in mountains, particularly in the west.

Fig. 105. Returning polar maritime, rPm.

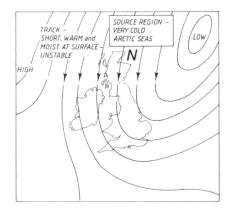

ARCTIC MARITIME

SUMMER: Very cold with frequent heavy showers.

WINTER: Very cold, strong winds from north and north-east. Heavy snow showers particularly in north and coastal areas. Cold and bright in Lake District and South Wales in lee of mountains to north.

Fig. 106. *Arctic maritime, Am.*

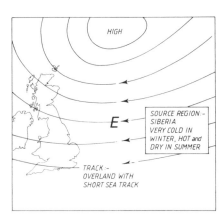

POLAR CONTINENTAL

SUMMER: Warm and dry, cloud-free, except perhaps near east coast where cool and showery.

WINTER: Snow near east coast in Kent. Occasional snow showers in west. Very cold and strong east winds.

Fig. 107. *Polar continental, Pc.*

Depressions

We have seen how the polar front separates two air masses with contrasting properties; cold polar air to the north and warm, moist 'tropical' air to the south. The line of this front is normally to be found across the North Atlantic, between Newfoundland and Iceland and it is here that the depressions, or low pressure systems, which dictate so much of our weather are born. Initiated simply as a wave in the polar front, a depression may deepen rapidly, developing a characteristic frontal pattern of its own.

It is important to appreciate that a depression is not simply a surface phenomenon and Fig. 108 attempts to illustrate its development in three dimensions. Notice how three kinds of motion are involved: the cyclonic

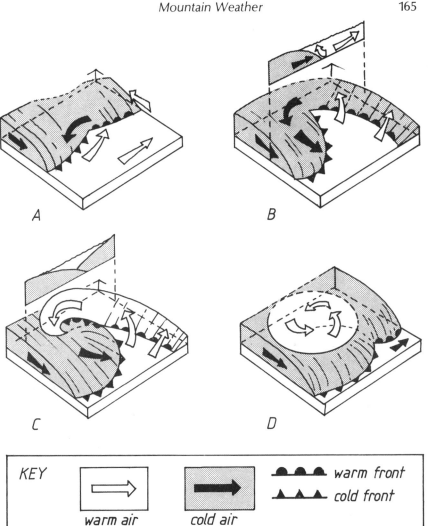

Fig. 108. *The development of a depression showing the vertical dimension, based on an illustration in* Mountain Weather for Climbers, *by D. Unwin.*

movement of air in an anticlockwise direction round the centre of the low pressure area, giving rise to the rule, 'that if you stand with your back to the surface wind, low pressure is on your left'; the upward movement of warm air drawn in at low levels (convergence) and spreading out at high levels (divergence); and the generally eastward movement of the whole system at a speed which varies between 20 km and 80 km per hour.

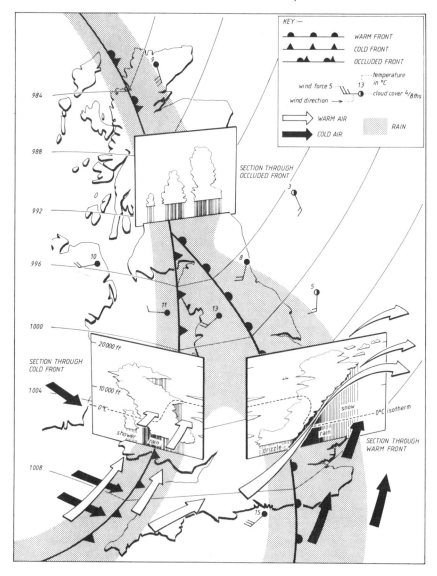

Fig. 109. *A depression crossing the British Isles—based on an illustration in* Know the Weather.

Because the cold front moves somewhat faster than the warm front, it gradually catches up and eventually overtakes it so that the warm air is squeezed upwards by the colder and denser air behind the cold front. The

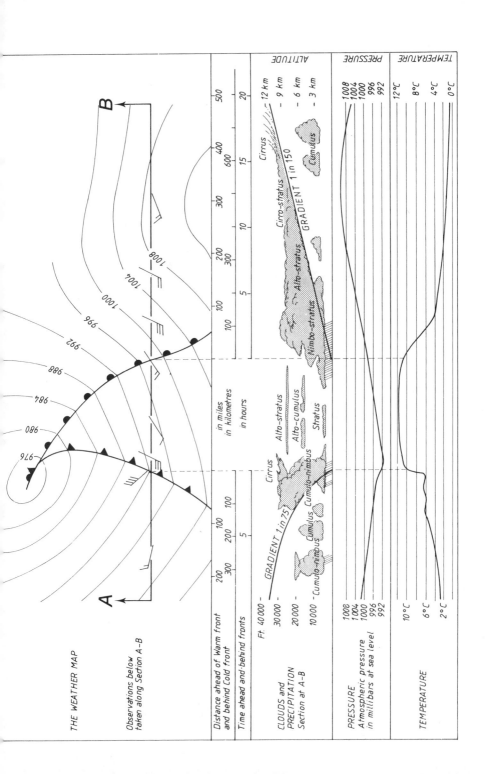

THE WEATHER MAP

Observations below
taken along Section A–B

Distance ahead of Warm front and behind Cold front		

in miles
in kilometres

Time ahead and behind fronts

in hours

CLOUDS and
PRECIPITATION
Section at A–B

Ft. 40 000 –
30000 –
20000 –
10000 – Cumulo-nimbus

ALTITUDE

Cirrus
– 12 km
– 9 km
– 6 km
– 3 km

Cirro-stratus
GRADIENT 1 in 150
Alto-stratus
Cumulus
Nimbo-stratus

Cirrus
Alto-stratus
Alto-cumulus
Stratus

Cirrus
GRADIENT 1 in 75
Cumulus Cumulo-nimbus
Cumulus
Cumulo-nimbus

PRESSURE

PRESSURE
Atmospheric pressure
in millibars at sea level

1008
1004
1000
996
992

1008
1004
1000
996
992

TEMPERATURE

TEMPERATURE

12°C
8°C
4°C
0°C

10°C
6°C
2°C

500
20
400
600
15
300
200
300
10
100
200
100
5
100

200
300
100
5
100

Fig. 111. *A satellite's view of a depression crossing to the north of the British Isles. Note the secondary depression already well established in the trailing cold front of the primary.*

Fig. 110. *Weather associated with the passage of a depression. An illustration of the weather pattern associated with a 'typical' depression moving eastwards at an average speed of 25 m.p.h. The width of the system is almost 1,000 miles, so it takes 40 hours to pass over a stationary observer. The vertical scale of the section along AB showing clouds and precipitation is greatly exaggerated in relation to the horizontal, with the result that the slope of the fronts appear much steeper than they really are. In fact, the gradient of the warm front in this example is 1 in 150, a slope of less than half a degree. One effect of this is that the first high clouds on the leading edge of the warm front may be seen by an observer many hours before the onset of rain associated with the passage of the front at the surface.*

new front so formed between the two masses of cold air is known as an occlusion. This process continues until the depression fills.

Such is the ideal life-cycle of a typical depression and it follows that certain more or less regular patterns of weather are associated with its various phases. In looking at these patterns it must be remembered that no two depressions are exactly alike. Not only do they vary in depth and character but their track in relation to the observer may be very different.

Crossed Winds Rules

It is convenient to distinguish between the lower wind which corresponds to the movement of the lowest clouds, roughly parallel to the isobars, and the upper wind as indicated by the movement of the highest clouds. It is the upper wind that is responsible for the general movement of the depression. Fig. 112 includes isobars for both these winds and it can be seen their relationship to each other depends on the position of the

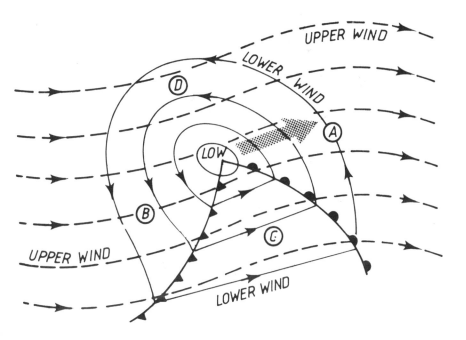

Fig. 112. *Weather map showing isobars for both upper and lower winds associated with a frontal depression.*

observer in relation to the depression. At position A, if the observer stands with his back to the lower wind the upper wind is blowing from his left. At B, if he stands with his back to the lower wind, the upper wind is from his right. At C the winds are parallel and in the same direction while at D they are parallel but blowing in opposite directions. By this means it is possible to tell where you are in relation to the centre of the depression and therefore to anticipate the next sequence of weather.

The crossed winds rules can now be stated:

(a) If you stand with your back to the lower wind and the upper wind comes from your left then the weather is likely to deteriorate. (Observer A in Fig. 112.)

(b) If you stand with your back to the lower wind and the upper wind comes from your right then the weather is likely to improve. (Observer B in Fig. 112.)

(c) If you stand with your back to the lower wind and the upper wind is behind you or ahead of you then there is likely to be little immediate change in the weather. (Observers C, D in Fig. 112.)

The wind at the surface in the vicinity of a depression blows at an angle of between 20–30° to the lower wind in the direction of the lowest pressure. So to find the lower wind turn 25° in a clockwise direction from

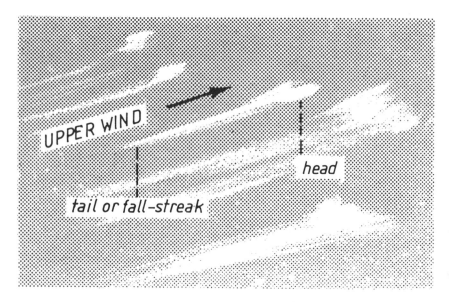

Fig. 113. *Cirrus clouds streaming in the upper wind at about 10 km altitude.*

the surface wind. The upper wind is more difficult to gauge but can be estimated by reference to medium and high cloud layers. Cirrus clouds are particularly useful indicators since they normally herald the approach of a warm front. Remember that the tails or fall-streaks stream behind and below the heads.

Some General Pointers in Anticipating the Movement of Depressions

In winter the polar front moves south, to lie roughly on a line between Florida and the south-west British Isles. The British Isles is therefore on the normal track of depressions.

If the Azores high extends northwards it pushes the polar front in the same direction. This results in better weather in the British Isles.

As a general rule, the centre of a depression will move parallel to the isobars in the warm sector and at the same speed.

A wide warm sector means that the depression is likely to continue to deepen.

Small depressions move quickly and tend to follow the main air streams.

Depressions move from areas of rising pressure tendency to areas of falling pressure tendency.

Depressions tend to follow the flow of air round large stationary anticyclones.

Families of depressions tend to follow the parent one, each new one starting further south than its predecessor.

A secondary depression tends to move with the main circulation round the primary.

Generally speaking, the future movement of a depression is an extension of its previous track.

A warm occlusion tends to follow the line of the warm front.

A cold occlusion tends to follow the line of the cold front.

As an occlusion progresses, the depression slows down and its movement becomes more erratic and may even cease altogether.

An occluded depression tends to move to the left of its original track.

Anticyclones

An anticyclone is a region of relatively high pressure, with light winds circulating in a clockwise direction in the northern hemisphere round the centre of high pressure. Two main types are recognised: cold anticyclones where the cold dense air is confined to surface levels, and warm anti-cyclones where the cold air is to be found at higher levels.

We have already seen that a semi-permanent cold anticyclone forms over Siberia in winter due to intense surface cooling. The cold dense air

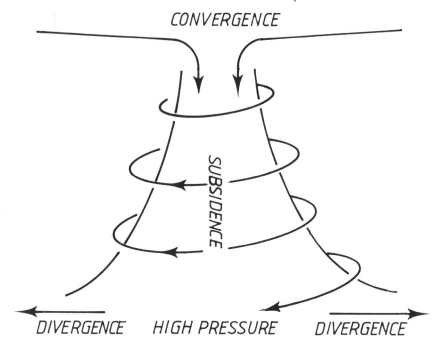

CONVERGENCE

SUBSIDENCE

DIVERGENCE   HIGH PRESSURE   DIVERGENCE

Fig. 114. *A model illustrating the main characteristics of an anticyclone.*

sinks and spreads out at the surface (divergence) while replacement air is drawn in at high altitudes (convergence). When this system extends to the British Isles it can bring bright cold weather to inland areas, although low cloud may persist round the east coast and further inland, especially in the north. Transitory cold anticyclones or ridges of high pressure commonly occur between a succession of depressions bringing a short respite from the normal pattern of frontal weather. In winter they may become established for longer periods if they extend over cold land surfaces.

Warm anticyclones are systems within the sub-tropical high pressure belt resulting from persistent convergent winds at high level. In contrast with the cold anticyclone the subsiding air within the system does not undergo any appreciable surface cooling. The Azores high is one such system and its position in relation to the British Isles has a profound effect on the type of weather we experience. In general a warm anticyclone is a stable, slow moving system, consisting of warm dry subsiding air and bringing long periods of fine clear weather. Temporary warm anticyclones can develop as extensions from the sub-tropical high or, more often,

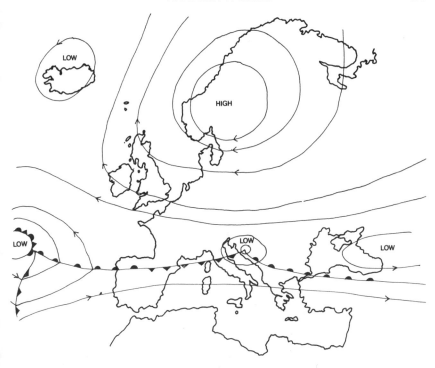

Fig. 115. *A 'blocking' high over Scandinavia which deflects the polar front and its associated depressions to the south of their normal track.*

simply as a development of a cold anticyclone where warming due to prolonged subsidence overcomes surface cooling.

Some Effects of Mountains on Weather

One of the very few reliable long term records of mountain weather in this country was compiled over a period of 21 years at the observatory on the very summit of Ben Nevis, from 1883 to 1904. It is instructive to compare this record with similar recordings made at sea level in nearby Fort William. On average Ben Nevis summit was 8·6°C colder, had only two-thirds of the sunshine and more than twice the rainfall. All this within a distance of 7 km. Combine this with an average daily wind speed of 48 k.p.h. and you have one of the most hostile environments in the world. So there is no doubt that mountains can and do have a profound effect on the weather.

Temperature

As a parcel of air rises or is forced up a mountain side, it expands because of the reduction of atmospheric pressure. Energy is required to effect this expansion and the parcel cools as it ascends. The rate at which it cools is known as the lapse rate and on average this is $-1°C$ for every 150 m of altitude. When the air is dry the lapse rate is greatest, $-1°C$ per 100 m. When the air is saturated, i.e. cloudy, it is at least, $-1°C$ per 200 m. These lapse rates are among the highest in the world and account for the very rapid fall-off in temperature with altitude, particularly in the summer months, on British hills.

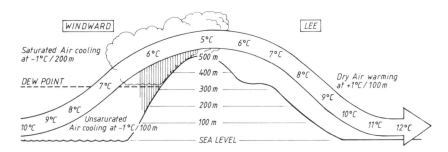

Fig. 116. *The Föhn effect. Because of the different lapse rates for saturated and unsaturated air, the air on the lee side of the mountain range is warmer than the air on the windward side. In the Alps this warm dry wind is known as the Föhn and is often associated with the onset of a wet avalanche cycle.*

Thus, if we follow our parcel of air up and over the mountain, it cools as it rises until it reaches the dew point, the temperature at which the water vapour in the air condenses into droplets. From this point upwards the air is saturated and it cools at the slower rate, possibly shedding moisture as it goes in the form of rain. Going down the lee side the air is dry and warms up as it expands at the dry lapse rate. The net effect of this passage over the mountain is that the air is both drier and warmer than on the windward side. In the Alps the difference may be substantial, but even in the British Isles the 'Föhn' effect can result in the air temperature being $1–2°C$ warmer on the east side of the highlands when a moist south-west wind is blowing.

Wind

Records from the automatic weather station on the summit of Cairngorm indicate that wind speeds are on average three times those in the adjacent Spey Valley. Wind in the mountains is indeed a force to be reckoned with, but it is not possible to establish any hard and fast relationship between altitude and wind speed. Much depends on the local topography, the direction of the wind and the atmospheric conditions prevailing at the time.

A range of mountains constitutes a barrier to the flow of air, particularly if it is orientated at right angles to the airstream. The air has only two options, to rise up and over the top of the range, or to flow round the obstacle. Both have the same effect: an increase in wind speed because of the 'overcrowding' of the air. If the airstream is stable, it will tend to flow round; if it is unstable, it will tend to rise over the range.

TEMPERATURE INVERSION

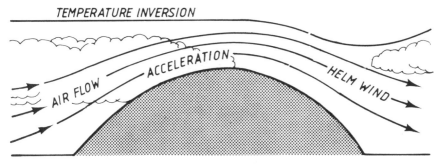

Fig. 117.   *The acceleration of air flow over a mountain barrier caused by the squeezing of air between the mountain top and the ceiling created by a temperature inversion.*

The funnelling effect of mountains and valleys is well known in the Lake District and other groups of hills, giving rise to greatly enhanced wind speeds particularly at the valley heads. Perhaps the best known example of this is the 'Mistral', a wind which blows down the narrow Rhone valley between two mountain blocks and out into the Mediterranean (Fig. 118).

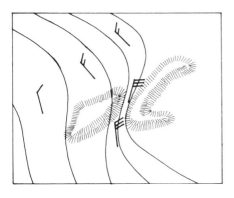

Fig. 118.   *'The Mistral', a strong northerly wind, captured by the mountain barriers on either side of the Rhone and funnelled into its valley.*

Battling against the Wind

Battling against a strong head wind greatly increases energy production and may lead to the early onset of exhaustion. It is not generally realised that a wind blowing against an object exerts a force roughly proportional to the square of its velocity. A light breeze of 5 m.p.h. exerts a force of 0·1 lb per sq. ft. But if the wind increases to 20 m.p.h., the pressure exerted is about 2 lb per sq. ft and rises to approximately 12 lb per sq. ft when the wind reaches 60 m.p.h. In simple terms if the wind speed increases by a factor of 3 from say, 10 m.p.h. to 30 m.p.h., then the force exerted by the wind increases by a factor of 9.

Local Heating and Cooling Effects

Air is warmed or cooled by contact with the ground. If the ground is warm, as it would be on the rocky mountain tops on a hot summer day, the surface air tends to rise relative to the colder free air at the same level. This causes a gentle upslope breeze from the valley known as an anabatic wind. Sadly, such winds are not frequent or of much significance in the mountains (Fig. 119).

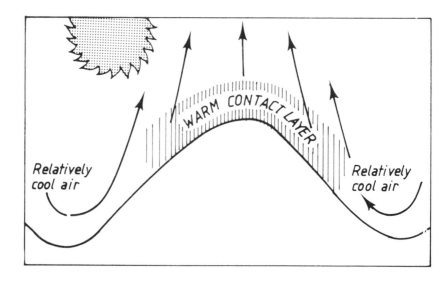

Fig. 119. *Anabatic or valley winds caused by intense solar heating during the day.*

Of much greater significance are the cold winds which pour off the mountains, usually at night, when surface air is cooled by contact with the cold ground which has lost heat by radiation into clear skies. In favourable circumstances these katabatic winds can attain gale force although in the British mountains speeds in excess of 5 m.p.h. are uncommon. Even very gentle down-slope movement of cold air is sufficient to cause it to accumulate in valley bottoms and hollows where the temperature may well reach many degrees below that on the hillsides above. These are the frost hollows and fog belts which the camper avoids if he wants a comfortable night.

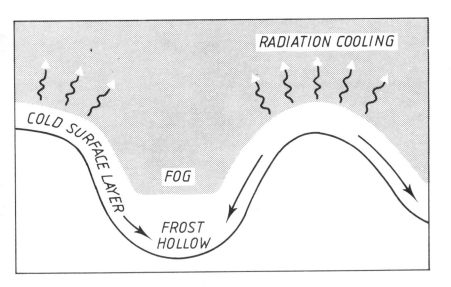

Fig. 120. *Katabatic winds pouring off the snow covered hills at night filling the valleys with cold air and causing intense frost and morning fog.*

Precipitation

You could be excused for thinking that Fig. 121 is a simple contour map showing the high ground in the British Isles. In fact, it is a map showing the average annual rainfall which almost exactly reflects the main mountain features. Increase in altitude not only means an increase in the frequency of rainfall, but also an increase in its intensity. For example, the yearly average of hours of rainfall in the north-west highlands is four times that in the Moray Firth area on the east coast. However, within this period, nine times the amount of rain actually falls. In other words, in the mountains

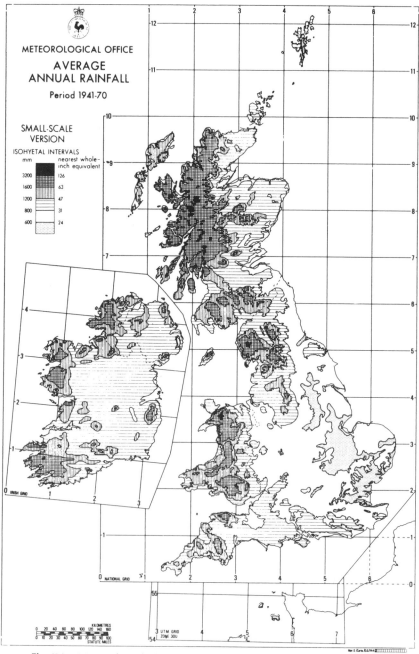

Fig. 121. *Meteorological Office map showing average annual rainfall, 1941–70.*
Reproduced with the permission of the Meteorological Office Crown Copyright.

not only does it rain more frequently but also much more heavily. Perhaps a more valid comparison can be made between the 4·35 m of rain which falls on the summit of Ben Nevis and the 2·05 m which falls at Fort William. In this case it is estimated that more than half the precipitation on the summit falls as snow.

The fundamental reason for the increase in rainfall with altitude is that moist air is lifted in its passage across a range of hills and in so doing is cooled to the point where condensation takes place and cloud forms. If the cloud is thick enough raindrops form, encouraged by turbulence within the cloud itself. This apparently straightforward process is, in reality, much more complex and local conditions and topography can have a considerable influence on the distribution and intensity of rainfall. A number of areas, such as the head of Borrowdale in the Lake District, are renowned for exceptionally heavy rainfall due to the convergence of air currents in the valleys leading to the mountain heartland. As we have seen the converse is also true when air spreading out and subsiding after crossing a mountain range can give rise to warmer conditions and clearer skies. When a cold front crosses the mountains and comes into contact with this warmer air, more severe conditions may be expected because of the heightened contrast between the two air masses. Following the same reasoning, a warm front would be weakened as a result of reduced contrast. In winter, the air in the lee of a mountain range tends to be colder because of clear skies and overnight cooling by radiation. Thus, more severe weather can be expected from the passage of a warm front and less severe from a cold front.

Quite often there appears to be a slowing down of a front as it crosses a mountain barrier, particularly if it happens to be a slow-moving occluded front. When this happens rainfall is likely to be more prolonged and intense on the windward side of the front than would otherwise be

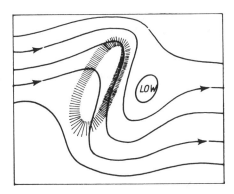

Fig. 122. *An orographic low forming in the lee of a mountain barrier.*

expected. Finally, it should be mentioned that under certain favourable conditions areas of low pressure can form in the lee of mountains.

Unlike normal depressions these 'orographic lows' are characterised by descending air warmed by the Föhn effect and are therefore likely to give rise to warm dry conditions in summer and cold frosty conditions in winter. They form most readily in the lee of the more substantial mountain ranges of Europe.

Weather Forecasting

There are many sources of weather information and the user should be aware of the limitations of various methods of presentation.

Press Forecasts

These are unsuitable for detailed up-to-date forecasts for individual localities and are only useful if they include actual weather maps giving the broad scale synoptic pattern, i.e. location of main centres of high and low pressure, weather fronts, etc. However, by the time you see a chart in a newspaper the synoptic features might have changed considerably and some totally new centre of pressure or front might well have appeared.

Television Forecasts

Again these are only of limited value in that the forecast is dealing with expected weather patterns some 24 hours ahead and can only give the generalised forecast for relatively large areas.

Radio Forecasts

Weather forecasts are broadcast regularly in the various BBC services. On the whole they are for short periods only, mainly designed to give general guidance and certainly not applicable to mountain areas without careful interpretation and supplementary data. The shipping forecast which is broadcast on BBC2, 693 kh long-wave, is exceptional in that it provides detailed information including actual observations from coastal stations, from which it is possible, not only to draw up a synoptic chart with isobars covering the whole of the British Isles, but also to draw a similar forecast chart for 24 hours ahead. This forecast situation can then be used to provide the base from which it should be possible to develop a clearer idea of what is likely to happen in the mountains.

Recorded Weather Forecasts

These are regional or local forecasts which can be obtained by dialling a number which is linked with an automatic answering service which supplies a pre-recorded forecast for a specific area. In general such forecasts should be used with caution when making decisions concerning mountain activities. This is particularly the case in periods of unsettled weather, but in some areas, such as the Lake District, there is a special Dial-the-Weather service provided for walkers and climbers, Even so, such forecasts should always be supplemented by further information if there is any element of doubt.

In some districts, such as the Cairngorms, mountain activity and climbing centres display forecasts which have been issued by the regional Meteorological Office (in this case the Glasgow Weather Centre) for the particular district. These forecasts can be very helpful, but it must be remembered that there is an inevitable time-lag between the weather chart(s) on which they are based, and the time when they go on display, so that the forecast becomes more and more out of date as each hour passes. When the weather situation is reasonably straightforward this is usually not very important but, during periods of unsettled weather and rapidly developing weather systems, a check should always be made if the forecast appears to be going awry.

The best way of obtaining weather information is a direct call to the Meteorological Office listed in the local telephone directory as the source of weather information. When making the call ask to speak to the forecaster and then outline briefly, but clearly, what you propose to do and when you propose to do it. This enables the forecaster concerned to phrase his reply in the most helpful way and to concentrate on the more important features of the forecast. It is a good plan to obtain a preliminary forecast the evening before and say that you will ring again at a certain time early the next morning to obtain an up-to-date forecast. Please remember to avoid duplication of requests for information caused by more than one person telephoning for what is basically the same forecast.

It must always be borne in mind that the network of reporting stations in mountainous regions is very sparse and thus it is sometimes difficult for a forecaster to be aware of the details of the actual weather prevailing at a given time over a mountainous area. If this is the case then obviously it becomes even more difficult to issue a detailed forecast. Thus it might well be that if you are actually up in the mountains at the time of the telephone contact, then you might be able to supply some very helpful clues about the actual conditions prevailing in your locality at that particular time. Any forecaster will welcome reliable information about current mountain weather within the district for which he forecasts and might well modify his interpretation of the situation in the light of such extra information.

Local On-the-Spot Sources of Information

Local people who have lived in a mountainous district for some time and whose daily activities take them out of doors, learn a great deal about local peculiarities of the weather. Their advice should always be listened to, especially when combined with an up-to-date appraisal of the synoptic weather chart situation as given by a Meteorological Office forecaster.

Lightning

Lightning can hardly be regarded as a major mountain hazard yet every year it claims the lives of two or three mountaineers. Like the winter avalanche it is commonly regarded as an Act of God and the very impartiality with which it chooses its victims encourages a fatalistic outlook among climbers and walkers. The actual physical process is now fairly well understood and this emphasises that there are certain simple precautions which can be taken to avoid a strike.

The first thing to realise is that to be 'struck' by lightning is by no means always fatal. True, a direct hit is likely to be so, but more often than not the victim receives only a part of the stroke, either by induction, because he happens to be standing near, or through the ground in the form of earth currents which dissipate, like the roots of a tree, from the source. Such partial shocks need not be fatal though they could, of course, cause death indirectly if the climber should fall off or be rendered incapable of fending for himself. The stroke itself is a variable quantity, being the product of a very large current (thousands of amps) and a very short time (thousandths of a second). In many cases a much smaller current in contact for a few seconds could cause considerably more damage.

Fortunately, there is usually some advance warning of the approach of an electrical storm and avoiding action can be taken, but once in the firing line decisions tend to be taken out of your hands. Anyone who has experienced the literally hair-raising preliminaries will vouch for this. Ice axes hum and spark, the skin tingles and local projections glow with a bluish light.

Lightning is usually associated with the towering cumulonimbus type of cloud which heralds the passing of a cold front. The occasional flash followed by a roll of thunder should be warning enough that an electrical storm is on its way. The sound will travel at a speed of 1 km per 3 seconds, so by timing the interval between the flash and the thunder you can estimate your distance from the storm.

During a storm, strikes tend to be concentrated on mountain tops or other natural projections from the general surroundings. At the same time, since such points 'service' a fairly wide area, there tends to be a shaded or

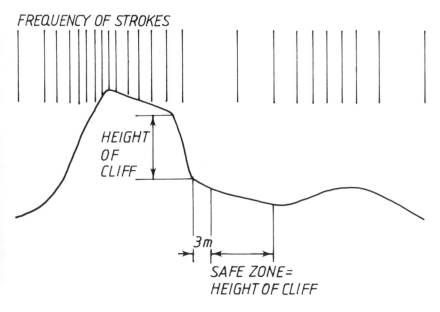

Fig. 123. *Frequency of 'strokes' in mountain area.*

relatively safe zone associated with them. The peak must be at least 7 m high and the relatively safe zone is of the same order horizontally (Fig. 123). Note that it affords no protection to be tucked in against the cliff or peak itself since in this position you are likely to receive earth currents shed from the peak.

The natural inclination in a really violent storm is to seek shelter, especially if rain is driving down. Unfortunately, this is quite the wrong thing to do unless you can find a cave which gives you at least 3 m head room and 1 m on either side. Such caves and hollows in the rock are often simply local expansions of natural fissures. These in turn are the likely conduits for earth currents, especially if they hold water and by sheltering in them you are offering yourself as a convenient alternative to the spark gap (Figs. 124 and 125).

Exactly the same argument applies to sheltering under large boulders. With reasonably waterproof clothing, remaining dry should not be a major problem and it is much safer to sit it out in the open. Try to find a broken scree slope, preferably in a safe zone and sit on top of a dry rope or rucksack with your knees up and your hands in your lap (Fig. 126). Do not attempt to support yourself on your hands or by leaning back. The object of these precautions is to keep your points of contact with the ground as

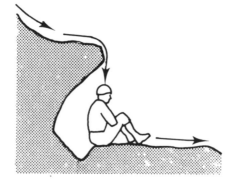

Fig. 124.   *Spark gap.*

Fig. 125.   *Danger under boulder.*

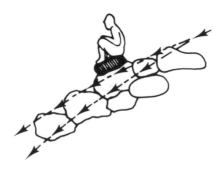

Fig. 126.   *Safe position.*

close together as possible and in such a position that a current flowing along the ground would tend to pass through a non-vital part of the body.

On a cliff face sit out the storm on the nearest ledge, but avoid chimneys and fissures of any kind. If a belay is necessary, try to avoid using the wet rope as a natural lead from a vertical crack to your body. On an exposed peak or ridge your position is much more serious and it is normally advisable to make some attempt to get at least part way down even at the height of the storm. Abseiling in an electrical storm is a risky manoeuvre, but it is normally preferable to a position on the lightning highway of an exposed ridge. In any event, one or two rope lengths may well take you to a position of relative safety. If you do abseil, use a dry rope if you have the choice and use a safety rope. Fatal accidents have often resulted from a non-fatal strike which, in the first instance, has merely stunned the victim.

It is fashionable, too, to discard pieces of extraneous equipment; cameras, rucksacks, crampons and even ice axes, under the mistaken impression that they 'attract' lightning. They don't, any more than you do yourself. The electrical resistance of the average wooden shafted axe between head and spike is almost five times that of the human body. If it is humming and sparking it may be prudent to lay it down carefully beside you, but no more. The axe is too valuable a tool to be tossed away in a storm. It may well be needed to deal with icy rocks on the retreat.

8 Mountain Hypothermia

Causes and Avoidance

Mountain hypothermia is the name given to the condition which arises when the vital core of the human body is cooled as a result of exposure to adverse conditions in the mountains. Formerly the complex of symptoms was known as 'exposure', but it is now suggested that this term is more properly applied to exposure to the environmental conditions which give rise to hypothermia.

It is a topic which has aroused a great deal of interest and research over the years, stimulated by a number of tragic accidents to young people involved in officially sponsored expeditions. On the whole, the young are particularly vulnerable to hypothermia. Their physical and mental reserves are less than adults and for this reason great care must be taken in the planning and execution of any expedition to ensure that they are not overstretched. There has been a welcome decline in recent years in the number of reported cases of hypothermia and some of the credit for this must go to those who have worked to increase the awareness of leaders of the dangers to groups of young people exposed to wet cold conditions on the British hills and moors. Such conditions are commonplace and can be every bit as lethal as the more obviously cold, dry arctic conditions, particularly when coupled with exhaustion. Improvements in the design and quality of clothing has also had a beneficial effect and it is fortunately rare nowadays to see parties setting out for the hills inadequately clad. Indeed, the converse is sometimes the case, with groups labouring under an unnecessary burden of 'emergency' gear, sufficient to ensure that it will almost certainly be needed.

Man is a homeotherm. That is to say, he endeavours to maintain a constant body temperature irrespective of the temperature of his surroundings. In a cold climate he achieves this by a combination of heat production and heat conservation, both processes being controlled partly by involuntary and partly by behavioural mechanisms.

The human body may be conceived as consisting of an inner 'hot' core surrounded by a cool outer shell. The core consists of the brain and other vital organs of the body, including the heart, lungs, liver, kidneys, etc., contained within the skull, chest and abdomen. The temperature of the core is maintained at a constant 37°C. The shell is what is left: the skin, fat, muscle and limbs, and is normally found to be 3°–5°C cooler than the core.

The CORE consisting of brain, lungs, heart, and other vital organs.

The SHELL consisting of the limbs, skin fat, muscle.

Fig. 127. *The core and shell concept of heat regulation in the human body.*

In a cold environment, therefore, the shell may be regarded as a buffer zone between the core and the outside world, protecting the organs of the body which are necessary for survival from any potentially catastrophic fall in temperature. It is helpful to visualise the boundary between these two areas as an elastic arrangement whereby in cold conditions the core contracts and in warm expands into the shell.

Hypothermia is the name given to the condition which arises when there is a progressive fall in core temperature which, if not checked, leads to unconsciousness, respiratory and cardiac failure and death. One of the quickest ways of cooling the human body is to immerse it in cold water and it is common knowledge that survival at sea in cold arctic water without special insulation can be measured in a matter of minutes. In the mountains the situation is different. Here, cold alone rarely kills, but combined with physical exhaustion it can kill just as surely as the arctic ocean. It may take longer, but the end result is the same.

It is the combination of exhaustion, cold, anxiety or mental stress which is especially dangerous. The elements in this combination will vary greatly with the individual, as will the individual's susceptibility to some or all of these factors. In considering exposure to cold, it is well to bear in mind what was written by the late Mr D. G. Duff, F.R.C.S., himself a mountaineer and rescuer of long experience. 'It is, I consider, the additional factor of physical exhaustion over and above cold which kills quickly. Death has

G

overtaken whole parties who, thinking they must keep moving at all costs, have "bashed on" instead of resting in some shelter before exhaustion supervenes. When the bodies of the victims are finally recovered, it is not uncommon to find that they carried the means of survival with them to their deaths: tents, sleeping bags, spare clothing, food. The essential is always to preserve a sufficient reserve of energy in severe conditions of cold and high wind.'

As a rider it may be added that, as with an injured and immobilised climber in the mountains, cold may kill a person who is not, as' such, physically exhausted. In this condition, however, the climber would certainly be suffering from shock and would therefore be much more susceptible to the effects of cold. Everything should be done to minimise shock and to allay his fears. It is emphasised that the risk of death from hypothermia is a real and often unrecognised danger among those, particularly the young, undertaking mountain expeditions in severe weather conditions.

Causes of Mountain Hypothermia

The causes of mountain hypothermia may be considered in two categories: those factors which relate to the individual and those which relate to the environment.

ENVIRONMENTAL FACTORS

Windchill
In the dry cold environment the factors to be considered are air temperature and wind speed, the combined cooling effect of which is known as windchill. For any given air temperature the cooling effect (windchill factor) increases rapidly with increasing wind speed. This is most marked at lower wind speeds, so that, in the range 0–24 k.p.h. (0–15 m.p.h.) even small changes in wind speed can have a profound effect on the degree of cooling. At wind speeds above 24 k.p.h. (15 m.p.h.) the factor changes more slowly. This does not mean that high winds can be discounted in other respects. A great deal more energy is required to fight against a 100 k.p.h. (60 m.p.h.) wind than a 24 k.p.h. (15 m.p.h.) one.

Charts such as this, however, should not be taken too literally. They serve to remind us that even a gentle breeze can have a dramatic effect on how cold we feel. Good windproof clothing is therefore essential if the worst effects of windchill are to be avoided.

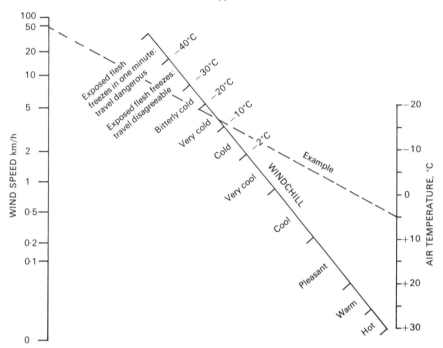

Fig. 128. *Nomogram showing effect of wind speed and air temperature on wind chill.*

Figure 128 illustrates the cooling effect of different combinations of air temperature and wind speed on a normally clad hillwalker. The degree of windchill is represented by the subjective sensation of cold experienced by the walker. In the example given, when the air temperature is +5°C and the wind speed 50 k.p.h. (31 m.p.h.) the windchill is described as 'very cold'.

This can be expressed in a different way by calculating how cold it would have to be if there was no wind at all, to achieve the same cooling effect. In other words the equivalent temperature in still air. These still air temperatures are shown on the chart opposite the descriptive classification. In this example, the temperature in still air would have to be − 12°C to have the same cooling effect as + 5°C in a 50 k.p.h. (31 m.p.h.) wind.

Wet Cold

Protection from the wind alone is not enough. Most cases of exposure in the mountains of the UK occur in wet cold conditions and it is astonishing that in a country with such a high annual rainfall more attention has not been directed towards remaining dry. Even the best clothing suffers an enormous loss of its insulating efficiency when it becomes saturated, and in a wind, heat loss is further accelerated by convection and evaporation. Complete waterproofing brings its problems, but these can, at least in part, be overcome by good design.

Individual Factors

Insufficient or Inadequate Clothing
It follows from the above that clothing should offer a reasonable degree of independence from the environment. A waterproof anorak (and therefore also windproof) is a 'must' and there are many well designed, inexpensive 'cagoules' on the market. Sweating can be a problem, but the design should allow for a considerable degree of ventilation: this keeps condensation to a minimum and at the same time allows for a complete weather seal in severe conditions Careful regulation of pace uphill and of the amount of clothing worn helps to avoid discomfort. In recent years a great deal of research has gone into the manufacturing of materials which are waterproof but which will allow the outward passage of water vapour. Such materials are now available and, though expensive, they do provide some solution to one of the most intractable problems for the mountain walker: how to keep out the rain and avoid getting wet from condensation at the same time. What you wear underneath your anorak is largely a matter of personal taste provided you have enough to afford the right level of insulation to match the conditions. The fundamental principle is that these underlayers should trap a layer of warm air next to your skin. For this purpose it is still hard to improve on wool, which has the added advantage of retaining most of its insulating qualities when wet. On the whole it is better to wear several layers of thin sweaters rather than one thick one. This allows you to ring the changes to suit the conditions as well as providing a kind of air sandwich which improves insulation.

A comprehensive range of clothing and equipment for different expeditions in summer or winter is given in Appendix III. It is, however, worth drawing attention to the fact that an enormous amount of heat can be lost from the thighs and also from the head, both parts of the body that are all too commonly ignored as far as adequate cover is concerned. Some fashion trousers provide minimal protection when wet. The range and design of protective clothing nowadays is such that it is inexcusable for groups to set out inadequately clad. It is the leader's responsibility to see that each person in his charge is wearing or carrying sufficient clothing to afford adequate protection in the event of bad weather.

It is important to realise that the clothing of growing children is rarely of comparable quality and fit to that of adults. Due allowance should be made for this and clothing and boots carefully checked before departure.

Exhaustion

This may be caused either by attempting too much or by not eating sufficient food to replace the energy used. Exhaustion in itself is a dangerous condition since it implies that the body is quite unable to mobilise any further reserves of energy either to do physical work, in other words to carry on, or even to maintain normal body temperature against the sapping of the environment. A man engaged in heavy manual work expends something between 16·8 and 18·0 megajoules (MJ) per day (1 MJ = approximately 250 kilocalories (kcal)). The mountain equivalent of this is a 20 km walk involving 750 m of climbing. In fact a fairly normal sort of mountain day.

Quite clearly, an expenditure of the order of 16·8 MJ (4,000 kcal) of energy per day is going to require good training and an adequate food intake, especially if this level of output is to be maintained for any length of time, as on an expedition, for example. This does not include any allowance for difficult terrain, weather and load carried, all factors which could add substantially to the total energy demands. There are, of course, energy reserves in the body but you cannot go on drawing on them indefinitely. Sooner or later they have to be topped up by a period of rest and recuperation. Over a period of time routes and expeditions should be planned so as to avoid making excessive overall demands, especially on young people whose working capacities may be as little as 50% of those of adults. Start in a modest way with expeditions in the 8·4 MJ (2,000 kcal) range or less and gradually build up to more ambitious projects. Exhaustion is always a possibility, but it becomes a probability if routes demanding more than 18·9 MJ (4,500 kcal) are tackled without adequate preparation and training. Know the individual capabilities of your party and plan accordingly.

Mention has already been made of the importance in time and distance calculations of making due allowance for weather, terrain, load carried and the general level of fitness of the party (Navigation, page 1). These variables can be accommodated in the chart (Fig. 129) (Aldridge, Waddell, Tranter), which offers a convenient method of estimating both the energy demands and the total time taken for expeditions of varying lengths. Note that it also provides a rough guide as to what is beyond the capabilities of parties with different levels of fitness.

A good balanced diet providing about 16·8 MJ (4,000 kcal) per day is essential and this should include a high energy lunch snack to be taken on the hill in addition to the personal emergency ration which, of course, must be kept in reserve.

Fat is the most energy dense form of food and the typical 'fry-up' breakfast will provide a significant proportion of these 16·8 MJ (4,000 kcal), but it must be borne in mind that fatty foods take longer to digest than

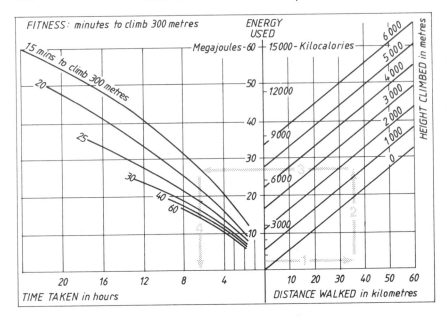

Fig. 129. *Expedition time chart.*
Condition lines: These represent different fitness ratings as measured by the time taken to climb 300 m in 800 m horizontal distance at a normal pace, i.e. 15 minutes is super-fit and 50 minutes is unfit.

Start at the bottom right-hand side of the chart with the 'corrected' distance, i.e. the total distance across country plus three-quarters of the total distance on roads. Follow the arrow vertically until you intersect with the line representing the total height climbed. From this intersection move horizontally towards the centre line and read off the energy expenditure. Continue leftwards to meet your particular 'Condition' line; adjusted, of course, to take account of load, terrain and weather (see 'Corrections to Naismith's Rule', page 37). If you run out of 'Condition' lines or if you do not meet your line because it stops short the trip must be regarded as too arduous. From this point descend vertically to the base line to read the estimated time in hours.

Note: To convert kcal to MJ, multiply by 0·0042.
To convert MJ to kcal, divide by 0·0042.

carbohydrates. Thus, a heavy fatty breakfast followed by violent exercise may produce adverse effects. Carbohydrate foods provide less energy weight for weight compared with fats, but their energy is made available more quickly. The best solution is to have a breakfast of carbohydrates and fatty foods followed up by a series of high carbohydrate snacks during the day. Sugars are absorbed more quickly than starches, so confectionery, chocolate, jams, honey, etc., should be included.

Sex and Physique

It is a fact that on the whole women are able to tolerate the effects of exposure better than men. This is due in part to better insulation provided by a thicker layer of subcutaneous fat and also to greater tolerance of physical stress. To a certain extent these advantages are offset by the fact that a woman's working capacity is, on average, some 30% less than a man's. Thin people and those with a poor strength-to-weight ratio are susceptible to hypothermia.

Lack of Training and Conditioning

The importance of training and of a gradual build-up towards more ambitious expeditions has already been stressed. Overestimation of fitness and underestimation of time are all too common causes of accidents. Where large groups are concerned it is obviously better to arrange people into fitness groups according to their condition times than to cater for all on the basis of the lowest common denominator. The latter policy, apart from being bad for the morale of all concerned, leads to the dangerous situation whereby the weak can be pushed too far and the strong barely kept at 'tick-over'.

In addition to improving the physical performance of individuals, training should be designed to familiarise the group with the range of difficult conditions which may be expected and so condition them to a certain extent both mentally and physically against hardship and discomfort. Such conditioning is of proven value in cold climates and there is no doubt that it helps to maintain a high level of morale in your own.

Dehydration

Perhaps because water is so plentiful in Britain we tend to ignore the fact that it is a vital ingredient of our diet. Normal consumption is about $2\frac{1}{2}$ litres per day, but in a hot climate and when engaged in hard physical work it can rise to five times this amount. There is a general reluctance among walkers and climbers to drink water on the hill. This seems to be due to vague fears of pollution, stomach cramps and other debilitating effects, most of which are imaginary. Water is required and the more work done, the more water is necessary. Roughly speaking about $\frac{1}{2}$ litre is required for each 1,000 kcal of energy expended in winter and about double this in summer. The 20 km mountain walk involving 750 m of ascent previously referred to demands an expenditure of 4,400 kcal and a water requirement in summer of 4 litres. It is of course possible to go into water debt and replenish stocks at the end of the day, but if the expedition is a long one this could be a dangerous policy. It is better to keep pace with the needs of the body and drink when the opportunity presents itself, 'little and often' being the best maxim to follow. On a long expedition, salt lost through sweating should also be replaced to avoid muscle cramp. Serious dehydration leads to a decrease in physical and mental efficiency and lowers resistance to exhaustion.

Morale
This is something of an unknown quantity. Certainly it cannot be measured and yet it is one of the most significant contributory factors to exposure. Apprehension, fear and a spirit of hopelessness can induce a state which, if not checked, can spread through a party like a bush fire. Apprehension itself is of some short term benefit in meeting a difficult situation, since its effect is to increase the activity of certain organs of the body, including the heart. However, if this keyed-up condition is sustained for a long period, it drains the energy resources of the body and leads to exhaustion. Furthermore, the improved peripheral circulation results in cooled blood being returned to the core, and in this way accelerates the loss of body heat. Confident and cheerful leadership should be the keynote with a wary eye and ear for the first sign of depression or panic. This does not mean that in a tricky situation the leader should pretend that nothing is wrong but rather that he should inspire the confidence and the willingness to co-operate among his charges that is necessary for a successful outcome.

Illness, Injury
A recent illness, such as an attack of 'flu, or even feeling a bit off-colour, predisposes a person to hypothermia and such people should not be put at risk. A period of running-in is essential before the full working capacity can be regained. Shock is present to some degree in each case of injury and it is important to treat the patient for this as well as for his injuries. A person in a state of shock is much less able to combat the effects of cold and maintain his body temperature. He is in fact halfway towards hypothermia already and must be protected from the rigours of the environment by all means at your disposal.

Recognition and Treatment

Symptoms of Hypothermia

It would be foolish to regard everyone who felt a bit cold or tired in the mountains as suffering from hypothermia. Nevertheless, the symptoms are ordinary enough at first, becoming more pronounced and easily recognisable as the condition becomes more severe. As the severity increases, so it becomes more difficult for the exposed person to be rational about his situation and take the necessary steps to halt the downward spiral. It is critically important to be able to recognise the early stages of hypothermia and take immediate action to reverse the process, even if that involves a delay or a change of plan. The more thoroughly the leader knows the individual members of his party, the more likely he is to separate the genuine from the feigned and recognise the warning signs for what they are.

At first, then, it is a matter of feeling cold and tired with perhaps some numbness of the hands and feet and intermittent bouts of shivering. Shivering is an involuntary response of the body to increase its heat production by a series of rapid oscillatory contractions of groups of muscles. None of these symptoms are in themselves particularly significant, but if left unattended they could progress towards true hypothermia. Continued exposure brings on more general and sometimes uncontrollable shivering. This is an indication of a more serious state of affairs and one or more of a range of other symptoms are now likely to appear:

Unexpected and apparently unreasonable behaviour, often accompanied by complaints of coldness and tiredness.

Physical and mental lethargy, including failure to respond to or to understand questions and directions.

Some slurring of speech. There is not necessarily early failure of speech and the victim may speak quite strongly until shortly before collapse.

Violent outbursts of unexpected energy with possible physical resistance to succour. Violent language. Failure to appreciate that something is wrong.

Lack of muscular co-ordination leading to erratic movements and falling.

Failure of, or abnormality in vision. It should be noted that some failure of vision, such as difficulty in focussing, is a very usual symptom, and when this does occur, the condition should be regarded with extreme seriousness.

It should be stressed that not all of these symptoms may be noticed, nor necessarily in this order. Other symptoms which may sometimes be observed are muscle cramp, extreme ashen pallor, light-headedness, and occasionally a fainting fit.

Symptoms of Deep Hypothermia

If left untreated the victim drifts into a deepening stupor. Shivering stops altogether and it becomes impossible to elicit any response. At this stage both pulse and respiration are feeble. Further cooling of the core leads inevitably to unconsciousness, coma and death. The time scale of these events varies but from recognition of the first serious symptoms to death may be as little as 2 hours. It should, however, be borne in mind that it can be almost impossible to tell whether the victim is actually dead or not, since virtually all signs of life, including the pulse, may be absent in severe hypothermia. Cases have been recorded of complete recovery following 1 hour's total cardiac arrest. It is safest then to assume that even an apparently dead person may be revived by resuscitative treatment.

Early Treatment on the Mountain

An observant and attentive leader should be able to recognise the early symptoms of hypothermia. Prompt action before the point of no return is reached may allow a retreat to be made in good order while the patient is still able to help himself. The immediate necessity is to seek shelter from the worst of the weather in the nearest convenient place. Once out of the wind every effort should be made to prevent further heat loss by changing out of wet clothing into dry spare clothing. Get the patient into a sleeping bag inside a bivouac sack and insulate him from the ground with anything which is available, rucksacks, etc. A hot drink and something to eat complete the treatment at this early stage. The remainder of the group should huddle round to provide additional shelter, natural warmth and moral support. Recovery may be rapid, but it is unlikely to take less than half an hour, even in ideal conditions. Insist on a proper rest period and do not proceed unless and until you are sure that recovery is complete. Dr Ieuan Jones has suggested a simple way of testing this. Ask the patient to subtract aloud 7 from 100 and then 7 from the remainder and so on until he reaches 2. He should be able to run through this mental arithmetic exercise in about a minute or less. If he takes much more than this or fails the test altogether then suspect the early stages of hypothermia. Even if recovery is apparently total, there should be no question of 'bashing on'. Relieve the patient of his rucksack and take the quickest and easiest route off the mountain.

The Dilemma

It is unfortunately the case that mountain hypothermia is often the final episode in a chapter of errors. It occurs when people are stretched beyond endurance, exposed to vile weather conditions and in all probability struggling to reach an objective that they are not confident of finding at the end of a long, hard day. It is all too easy to give sensible advice on what to do in such a situation and, alas, all too difficult to put into practice. The temptation to press on is very strong indeed, fueled by the thought of a night out in an exposed situation without proper bivouac equipment. The leader of such a party is in an unenviable position, having to choose between two equally hazardous alternatives. The moral is surely obvious. Do not allow yourself to be trapped into this situation.

Rewarming on the Mountain

However, let us assume the worst. You have diagnosed mountain hypothermia in a member of your party and he has not responded to the initial treatment. You decide that to attempt to move him down the mountain would be too risky and therefore you must summon help and do what you can with what you have on the spot. The essential and immediate treatment is to prevent further heat loss by providing comprehensive insulation round the victim. Given really good insulation, protection from the weather and rest, all but the most severe of cases will survive. Any positive contribution that can be made to his heat balance can be regarded as a bonus.

The body itself acts to maintain core circulation and temperature by restricting the flow to the exposed periphery so that core blood is not cooled at the surface. In any treatment, therefore, the importance must be realised of not increasing peripheral circulation unless there is minimal loss of heat at the skin surface. Further heat loss from the core must at all costs be avoided. Sudden local surface warming such as may be produced by hot water bottles, rubbing or alcohol intake could be disastrous.

Methods will vary according to conditions and the equipment immediately available. An outline of what should be done, if at all possible is:

Find the most sheltered spot in the vicinity or a place where some sort of shelter could be constructed or a tent pitched.

Get the victim into a plastic bag and then into a casualty bag or wrap sleeping bags round him, not forgetting to provide insulation below as well as above his body. This plastic bag will prevent the clothes from wetting the sleeping bag which will therefore retain their insulation properties. He should lie in the 'foetal' position with his head downslope. It is usually impracticable to remove the victim's wet clothes and a considerable amount of body heat may be lost in the process.

If there is room enough, put a fit companion into the sleeping bag alongside him, to give him bodily warmth. To be of much value there must be skin to skin contact especially in the area of the chest. Exhale warm air near the victim's mouth and nose.

There should be a windproof and waterproof covering (e.g. polythene) around the bag and the victim. The insulation between him and the ground is most important.

- Meanwhile, get the rest of the party to pitch a tent over the victim to provide fuller shelter. If the tent has a sewn-in groundsheet, carry him inside the tent. Light a stove, if carried, and get as many people inside as possible, but ensure adequate ventilation.
- If the victim can still take food, sugar in easily digestible form (e.g. condensed milk or in solution) may be given. A hot sweet drink may be prepared later if available.
- If respiration falters or ceases altogether, perform artificial respiration continuously by mouth to nose/mouth method.
- Be alert for failure of the heart (no pulse, blue lips, dilated pupils). It is important to continue artificial respiration and this can be administered by a second person at the rate of one inflation after every five compressions.

There will then normally ensue a period of some hours duration, before the rescue party with stretcher that has been summoned can arrive. Even if, during this period, the patient apparently recovers, and even if he insists that he is quite fit, he must still be treated as a stretcher-case, however unwilling or ashamed he may be, and the full normal rescue drill must be enforced. During this waiting period, once the patient has been insulated, a brew-up should be started, and hot beverages and food should be given to him, according to what he can take. Food and hot drinks should also be taken by those members of the party who have remained with him, and whom it is safer to regard as themselves suffering in some degree from shock and exhaustion.

Evacuation

The stretcher party, when it arrives, should preserve all the insulation around the patient during the carry. It is important that his face and mouth should be protected, to minimise heat-loss, without interfering with ventilation and ease of breathing. It is imperative that in descent the patient should be evacuated in the head down position and that someone (not a stretcher bearer) is detailed to keep an eye on him in case of vomiting, respiratory or cardiac failure. The evacuation is a critical phase of the whole operation and great care must be taken in handling the stretcher, particularly in the case of an unconscious patient.

If a case of hypothermia occurs in a very distant and isolated spot, and the delay before the arrival of the rescue party is likely to be inordinately long, the leader may face the very difficult decision as to whether to start removing the casualty towards the rescuers and safety. But before any such attempt is made, all the measures of immediate treatment in the field, as outlined above, should be taken first. And only if considerations of time, distance, and bad weather then clearly make it less of a risk to carry the patient towards safety, than to keep him, insulated and cared for, where he is, should the risk of carrying him be accepted. On no account should improvised carrying techniques be used which keep the patient in an upright or semi-upright position (e.g. pick-a-back). The improvised stretcher should be made as rigid as possible and the patient evacuated in the head-down position with as little movement as the terrain allows.

If, on the other hand, there is a good possibility of getting the patient to hospital within 1 or 2 hours, such as would be the case in a helicopter rescue, he should be taken there immediately without any attempt being made to treat him in the field, other than the provision of more clothing and plenty of insulation. The sophisticated rewarming techniques available at a hospital make recovery of the severely hypothermic patient, who has been kept alive by artificial respiration and cardiac massage, more likely. Until the treatment, the low body temperature due to hypothermia will keep demand for oxygen by the brain and other vital organs to a minimum.

Treatment at Base

It must be emphasised that an unconscious victim of mountain hypothermia is in a critically ill condition. If at all possible, treatment should be undertaken by qualified medical staff in hospital. However, since such facilities and expertise are not always available it is important to understand the rewarming process so that the correct and safe procedure can be followed.

The need to avoid any measure which causes relatively warm core blood to flow through the cold outer shell of the body and so cool the core still further has already been mentioned. In the past, rapid rewarming by immersion in a hot bath, *circa* 40°C, has been the treatment of choice and still is for patients suffering from rapid-onset immersion hypothermia. For the victim of mountain hypothermia the hot bath treatment involves some degree of risk and the more serious the condition the more likely 'rewarming collapse'.

After removal of the patient from the cold environment there is usually a continued fall in core temperature for a period of 10–20 minutes. This is the so-called 'after-drop'. Its significance lies in the fact that the core temperature may fall to the lethal zone. It is therefore essential, whether rewarming is spontaneous or imposed, that someone should remain with the patient at all times to monitor breathing and pulse which may, in a severe case, be hardly perceptible. In the event of respiratory or cardiac failure, the first priority should be artificial respiration followed by cardiac massage and, once these functions have been restored, slow rewarming, preferably in a warm room and bed, but without hot water bottle or pillow.

Recovery can sometimes be quite dramatic. Insist on complete rest and examination by a doctor as a matter of urgency.

THE HOT PACK

The International Commission for Alpine Rescue, IKAR, recommends the use of a 'Hot Pack' on hypothermic patients, both on the mountain and at base. The treatment involves making a thick pad out of a sheet or items of clothing, soaking the inner surface of this with hot water and placing it on top of the patient's underwear to cover his chest and abdomen. The compress is itself covered by more articles of clothing and the whole trunk then enveloped in foil or a space blanket leaving the extremities uncovered. Finally, the patient is wrapped up tightly in blankets, tucked in securely round the neck and placed inside a sleeping bag. The Hot Pack should be renewed after 1 hour. The removal of clothing which this method entails and the necessity to have hot water available, make it unlikely to be the treatment of choice on the mountain. However, it is a proven lifesaver and is the preferred treatment at the camp or bothy or whenever conditions make it a practicable proposition.

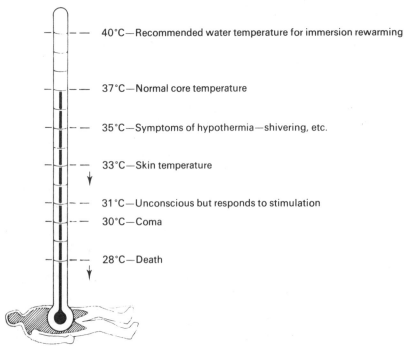

40°C—Recommended water temperature for immersion rewarming

37°C—Normal core temperature

35°C—Symptoms of hypothermia—shivering, etc.

33°C—Skin temperature

31°C—Unconscious but responds to stimulation

30°C—Coma

28°C—Death

Fig. 130. *Core temperature in hypothermic patients.*

HOT BATH

Rapid rewarming by immersion of the patient in a bath of hot water kept at 40°C is an effective treatment for the early stage of hypothermia. It is not appropriate for severe cases, or for the unconscious, the very old and the very young or for those who for any reason are frail or unwell.

Strip or cut away the outer garments and immerse the patient in the bath taking care to exclude any frostbitten part which should be dealt with separately. The legs and arms should be left out and the trunk maintained in a horizontal position with the head held just out of the water. The bath temperature will fall immediately and therefore hot water should be added at regular intervals and the water agitated to maintain the temperature at 40°C. After 20 minutes or when the patient begins to sweat, remove him in the prone position (i.e. do not sit him up) and transfer him to a previously warmed bed.

AIRWAY WARMING

Heat lost through the expiration of warm moist air forms a substantial proportion of the total heat loss in a cold environment. Dr Lloyd has developed an ingenious apparatus to minimise this loss by providing the means to warm and humidify the inspired air. The equipment, which requires expert handling, has been adapted for use in the field by mountain rescue personnel.

Conclusion

It is said that an Eskimo, immersed in cold Arctic water, will die from hypothermia just as quickly as the rest of us. His ability, not only to survive, but to live comfortably in a hostile environment is almost entirely due to the fact that he keeps fit, dresses well and is highly experienced in avoidance. This, perhaps slightly unfair comparison, sums up all that is necessary to know as regards prevention. Better by far that you should know how to avoid getting a case of exposure than to cure one. Therefore:

See to it that the equipment and clothing worn by the party is sufficient for the route chosen and takes cognisance of sudden and unexpected changes in conditions. Waterproof clothing is a must whether it be worn or carried in the pack. It is effective even when worn over wet clothes as it reduces the windchill/evaporation effect.

Adequate food and water should be taken before and during any mountain journey.

A minimum of emergency food and equipment must be carried by the party. In winter time, at high level, this may include a lightweight bivouac tent sufficiently large to accommodate the whole party.

Progressive training is important as is the careful regulation of pace throughout the day. Arrange large groups according to their fitness and capabilities.

Loads in excess of 40 lb are unnecessary, as well as being heavy. As a rough guide on a camping expedition loads should never exceed one-third of the body weight of the individual.

Good morale means increased safety.

Safety first—seek shelter or turn back in good time.

Good leadership involves good planning.

Finally, it must be said that good leadership is also an awareness on the part of the leader of each member of his party as an individual; an awareness amounting almost to a premonition of possible hazards and dangers that may arise and above all the ability to take avoiding action before circumstances dictate their own terms.

9 Effects of Heat

It is often said that man is a tropical animal, and it is certainly true that in general it is a good deal easier to lose heat than to conserve it. However, in a cold climate, heat conservation is achieved by the relatively simple expedient of improving the insulation, whereas, in a hot climate, heat loss is largely controlled by physiological adjustments which are outside the control of the individual. It is easier to wear an overcoat than a refrigerator. Exposure to heat is, in any case, a rare phenomenon in this country. However, cases of quite serious sunburn and mild heat exhaustion have been known, and the mountain leader should be familiar with the main heat disorders and their avoidance.

Water Requirements

Since most of these disorders are due to water depletion, rather than the direct effects of heat, an appreciation of the water requirements of the body is necessary. As a rough guide, $2\frac{1}{2}$ litres may be taken as the average daily requirement, broken down as follows:

	ml per 24 hours
Urine	1400
Respiration	400
Insensible perspiration	600
Faeces	100
Total	2500

This requirement is greatly increased by hard physical work, especially in hot weather, when an additional 750 ml may be required for every 1,000 kcal of energy expended. Most of this water is evaporated as sweat, and in this way, serves to cool the body surface. The evaporation of 1 litre of sweat results in a heat loss of about 600 kcal. In really hot climates the water requirement may be as much as 8 litres per 24 hours.

Salt Requirements

Normally our salt intake is a good deal more than our actual requirements, but prolonged sweating can lead to substantial salt losses, particularly in those who are unacclimatised. For every litre of fluid lost, 2 grams of salt is lost. Fortunately, acclimatisation to salt depletion in a hot environment takes place fairly rapidly and the immediate effects can be countered by the simple expedient of taking salt, solid or in solution, and by cutting down on water intake.

Acclimatisation

Very little is known about long-term adaptation to heat and one is left with the impression that, as with the Eskimo in the cold environment, experience in avoidance is the best protection against the harmful effects of a hot climate. There is no doubt that short term adjustments take place in a matter of several days of exposure to heat and these include: a less marked increase in heart rate when working, a lower skin and body temperature, greater efficiency of the sweating mechanism (sweating is more rapid in onset), a reduction of salt in sweat and urine and a marked increase in tolerance of the conditions.

Sunburn

This can be very severe particularly to those with sensitive skins. In addition, sunburn can interfere with sweat secretion and lead to further heat complications. It is usually caused by sudden and prolonged exposure to sunlight without adequate protection. The length of exposure should be carefully regulated to build up a protective tan and initially, at any rate, an efficient barrier cream used which does not interfere with sweating and which cuts out most of the harmful ultra-violet radiation. In applying the cream it is important to remember the lips and also those areas of the face which receive a lot of reflected light from the ground or snow: under the nose and ears, chin, etc. Sunburn can be effectively treated with calamine lotion.

Effects of Glare

Snow blindness is considered briefly in the winter section (page 330). Here we are concerned with discomfort and strain, as a consequence of inadequate protection of the eyes. The remedy is simple: wear sunglasses. These must be of good quality and reduce the amount of ultra-violet without cutting down too much on the total transmission of light. In snow conditions, especially at high altitudes, it is essential to shield the eyes as well from light entering round the sides of the lenses.

Heat Disorders

Prickly Heat

This is an irritating rash of tiny blisters, usually caused by constant sweating in a hot climate. The only real cure is to get out of the sun and rest, although various measures can be adopted to relieve the symptoms.

Heat Syncope

Unacclimatised people exposed to heat frequently suffer periods of acute fatigue associated with fainting or a feeling of giddiness. This is a common condition and it can be counteracted effectively by rest.

Heat Exhaustion

When due to water depletion, this can be a very serious condition, leading ultimately to death. The symptoms include, thirst, fatigue, giddiness, a rapid pulse, raised body temperature, low urine output and later on, delirium and coma. The only remedy is to re-establish water balance.

When due to salt depletion, similar symptoms are manifest though without any marked rise in body temperature, but almost always associated with severe muscle cramp. It can be serious if not treated by the addition of salt to the diet. There is no such thing in man as a craving for salt and therefore the victims are unaware that they are suffering from a deficiency.

Heat Stroke

Mistakenly referred to as sunstroke. This is by far the most serious of the heat disorders and is caused by a failure of the body's temperature regulating system. It is associated with a very high body temperature and absence of sweating. The skin is hot and dry to the touch. Early symptoms show a remarkable similarity to the symptoms of hypothermia, such as aggressive behaviour, lack of co-ordination and so on. Later on the victim goes into a coma or convulsions and death will follow unless effective treatment is given.

In the field, the treatment consists of sponging down the patient, or covering him with wet towels, accompanied by vigorous fanning. It is imperative to begin treatment immediately, unless of course the shortage of water is so acute that other lives may be endangered. When facilities permit, immersion in a cold bath (10°C) is the treatment of choice.

Precautions

It is wise to remember that it is not possible to acclimatise to a low intake of water. A certain minimum quantity is required for survival. Most of the recommendations, therefore, concern conservation of water:

Keep fit. Fitness is very important, especially when travel is involved.

Do the minimum of work consistent with the achievement of the expedition's aims.

Keep out of the sun as far as possible and certainly during the hottest part of the day.

Drink more than you need when water is readily available; a little and often being the best maxim to follow. Thirst is a poor indicator of your actual requirement and a reserve will be useful on a long journey.

Don't hoard water till collapse is imminent.

Be prepared to collect rainwater by tapping as large a surface area as possible, e.g. with a polythene sheet. A plastic straw can be used to extract water from rock pools.

A high calorie diet, short on protein, is desirable.

Wear loose, lightweight clothing, permeable to sweat and light in colour; also a shady hat and sunglasses. On no account labour uphill in hot conditions wearing fully waterproof clothing.

If salt tablets are taken they must be dissolved in a sufficient quantity of water.

10 Mountain Rescue

Introduction

Not too very long ago there were no mountain rescue teams, no heli- copters, and a good deal fewer people walking and climbing in the mountains. If an accident occurred there was no professional organisation ready to swing into action as soon as the alarm was raised. Mountaineers had to rely on their own resources to get themselves out of trouble and if, for any reason, this was not possible then they had to call on such help as was available from other parties walking or climbing in the neighbourhood. It is a tradition of self-reliance and mutual support that is well worth preserving, even in this day of sophisticated rescue aids. It is a cardinal mistake to rely on someone else to come and bail you out should things go wrong. You should set out on the clear understanding that you are an independent, self-reliant party, able to deal competently with most eventualities and ready and willing to offer assistance should this be required by others in distress.

Today, of course, with greatly increased numbers of people taking to the hills, many of them relatively inexperienced, such a system of self-help is no longer enough on its own. It has, of necessity, been reinforced by a more professionally orientated organisation comprising local mountain rescue teams which are well equipped, highly efficient and are supported by the search and rescue helicopters of the RAF. Inevitably, such a sophisticated service brings with it the danger that we may come to rely on always having a back-stop should things go wrong. This is an extremely dangerous attitude of mind which may encourage those who have it to overreach themselves. It is as well to remind ourselves that when conditions are really bad, helicopters cannot fly and even efficient rescue teams are greatly restricted in what they can do.

The only thing is to be self-reliant in attitude and, as far as possible, self-sufficient in terms of equipment and skills. Accidents happen, often when you least expect them, and the mountain leader should be confident that he can make right decisions and act on them competently. Accidents in the mountains have a nasty habit of escalating. A relatively minor mishap, through a series of wrong decisions can, and often does, develop into a major incident involving possible threat to life. Making the right decisions at an early stage in an incident is of paramount importance. To do this you need a cool head, the right kind of experience and a liberal dose of common sense; none of them easy to acquire!

Accident Procedure

In the event of an accident—do not rush. It is essential that you keep a grip of yourself and assert your control over the party at an early stage when your natural concern for the victim may encourage you into some precipitate action. Keep other members of the group back; get them doing something useful. Approach the casualty with caution and never from above when there is a chance of loose rock being dislodged and falling on to the victim.

Make a rapid examination of the casualty checking for life-threatening conditions; failure of breathing, no pulse, arterial bleeding. You should be thoroughly familiar with methods of resuscitation and life-saving first-aid.

See to it that no immediate danger threatens the victim or the rest of the party. If it does then it may be your first priority to move to a safer area nearby where you should make a more comprehensive examination followed by first-aid treatment as required. Remember that no treatment is better than unnecessary meddling. Make the casualty as comfortable as possible and provide warmth and shelter as far as circumstances and equipment allow. Be particularly careful to provide adequate insulation from the ground. If there is no spinal injury it may be advantageous to move to a more sheltered site provided this can be accomplished without undue discomfort or aggravation of injuries. If you decide not to move then build a shelter with whatever materials are to hand.

Plan of Action

This is an absolutely critical stage in the whole operation, so take your time and do not be rushed into making over-hasty decisions which you may regret later. You have to decide whether you can deal with the incident within the resources of your own party or whether you are going to need outside help. In either case you will have to work out a detailed plan taking into account the following factors:

The Nature of the Casualty's Injuries   Very few injuries require immediate evacuation as an absolute priority, although there are one or two conditions where such action would be justified, e.g. acute appendicitis, diabetic coma. On the other hand, there are quite a few where the specialised expertise of a rescue team, probably with a doctor in attendance, would be virtually essential, e.g. head and spinal injuries, severe internal injuries, heart attack, stroke, severe hypothermia.

The State of the Party   It is very understandable, but also dangerous, to focus all your attention on the casualty. Remember that you have a responsibility to the rest of the party and that they are particularly vulnerable to cold and fear at this time. If you fail to attend to them you may well find yourself with more than one casualty on your hands. Discuss the situation frankly, but optimistically, with them and consult them before finalising your plan of action. As far as possible keep them busy and involved in providing succour to the patient.

The Time Available   There is very rarely enough time to do all that has to be done. Time spent in making the patient comfortable is time well spent. Make sure that he understands what you intend to do. You will have to make an estimate of the time required to complete each of the possible alternatives taking account of the fact that part of the rescue operation may have to be conducted in darkness.

The Weather   Bad weather conditions are frequently associated with accidents. It may be so bad, or you may judge that it will become so, that immediate evacuation to a lower, more sheltered, location overrides all other considerations. In winter, snow conditions underfoot may rule out the possibility of evacuation using improvised material and techniques.

The Availability of Assistance   Sometimes, with the support of other groups walking or climbing in the neighbourhood, it may be practicable to evacuate the casualty. Advice on how to attract attention is given in the next section. You must, of course, be familiar with the location of the nearest mountain rescue post and the most convenient place from which the rescue services can be summoned.

The Terrain   You will have to determine the best route out for the messengers who may be sent to summon help.

Finally, you must evaluate the human and material resources available to you at the accident site and decide whether or not you have the capability of evacuating the casualty without outside assistance.

Calling for Help

Whatever you decide to do you will almost certainly want to attract the attention of any other parties in the vicinity to seek whatever help they

Table 8. Agreed signals used in Mountain Rescue

Message	Flare signal	Audible signal	Light signal
HELP REQUIRED	Red Flare(s)	6 blasts etc. in quick succession, repeated after a 1 minute interval. SOS: Three short, three long, three short blasts etc. in quick succession repeated after a 1 minute interval.	6 flashes in quick succession, repeated after a 1 minute interval. SOS: Three short, three long, three short flashes, repeated after a 1 minute interval.
MESSAGE UNDERSTOOD	White Flare(s) (also used for illumination)	3 blasts etc. in quick succession, repeated after a 1 minute interval.	3 flashes in quick succession, repeated after a 1 minute interval.
RETURN TO BASE	Green Flare(s)	A prolonged succession of blasts etc.	A prolonged succession of flashes.
POSITION OF BASE	White or Yellow Flare(s)		Continuous light.

N.B. FIXING POSITION. As soon as a signal is seen (or heard) a compass bearing must be taken on it. Two such bearings, if taken from different positions, will give a reasonably accurate fix on the position of the signal.

can offer. There is an internationally recognised code of signals, both audible and visual and this is summarised in the table above. It should be borne in mind that a single signal can easily be missed so keep repeating it until it is acknowledged.

There are really only two options open to you. Either you send for help or you evacuate the casualty yourself using whatever assistance you can muster at the accident site. You may decide, of course, to leave one or more of your group with the injured person and lead the rest down to safety yourself.

Sending for Help

At least two fit and reliable members of the party should be sent for help and they must be thoroughly briefed as to what is expected of them. The safety of the whole party and the success of the rescue operation depends on them getting the call for help through to the proper authorities. No matter how serious the circumstances appear, speed must not be achieved at the expense of safety. The messengers should carry a written message. This is important because it is very easy under the pressure of events to omit or forget some vital piece of information. A written note, or better still an accident report form, imposes a disciplined consideration of all the relevant factors. At the very least the written note should give the following particulars:

The precise location of the accident including a six-figure grid reference.
A description of the accident and the time it occurred.
The name of the casualty and his/her next of kin, if known.
The nature of the injuries sustained.
An outline of the plan of action, including details of the other members of the party.
Any relevant information about the terrain and the best approach route.

The messengers should take note of the terrain on the way out. They may have to lead the rescue team back in the dark. When they reach the point from which the alarm can be raised it is vital that they speak to, or get the message into the hands of, the competent authority, preferably the leader of the rescue organisation. If the message is to be relayed, they should make sure that they are standing by the telephone, ready to respond to any request for further first-hand information. Normally the first point of contact is the police, dial 999.

If the victim is to be left on his own, and it must be said that it is only in the most dire circumstances that such action should be contemplated, then he must be told to 'stay put' at all costs. He should be given all the spare food and clothing and provided with a whistle and torch if these are not required by the messengers. Mark the spot with a brightly coloured garment held on top of a cairn of stones. A safety rope, if not otherwise required, may be extended out from the victim to act as a marker-guide. Remember that the rescue party may have to find the exact spot in the mist or in the dark and in winter the victim may well be covered with drifting snow. An unconscious patient must never be left alone. In a party of two, it is safer for the uninjured person to stay with the victim to render help when necessary and to attempt to attract the attention of other climbers and walkers. Only as an absolute last resort should the victim be left and in that event he should be tied securely to the rock if in an exposed situation and a note left explaining what action has been taken. It is worth remembering that an injured person will normally attempt to untie himself.

Self Help

At the outset it should be appreciated that improvised 'carries' and 'stretchers' are of short range value. It would be exhausting and possibly dangerous to attempt a long evacuation by such methods. Their main use is in moving an injured person to a more sheltered situation or in evacuating someone with relatively minor injuries or, of course, when evacuation by any method is preferable to leaving the victim where he is.

A number of different techniques are illustrated in the following pages, some of which look deceptively straightforward to improvise and effective in operation. Do not be misled. They all need practice so that you become aware of the limitations of each method in terms of material, manpower and effective range and, more important still, you become aware of your own physical limitations.

Improvisation

Fireman's Lift, using two, three or four hands. Methods are unsuitable for distances over 50 yards.

METHOD:
  Piggy Back
PEOPLE REQUIRED:
  One

EQUIPMENT AND MEANS:
  Nil
COMMENT:
  Exhausting

METHOD:
  Rucksack Carry
PEOPLE REQUIRED:
  One
EQUIPMENT AND MEANS:
  Rucksack and padding. Casualty sits on padding, legs through rucksack straps
COMMENT:
  Depends on shape of sack

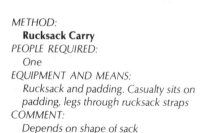

Fig. 131. *Rucksack carry.*

Fig. 132. *One-man split rope carry.*

METHOD:
 One-man Split Rope Carry
PEOPLE REQUIRED:
 One

EQUIPMENT AND MEANS:
 Rope and padding. Casualty sits on
 padding with coils of rope
COMMENT:
 Moderately comfortable

METHOD:
 Two-man Split Rope Carry
PEOPLE REQUIRED:
 Two
EQUIPMENT AND MEANS:
 Rope and padding. Split into two over
 outside shoulders of carriers. Casualty
 sits on rope (padded) in between
COMMENT:
 Not good on rough terrain. Unstable
 fore/aft

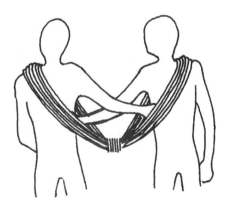

Fig. 133. *Two-man split rope carry.*

METHOD:
Two-man Rucksack (or Crossed Sling) and Pole Carry
PEOPLE REQUIRED:
   Two
EQUIPMENT AND MEANS:
   Two rucksacks (or four slings) and pole
   or long ice axe. Pole slotted through
   rucksack's straps (or crossed slings)
   behind carriers' backs. Patient sits in
   between on pole
COMMENT:
   Uncomfortable for casualty

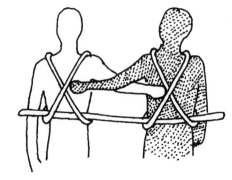

Fig. 134. *Two-man sling and pole carry.*

METHOD:
Sedan Chair
PEOPLE REQUIRED:
   Three
EQUIPMENT AND MEANS:
   One rucksack, two poles or long
   ice axes, one anorak. Anorak
   sleeves inside out, poles slotted
   through to form seat.
   Front carrier wears rucksack,
   poles slotted through straps.
   Casualty sits back to back with
   front carrier. One carrier either
   side at rear of poles
COMMENT:
   Good. The more helping to
   carry the better, provided they
   can see 4–5 ft in front of them to
   place feet

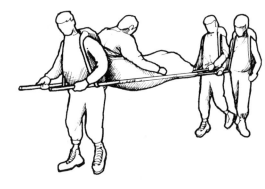

Fig. 135. *Sedan chair.*

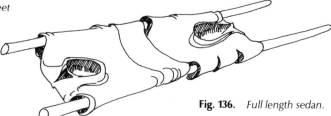

Fig. 136. *Full length sedan.*

METHOD:
Full-length Sedan
PEOPLE REQUIRED:
   Six or more

EQUIPMENT AND MEANS:
   Long poles (tent), four anoraks. As above
   only casualty lies prone. The bed can be
   made with anoraks, tent, poly bag
   or rope
COMMENT:
   Excellent. Rigid sides easier to carry

METHOD:
Poly-bag Stretcher
PEOPLE REQUIRED:
  Six or more
EQUIPMENT AND MEANS:
  One 8′ × 4′ survival bag, tent or similar.
  6 round, plum-sized stones.
  6 slings, straps, belts, etc.
  The stones are placed in position inside
  the polythene bag and each one tied off
  with a clove hitch
COMMENT:
  Simple and quick to make. A bit fragile
  and floppy for the casualty. Excellent for
  sliding on snow if injuries permit

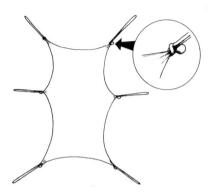

Fig. 137.   Poly-bag stretcher.

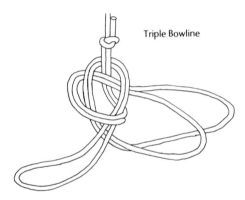

Triple Bowline

Fitted as a sit sling

Fitted as a full harness

METHOD:
  The Triple Bowline
PEOPLE REQUIRED:
  One or more to lower casualty
EQUIPMENT AND MEANS:
  Rope only
COMMENT:
  Easy to tie, but difficult to adjust,
  particularly the single loop which goes
  across the casualty's chest

Fig. 138.   The triple bowline.

Rope Stretchers

It takes a lot of patience and a lot of practice to make a good rope stretcher, but for those who are prepared to put the time into it, it can be a worthwhile and useful technique. Constructed incorrectly, it can be worse than useless. The original Piggott stretcher has been extensively modified and the method illustrated here is considerably easier to tie and adjust.

ROSCOE ROPE STRETCHER

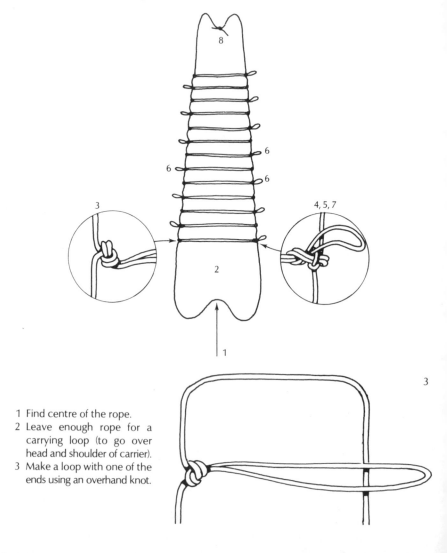

1 Find centre of the rope.
2 Leave enough rope for a carrying loop (to go over head and shoulder of carrier).
3 Make a loop with one of the ends using an overhand knot.

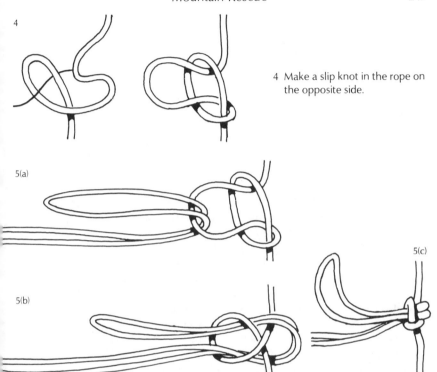

4

5(a)

5(c)

5(b)

4 Make a slip knot in the rope on the opposite side.

5 Thread the loop through the slip knot, then pull the slip knot inside out, to form a sheet bend. (The end of the loop should be long enough to tie a half-hitch, once the stretcher is finished, and be used as a small handle.)

6 Repeat this, taking loops from alternate sides, until the stretcher is the required length. The knots should be about 4″ apart at weight bearing parts of the stretcher (where shoulders, head and hips will be); if short of rope they can be further apart on legs.

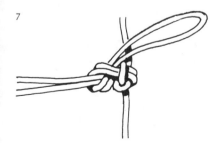

7

7 Adjust width of stretcher to fit patient. Tie off ends of loops with half-hitches. (These can then be used as small handles.)

8 Tie ends of rope to form a carrying loop at foot of stretcher. Pad stretcher before loading patient.

Fig. 139.   *The Roscoe rope stretcher.*

Bivouac Techniques

There is a world of difference between a planned bivouac and an un-
planned one. If you deliberately set off with the intention of spending
the night out you can, to a large extent, choose when you will bivouac and
also ensure that you have with you the means to spend a reasonably
comfortable night: a down jacket or even a sleeping bag, a piece of foam
for insulation, a change of clothes, some food, a lightweight stove to make
a hot brew and perhaps a bivy-sac or polythene bag to provide protection
from the wind and rain. In an emergency situation you may have none of
these things and you will have to make do with what you normally carry
on a hill walk.

To what extent, then, should you 'be prepared' to deal with and survive
an unexpected night out? There is more than a grain of truth in the
observation that if you burden yourself with all the gear required for a
comfortable 'emergency' bivouac you will almost certainly ensure that
you have one. What you carry in the way of emergency gear is very much
a matter of judgement, taking into account the nature of the expedition,
the composition of the party and the likelihood of being caught out. The
obligation on the leader of a party of inexperienced people to adopt a
fail-safe approach is clearly much greater than on a similar party of
independent experienced hillwalkers. The possibility of an emergency
must be considered seriously and some provision made in the equipment
to be carried among the party. Individual protection from the wind and
rain is the primary requirement and this can be achieved by each person
carrying an 8' × 4' polythene survival bag. Some condensation is inevitable,
but for a single night it is surely a tolerable alternative to exposure. A
Goretex bivy-sac, large enough to accommodate six to eight people, is a
very satisfactory alternative allowing all to benefit from sharing body
warmth as well as the companionship of being under one roof. The
amount of spare clothing to be carried will depend on the season and
circumstances but an extra sweater and a spare pair of socks (which can
double-up as spare mitts or even a hat) should normally be carried in
reserve. An emergency ration, over and above the day's supply, is a
sensible addition, as much for its psychological as for its nutritional value.

'Howffing' may be defined as the art of making oneself comfortable with
the natural material to be found in the wild. To some it is an end in itself, to
others a means to an end, but there is no doubt that necessity is the
mother of invention and inventiveness is the foremost attribute of the
'howffer'. He will choose a site, sheltered from the wind, perhaps in the lee
of, or under, a boulder, and make an insulating mattress of heather, stop up
cracks and draughts and get a fire going. All these skills come into play, but
the most important of all is likely to be maintaining the morale of the party,

especially in an emergency situation where the shortage of time is likely to preclude all but the most rudimentary preparations. In winter conditions an emergency bivouac is a much more serious proposition where the risk of frostbite and exposure is very real. A bivouac under these circumstances should not be contemplated unless there is no other possible alternative.

Mountain Rescue Teams

There are over 100 mountain rescue teams in the British Isles and a similar number of official mountain rescue posts. The work of the teams is co-ordinated by the Mountain Rescue Committee through its various regional associations and by the Mountain Rescue Committee of Scotland and the Northern Ireland Mountain Rescue Co-ordinating Committee. These committees work closely with the police and with the RAF mountain rescue teams and rescue co-ordinating centres. Detailed lists of teams and posts are contained in the Mountain and Cave Rescue Handbook published by the Mountain Rescue Committee each year. You should be familiar with the general contents of this and be aware of the teams and the location of rescue posts in the area you are in.

Mountain Rescue Posts and Equipment

Mountain Rescue Posts have been established at strategic locations in the mountainous areas of the British Isles. They are identified by the MR sign and contain sufficient equipment to enable a simple rescue operation to be mounted quickly by whatever help is first available. In many cases posts are used and maintained by the local rescue team, but in some remote areas such support is not available. It is expected that you should be familiar with the contents of the rescue posts and how to use them in an emergency.

Authorised List of Equipment

1 or more stretchers (with head shield for selected posts).
2 rucksacks, including one medical rucksack.
1 casualty bag and 1 large polythene bag, 2 m long.
1 Thomas splint or equivalent.
6 triangular bandages. 12 × 15 cm Dommette bandages.
2.5 cm zinc oxide strapping.
7.5 cm elastic adhesive bandage.
2 straight aluminium arm splints or Kramer wire splints.
1 inflatable leg splint, 1 inflatable arm splint (for selected posts).

H

1 Airway Brooks, Hewit's or modification (Ambu respiratory apparatus for very busy posts only).

1 protective helmet (for selected posts).

1 container of antiseptic powder or liquid.

6 factory dressings or equivalent.

1 packet gauze.

1 $\frac{1}{4}$-lb cotton wool.

1 pair surgical stainless steel dressing scissors.

2 dozen safety pins.

1 electric hand lamp (for selected posts).

3 cups, including 1 feeding cup

2 Thermos flasks.

3 ampoules of Morphia (Omnopon) containing 15 milligrams (5 year shelf life). Not at unmanned posts or kit boxes, being replaced by Pantapon containing 10 mg.

1 pair stainless steel dressing forceps.

1 packet disposable gloves.

1 packet J-cloths.

For Selected Posts

Sphygmomanometer (anaeroid blood pressure apparatus).
Vitalograph suction apparatus (with Yankaver disposable suction end).
Plastic water bottle.
1 non-stretch rope.

The decision whether or not to use Post equipment will depend on the circumstances of the accident and your assessment of your capability to carry out a successful rescue operation without calling on the resources of the local mountain rescue organisation. Do not make the mistake of underestimating the difficulty and sheer physical endeavour required to evacuate a casualty over rough terrain. It is almost certain that you will need help, although you may well decide that something can be done while this help is on its way. If you do use Post equipment it is vital that you inform the Post Supervisor immediately afterwards so that he can make arrangements for its return or replacement.

Radio Communications

All teams are now equipped with portable transceivers. Most of these are on the Mountain Rescue frequency, but call signs should be checked before departure and procedure, including time on and off the air, established. Good communications can be a tremendous asset in any search and rescue operation, but their maintenance should not so dominate the conduct of affairs that other vital considerations, such as speed and efficiency of search, are neglected.

It is important to be aware of the limitations of radio communications in the mountains. Broadly speaking VHF transmission is only possible between stations within line of sight of each other and therefore communication across intervening ridges and hills is not practicable. It is possible, of course, to position an operator on the intervening feature and relay messages from one side to the other. In some areas a 'relay' station has been permanently sited on top of some strategic high point which automatically relays transmissions over a wide area.

Stretchers

There are three types of stretchers in common use, the Thomas, the MacInnes and the Bell. You should know how to assemble each of these and be able to secure a casualty safely and comfortably in preparation for evacuation. The main features of each type are described briefly.

Split Thomas

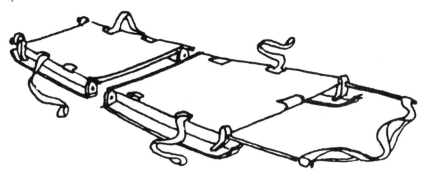

Fig. 140. *Split Thomas stretcher.*

This stretcher splits in two sections for easy carrying. The carrying straps serve as rucksack-type straps. The stretcher bed is made from either plastic coated wire mesh or canvas duck. The shafts are telescopic and the complete stretcher weighs over 18 kg (40 lb). The two sections are locked together with a bolt. A mesh headguard is also available. This stretcher may be fitted with a Thomas splint which enables a fractured leg to be immobilised under traction. If you are unfamiliar with this technique use some other method, such as an inflatable splint, Kramer wire splint, wooden slats, etc., to immobilise the limb.

MacInnes

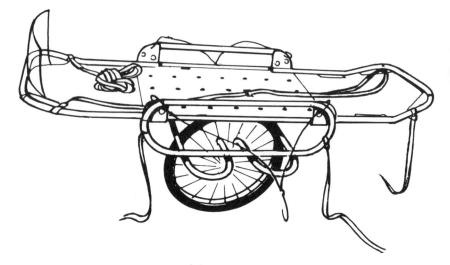

Fig. 141.　*The MacInnes Superlight.*

The Split model is based on the design of the folding model, but with the two sections being held together with stainless steel pins and locking plates. The alloy patient bed is covered with closed cell foam. There are four side-bearer straps, a patient stirrup and a long patient wrap-round security tape. The shafts are telescopic and lock into position. The transport is secured by four hook bolts and is fitted into a heel brake. The complete stretcher weighs 22 kg (48 lb).

The MacInnes Superlite has been developed especially for use with helicopters. It weighs 11 kg (24 lb) and can take a standard transport wheel. The two ends of the stretcher fold in to make a compact load for carrying.

Bell

The Bell Split Rescue Stretcher is supplied in two halves, each with its own carrying pack frame. Assembled and with the hinged handles inboard it measures 2 m × 60 cm. It is constructed from square section stainless steel tube and weighs approximately 20 kg when ready for use. Plastic ski runners and a headguard can be fitted as and when required. The patient bed is of reinforced steel mesh strengthened by cross wires.

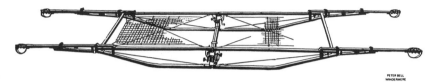

Fig. 142. *The Bell stretcher.*

Securing Casualty to Stretcher

Different types of stretchers have different means of securing the casualty, but the essential elements are:

That he should be warm and comfortable. The use of a casualty bag makes the whole process very much easier.

That he should be securely attached to the stretcher by adjustable straps which can be positioned to avoid pressure on injuries. A single, long (8 m) nylon tape wrapped round both patient and stretcher bed is very effective.

That he should have the necessary support such as a foot stirrup or chest harness. A decision on this will have to be taken before the casualty is sealed up in the casualty bag.

That he should be provided with head protection if necessary. Most stretchers have some sort of headguard.

Other Items of Equipment

Casualty Bag

Many posts and teams are now equipped with specially designed casualty bags incorporating sleeping bag, mattress and carrying handles. Their main advantages are that they allow minimal handling of the patient to get him into the bag, they provide a convenient method of transport to and from the stretcher and they offer excellent insulation from the ground or on the stretcher itself. Sleeping bags should be carried by teams not equipped with a casualty bag, although it will be appreciated that it can be exceedingly difficult to get a severely injured person into a bag which does not have a full length zip.

Personal Clothing and Equipment

Refer to the kit list, Appendix III, but be particularly careful to ensure that you have adequate lighting. A pocket torch or head lamp may last less than 1 hour so take plenty of spare batteries. Long life cells should be used.

Lightweight Tent

This is not part of the official post equipment but it could prove a life saver especially if the victim is suffering from exposure. On wide scale searches in bad conditions a tent with each search party is a must. Some teams have a complete bivouac unit which will accommodate the whole party including the casualty.

Search Lamps

At night each team should carry at least one search lamp capable of providing wide and narrow beam illumination continuously for at least 4 hours. It must be backed up by first class personal lighting and, if available, by illuminating flares.

Signalling Devices

Rockets, maroons, miniflares and so on may be of use in favourable conditions. The agreed code is as follows: Red—help wanted here; Green—recall to base; White—message understood. Do not rely on a single flare. Release several at intervals till acknowledged. A thunderflash or other loud noise will help to attract attention before releasing flares.

Food and Drink

Adequate supplies of food and hot soup or other liquids should be carried to meet the needs of both rescuers and rescued. If the search is likely to be a long one then a stove, fuel, billies and the necessary material (tea, sugar, etc.) may ease the weight problem.

Specialised Equipment

Depending on the circumstances of the accident certain items of more specialised equipment may be required: climbing ropes, crash helmets, pitons, slings, karabiners and so on. In any event at least two ropes should be carried by each team since these may be required to deal with a host of unforeseen problems.

Organisation of Search

It is not expected that mountain leaders will be concerned with the organisation of a major search and rescue operation. This is the responsibility of the local team leader in co-operation with the police. Nevertheless, it is important they they should have a clear understanding of the system so that they can offer competent assistance in an emergency, perhaps as the leader of a smaller search unit.

Big searches are costly affairs, in terms of man-hours as well as in hard cash. An efficient organisation makes the best use of all available resources, minimises delays and frustrations and greatly increases the chances of a successful outcome. Just as it is vital that each small group should have its appointed leader, so it is vital that an experienced mountaineer should take overall responsibility for the control and conduct of the search. In a large scale operation this can only be successfully done from a fixed base in contact with all aspects of the search, both in the field and behind the lines.

The rescue co-ordinator should:

1 Interview the person bringing the news of the accident. This is best done away from the crowd which invariably gathers at the mention of the word accident. Reliance should not be placed on second-hand information. This may be coloured and omit some vital piece of information concerning the circumstances.
2 Establish precise details of the accident, including location, time, number involved and the nature of the injuries. This is greatly facilitated if a written accident report has been sent down by the party leader.
3 Once this information has been given act speedily—not hastily. Inform the local police and doctor. They will make arrangements for an ambulance, but will require an indication of the expected time of arrival at the nearest road.
4 Each area has devised its own call-out system, but it is worth remembering that it is better to have a team on 'stand-by' if there is any likelihood of their being required, than to call them out at the very last moment without warning.
5 No two search and rescue operations are ever the same and therefore the plan must be adapted to the circumstances. It should be drawn up immediately in consultation with the team leaders and the police. Contact the Meteorological Office for an up-to-date weather forecast and inform team leaders.

It is important that:

Team leaders are fully briefed on the circumstances of the accident and the responsibilities of their groups. Check on the experience and personal equipment of their members. Radio call-signs and an agreed communications system should be established.

A record is kept, giving the names of the members of each party and their leader, the route to be followed, special equipment carried, radio call sign, time out, and expected time of return. This information could be of vital importance if a claim on insurance is to be made.

Each party should carry sufficient equipment to render positive assistance to any casualties, i.e. first-aid kit, spare clothing, food and drink, together with the means to provide adequate shelter. Other equipment carried will obviously depend on the circumstances known about the accident.

Night Search

It is hazardous and a waste of manpower to send all parties out on a general search at night unless fairly precise information is available. However, some immediate effort must be made and this should take the form of checking mountain huts and other known refuge points.

Search Methods

If the locality is known a small party is sent ahead with an emergency first-aid pack. This should contain sufficient material to deal with most injuries. There is also tremendous psychological value in having help arrive as quickly as possible. If the stretcher party is inexperienced it is better to have the patient tidied up before the party arrives.

A stretcher party is organised to follow up the advance party. This should be at least 12 but preferably 18 persons. All members must be properly clad and equipped. If there is any doubt, they should not be allowed to proceed.

If the location of the accident is unknown, but the general area fairly well defined, the stretcher(s) and other heavy gear may be left at some convenient advanced base where it is reasonably accessible to the various units and in radio communication with them. This base can be moved as the search progresses. Some teams, of course, will be carrying lightweight stretchers.

Four main methods of search are recognised and their use obviously depends on the number of searchers available, their experience, the nature of the ground and the information available to the controller.

Reconnaissance Search

Small fast units, consisting of three or four experienced men, are sent out with the minimum of gear with the object of locating the casualty as quickly as possible. Helicopters and dogs are tremendously useful in this sort of preliminary scouting operation and may save endless work later. They should follow the intended route of the missing party if this is known and check any huts or other likely places where they may have taken shelter. The rescue party should carry a first-aid kit and the means to provide basic shelter and sustenance. A radio link with base completes the essential equipment.

Area Search

This is the normal method of covering a fairly large area. Each team is allotted a piece of ground bounded if possible by natural features such as streams or ridges. It is then up to the team leader to choose the detailed method of search best suited to the terrain in his area. In most cases this will involve some sort of sweep in line across the area together with a more detailed search of particular features.

Sweep Search

As the name implies this method of searching involves spacing the members of the party out in line across the area to be searched and then sweeping to and fro across it. The spacing of individuals will be determined by the nature of the ground, the visibility, the number of people available, the size of the area to be searched and the hours of daylight left. Discipline and concentration are prerequisites for an effective operation.

Contact Search

This method is designed to concentrate the search over a relatively small area, perhaps at the foot of a cliff or in an area where there is good reason to believe that the missing person(s) may be found. The spacing between searchers is dictated by the ground and may vary from 50 m in open country to 1 m in thick bush. The important point to bear in mind is that this type of search should be conclusive. An area searched in this way must be clearly marked.

Search and Rescue Dog Association

S.A.R.D.A. was founded by Hamish MacInnes in 1965 when the first training course was held in Glencoe. Now the Association has handlers and dogs in all the main mountain areas in the British Isles whose services can be called upon to assist in the search for missing persons and to locate people buried in avalanches in winter.

The dogs and their handlers attend a selection course in December and if successful, a follow-up course in March at which 'novice dogs' are selected. The dogs are reassessed after a year, qualifying as 'Search dogs'. Search dogs are retested every 3 years.

The requirements in Britain are quite different from those in Alpine countries in that large tracts of mountain country may have to be searched both in summer and winter conditions. Dogs may have to operate at some considerable distance from their handlers in order to cover as large an area as possible. In the Alps dogs are primarily used at close quarters to search avalanche debris for buried victims.

To make the best use of a trained dog it should be allowed to search the most likely areas before large parties of searchers move in. If a dog is not immediately available the search must be pursued using whatever resources are available. Wherever possible dogs should be allowed to work into the wind where any scent will be carried towards them. They rely very little on sight and indeed one of their great advantages is that they will operate equally well at night, when other search work is greatly curtailed. As a very approximate guide a trained dog is capable of doing the work of 20 searchers and in some conditions, such as after a fall of new snow, considerably more. Nevertheless it should be borne in mind that dogs cannot work miracles, but when used properly and in good time they can be an invaluable asset in a search operation.

Helicopters

Helicopters are frequently used in rescue operations and have been instrumental in saving many lives. However, it is important that their use is seen as being complementary to the mountain rescue teams, not a substitute for them. There are many situations where the deployment of a helicopter is difficult or impossible, such as in dense cloud, darkness or in very severe weather conditions. Under these circumstances the ground team is the only reliable source of help. When lives are at stake, sympathetic consideration is always given by the Service authorities to a request for a helicopter, although it should be appreciated that Service requirements must have first priority. Any such request should be made through the police who will contact the Rescue Co-ordination Centre.

Signalling from Ground to Air

If you have to communicate with a helicopter or other aircraft from the ground there is an internationally recognised code of signals, making use of whatever materials are to hand, to convey simple messages. Characters should be 3 m in size and offer as much contrast as possible with the background.

'Help Required' Hand Signals

Here are just a few of the more important ones:

△	Safe to land here
I	Require a doctor
↑	Proceeding in direction of arrow
X	Unable to proceed
NN	Nothing found
II	Require medical supplies
IIIII	Require assistance
LL	All well

Normally the pilot will select a safe area to land. The clothing of the ground party should be sufficient to attract his attention, but if a marker of any kind is used it should be firmly pegged or weighted down in the centre of the landing area. Clear away any loose debris and stamp down dry snow. The aircraft will approach into the wind, so assemble your party well clear and to windward of the landing area.

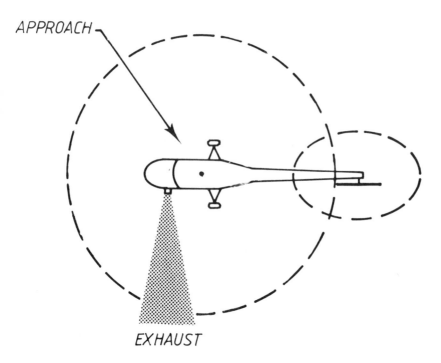

APPROACH

EXHAUST

Fig. 143. *Approaching a helicopter.*

Safety Precautions

Do not approach the helicopter until you are signalled to do so by the pilot. When you do, proceed with caution in the direction indicated, usually from the front and on the pilot's right hand side, so that you remain in his sight at all times. Do exactly as you are told by the crew.

Evacuation of Victim

With the main party, proceed to the scene of the accident at a steady pace. Do not rush, as the time is being put to good use by the advance party in making the patient comfortable and rendering the necessary first aid. Remember that there may be a long carry back and energy must be conserved. If there is the prospect of a very long carry make arrangements for a support party to bring food and drink.

On the way in, examine the ground for the best evacuation route and mark it if necessary.

The arrangement of the victim on the stretcher will depend on the nature of his injuries and the type of stretcher in use. Freedom from pain on the move should be the aim. Remember that a helmet may be necessary if steep ground or screes have to be crossed. Be particularly careful in the case of suspected spinal injuries to avoid any movement of the spine itself. A rigid stretcher is essential for the safe evacuation of such cases.

Unconscious, or seriously injured casualties are best carried in the three-quarter prone position with the head tilted to one side. Someone must always be in attendance in case of vomiting, cessation of breathing or other emergency.

A stretcher-bearing party normally consists of 16–20 persons working in two teams and changing shifts every 10 minutes or so depending on the terrain. A third team is useful if the carry is to be a long one.

If the route is not obvious and has not been previously marked, someone should be sent ahead to select and mark the best line. This is, of course, particularly important at night.

It is the job of the Rescue Controller or of the police to give information to the press. If asked, the facts should be given, but on no account should any information be divulged about the victims, their names, addresses and so on. Even apparently harmless information about place of work, relatives or friends may be used by the media to identify injured persons before the next of kin have been informed. These details will be given at the proper time by the police.

Report to the Rescue Controller on return to base.

The Mountain Rescue Committee and the Mountain Rescue Committee of Scotland keep a record of all accidents in the hills. It is important that a full report on every incident is submitted to them.

Accident Report Form

ACCIDENT REPORT	Date:			Time	AM	PM

	Nat Grid Ref:

LOCATION	Exact Location (include marked map):

	Terrain:	Snow	Moor	Forest		Rock	Path
		Heather	Easy	Moderate		Steep	Other

COMPLETE DESCRIPTION OF ACCIDENT			Ascending Roped Rock Fall Avalanche Equipment Failure	Descending Unroped Illness Cold
	Witnesses:		Other	

INJURED PERSON	Name:		Age:	
	Address:		Male	Female
	Phone:			
	Whom to Notify:	Relationship:	Phone:	

INJURIES	Overall Condition:	Good Unconscious: If yes, length of time:	Fair	Serious Yes	Fatal No
	Injury 1	Location on Body: Nature of Injury:			
	Injury 2	Location on Body: Nature of Injury:			
	Other Injuries:	Location on Body: Nature of Injury:			

	General:	Bleeding Stopped Artificial Respiration Treated for Shock	Shelter Built Warm Fluids Given Evacuation

Accident Report Form (*Continued.*)

FIRST AID TREATMENT	Injury 1
	Injury 2
	Other Injuries:

ON-THE-SCENE PLANS	Will stay put Will evacuate to road Will evacuate a short distance to shelter Will send some members out Others:

PERSONNEL	Number: Inexperienced Intermediate Experienced Advanced Capability for a bivouac: Yes No
	Attach the pre-trip prepared LIST OF PARTY MEMBERS including names, addresses and phone numbers to the ACCIDENT FORM BEING TAKEN OUT.

EQUIPMENT AVAILABLE	Tents Sleeping Bags Flares Ice Axes Hardware Stove and Fuel Ropes Other:

WEATHER	Warm Moderate Freezing Snow Wind Sun Mist Rain Other:

TYPE OF EVACUATION RECOMMENDED	Lowering Operation Carry-Out Helicopter Rigid stretcher None until specialised medical assistance Specify:

PARTY LEADER	Name:

MESSENGERS SENT FOR HELP	Names:

FURTHER INFORMATION, IF ANY	

11 Thoughts on Party Leadership

One of the unavoidable illusions created by any handbook of this type, is the impression of a mass of material all in watertight compartments, any one of which a leader may be required to recall from time to time. What such handbooks cannot easily convey, is the need for all these items of skill and knowledge to have been so well absorbed that they no longer exist in isolated compartments. It is necessary for them to have meshed with all the others in an integrated manner similar to the way in which tapestry threads interweave to form a pattern or picture. This mingling of threads underlines the fact that each of them has a relationship with all the others. The nature of these interdependent relationships must be understood by the leader so that when he is faced by situations, minor or major, requiring his skills, the interaction of all the factors will have occurred almost intuitively and spontaneously to the point where the key factors influencing the situation are identified. Identifying the key factors in a situation is a crucial leadership skill for it is these factors which influence judgements and subsequent decisions. The ability to juggle them all in the air and quickly select the appropriate skills from the armoury to deal with a situation should be an important aim for all aspirant leaders.

The handbook cannot tell you how to 'get it all together' so that you can apply all you have learned in the right sequence; pitch it all at the right level; deliver it all at the right moment in the manner most appropriate for a group in the course of a day in the hills. Depending upon your experience and your point of view it is either a very simple or a very complex business. The notes in this section attempt to give some intimation of the nature of that task when the job of leadership is actually being carried out.

Aims and Values

In the hills with a group of people, the party leader has one big paradox to resolve: he has to find the right balance between what is dangerous (exciting), and what is safe (perhaps dull). This is, admittedly, oversimplifying the situation but the problem lies at the heart of the most fundamental questions: 'Why are you doing it? What is it all for? Why bother taking a group into the hills when you could be doing your own thing with friends? If you have bothered to saddle yourself with a group, just what are you hoping to achieve? For what overall purpose are you really taking the group out into the mountains? What is it all about? What are you all about?'

If you have not really attempted to find an answer to these questions for yourself there will be something lacking in the way you approach both your group and the mountains. The answers to these questions will colour and shape all your subsequent behaviour and actions in the working situation. No one else can tell you the answer. Discussing it and exchanging opinions about it will help, but the final amalgam of ideas must necessarily be of your own making and be peculiar to you.

The leader's problem then in trying to find the right balance between danger and safety, is trying to find the balance between on the one hand, excitement, pleasure, interest, spontaneity, enjoyment and freedom; and on the other hand, too much discipline leading to regimentation and monotony or the sterile rigidity that comes from over-planning and over-preparation. The leader should always try to be aware of whether the balance is being tipped in one direction or another through his own arrogance or anxious lack of confidence or through sound judgements or optimistic inexperience.

He has to know when it is permissible to prevent the considerations of safety from intruding too strongly on his party to the point that they detract from the experience he wants his party to have. He has to know when it is necessary for such considerations to be paramount to all others. If he can so control the safety factors that they are a discrete background framework of good practice working for, rather than against, feelings of excitement, interest, curiosity, exploration, adventure, achievement and a general enjoyment of the hills, he is on the right lines.

The mountain leader training scheme does not set out to teach you how to become infallible. It cannot even give you (and never will) a set of rules and procedures that will work in every situation to give you the right answer. It can only give you, as it were, a set of tools and show how they might be used in certain specific instances. How you might use them in other instances can only be learned through experience by you. It is more a question of developing a total awareness of the mountain and group situation (experience helps here) so that one is able to weigh up all the various factors and come up with an answer for a particular party in a specific situation. It should be obvious that the quality of your own personal experience is going to be a crucial factor here. Considerable demands may be made on your powers of judgement and decision-making at times. To be effective, these must be able to rely on a sound foundation of solid experience.

Personal Experience

There is no substitute for actual personal experience and there are no shortcuts to the gaining of it.

You cannot hope to become an effective party leader unless you are prepared to spend a considerable amount of time on it and until you have the adequate background of personal experience that will enable you to make accurate assessments of situations and therefore sound decisions regarding action to be taken. These assessments and decisions must then be tempered by what you know your group can take or is capable of doing. If you have a new group about which you are not sure, your safety margins must be greater. Amongst other things this means that:

(a) You must be able to distinguish between real and apparent danger.

(b) You need to know what your own strengths and weaknesses on the mountains are, so that you can recognise and avoid situations where you will be more concerned for yourself than your party. You may also possibly be taking unjustifiable risks with your party in such situations.

(c) You need sufficient depth of experience to enable you to recognise those exceptional situations when the text book answer should be disregarded because it is unsuitable for a particular set of circumstances. It then becomes a question of using past experience to help you judge what needs doing and what should be guarded against and applying intelligence as to the best way of doing it with the means at your disposal. Mountaineers have a rather vague name for this which they loosely term, 'having mountain sense'. There are times when it is intuitive and almost subconscious in nature and other times when it is strongly conscious and insistent. It probably has its roots in past experience.

Leadership Styles

The term 'leadership' is capable of so many widely differing interpretations that it tends to be a stumbling block to the understanding of many people both inside and outside the mountain leader training scheme. Some leadership styles are easily identifiable.

(a) There is leadership by example—a force pulling the group along from the front. Unless care is taken the tail-end may suffer. If this type of leader is himself highly skilled and competent he may be so far removed from the level of skill in his party that he is unaware of, or unsympathetic to, the difficulties his party may be experiencing. Being at the front, he will tend to take all the decisions all the time.

The group will not be involved in the experience as much as they might be. They will tend to be tagging along blindly without any real idea of what is happening or of the whys, wheres and hows of it all.

(b) There is leadership from the rear—a force pushing the group from the back. The concern here may be to allow those at the front to feel they are involved and exercising some initiative in the shape of the day. There is also present a humane concern to encourage the weaker ones who tend to be in the rear. The danger here is the leader's loss of control at the front unless some thought has been given to the problem. You need to know the ground quite well so that you can anticipate when you need to return to the front to cope with any tricky sections. You need to know your party well enough to be able to rely on them not moving on beyond the contact range of eye, ear or voice, as necessary to the situation. You can set recognisable points at which the front should halt to allow the rear to catch up. A more experienced party may be content to go at the pace of the slowest, but techniques need devising to cope with the impulsiveness of novice groups. The skill is to maintain enthusiasm and enjoyment without losing control. To regard your role as maintaining control without killing enthusiasm is a negative way of approaching the situation.

(c) There is leadership from the centre which is symbolic of the modern sociological concept of leadership. Such a leader is a combination of both the styles mentioned above. He will only be authoritarian and almost military at those times when occasion or situation demand it. This style will be used sparingly and only when physical safety is threatened by ignorance or foolhardiness in the group. During the day he will be at the front, centre or back according to the indications he picks up from the physical environment and his group. He tends to work democratically as far as possible, helping (but not generally dictating) his group to resolve their different impulses and inclinations, to decide for themselves, to adapt and to carry through their plans. He is watchful to give support, encouragement, sympathy, guidance or advice to those individuals who need help to cope. He is tuned in to signs of discomfort, stress or anxiety. He is alive to possibilities that will arouse interest in and enthusiasm for the mountain environment. He is at once consultant, counsellor, guide, mentor, chaperone, and a source of information, knowledge, skill and experience. He sees himself less as a leader and more as a person whose experience is at the service of the group. In short, he helps a group to lead itself as far as he judges it is capable of doing so.

I would suggest this style as being the most desirable one.

Leadership Awareness

Leading a formal party in the hills is a very different 'game' from the 'walking informally with friends' situation. With friends of ability equal to your own, responsibility and decision-making is shared in a very casual almost carefree, way. Each is tacitly understood to be more or less master of his own destiny (and for adults this is the legal interpretation too), having the skill, experience and knowledge to look after himself. If one of them has a problem it is assumed he will have the sense to speak up.

Once you begin formally to lead a party you enter a different world of hillwalking with a new, extra, second dimension containing an additional set of factors to become aware of and take into account. These factors are mostly concerned with managing people and maintaining good working relationships.

(a) Although you will have a group with you, you are virtually walking 'solo' in the sense that there may be no other person with whom you can in extremity, share the responsibility of decision-making and navigating. You may encourage the group to participate in these activities but the onus is still on you to check they are correct or acceptable.

(b) The whole group is dependent on you to the extent that, in the final analysis, you are responsible for its enjoyment, comfort and safety.

(c) You may have to do all the thinking about everything for each and every one of them (especially if they are novices).

(d) You may not assume that what you can do, they can also do.

(e) You may not assume that what you want to do in the day will coincide with their desires and aspirations. This is one aspect served well by the democratic style of leadership which keeps channels of communication open and gives you vital feedback on how the group reads the situation.

(f) You may not assume that how you feel at any given moment (e.g. too hot, too cold, comfortable, relaxed, confident) is how they feel (e.g. thirsty, hungry, miserable, overawed, anxious, tense, bored, fed-up, etc.). Watch for 'signals' coming your way. Be aware of your group.

(g) Safety should be more a matter of good practice used discreetly so as to detract minimally from enjoyment.

Leadership Attitudes and Approaches

To deal successfully with these factors, outlined in the previous section, an attitude and approach is required that is rather different from the hillwalker who climbs for personal satisfaction and pleasure. Refer again to the first section about aims and values.

(a) You need to have examined within yourself your own reasons and motives for wanting to take groups into the hills. You need to have clarified for yourself why you are wanting to do it at all, and to what ends. There needs to be a clear realisation that the responsibilities of leadership impose a discipline that allows no room for your own wishes, ambitions or aspirations. Leadership in this context is a state of mind that is largely selfless.

(b) Leadership used for selfish ends is both empty (i.e. non-creative) and sterile. Leadership used to inflate your own ego, such as needing to demonstrate your own 'superior (?)' powers to the group, is a destructive exercise without value to your group. The group should be approached with humility rather than arrogance. Do not assume you will always know what is best for them. Do not think you understand their needs so well that you do not need ever to consult them or ask for opinions. How could you otherwise ever hope to pitch things at their level of expectation, motivation, interest and capability?

(c) A leader should be concerned that his interest in mountains does not overshadow his interest in the group. If getting into the hills means more to you than having a group with you, you should think twice before taking it on. By this I mean that if your satisfactions derive primarily from personal reasons (i.e. so many miles covered or peaks climbed) you are going to be a disappointed, frustrated person who is unsympathetic to the group and a rotten leader. Very rarely will the motives, ambitions, interests and capabilities of the group coincide with yours.

(d) If your concept of your job consists solely in imparting as much technical know-how to your group as you can, think again! There is more to mountains than teaching the skills and techniques of mountaincraft. These things are essential aids and tools, but such a day so spent may be too clinical, too mechanical, and so without life. The essential nature of the mountain experience may be missed. Under the mass of time-calculations, distances, bearings, conventional signs, contour lines, do's and don'ts, the mountains may be so obscured that they never have the chance to reveal their inherent attractions to the group. If the garnering of your own experience was a chore, you will never be able to set the atmosphere so that a love and feeling for mountains can be transmitted to the group. Time should be given for the aesthetic and spiritual feelings to impinge on the awareness of those in the group for whom such things will have meaning and great importance.

(e) Colour, light and shade, shape and form, textures, sounds and scents are all part of the mountain scene. Sometimes they will work their own magic unassisted. At other times the leader may find he is able with benefit to heighten the group's awareness of them. The ability to interpret the mountain scene is of enormous value, for walking can be a monotonous business for many children. They sometimes need to have been exposed to the hills a number of times before they come to appreciate that a good deal of the charm lies in their contrasts and infinite variety. Any snippet of information about flora, fauna, natural and man-made features, is grist to the leader's mill. Curiosity, starved, often dies quickly. Feed it and the results are often very surprising and fruitful.

(f) Because of the serious nature of your responsibilities, however, your approach to the leadership situation must be systematic—the 'woolliness' of the 'walking with friends situation' will no longer suffice. All the detailed factors relating to good practice and comfort (i.e. safety) must be identified, and in this context, there must be a reason for everything you do and say and you must be conscious of the reason. There will be many things you learned in the early days by experience which you now do unconsciously without thought (e.g. the way you walk and pick your way up a path). All these things now have to be brought, as it were, from the back of your head to the front and consciously stored ready for use. In those areas which relate to safety and comfort you must be able to justify in every minute detail everything you do or choose not to do. This implies a very articulate grasp of the mountain situation which only a process of self-analysis and self-questioning about your own experience (mountain and otherwise—both are relevant) will give. It is not enough to know the right thing to do. You must know why it is right and what the consequence will be if it is done incorrectly or differently.

Leadership Skills

All the foregoing sections may seem to present a rather formidable challenge to an aspirant leader. But there are a number of skills he can employ to help himself. Indeed he should try so to develop these skills that they become ingrained habits rather than skills.

(a) *Recalling Past Experience*
One of your most invaluable aids will be *the ability to recall clearly past experience*, particularly your own feelings as a beginner. It will enable you to appreciate and be more acutely aware that if there

are occasions now which you feel are extending you the slightest bit, there will be some in the group in whom these feelings will be greatly magnified. This is called 'insight'. Develop it. Possible examples are when negotiating sections of rocky scrambling; narrow paths across steep slopes; steep descents; feelings of cold, hunger, thirst, fatigue to which you are more acclimatised than they are.

(b) *Planning and Forethought* (Anticipation)
   (i) This is a skill which will enable you to meet difficulties in a state of greater preparedness.
   (ii) It will often provide you with a ready-made course of action when emergencies arise.

   Do not, however, continually go about expecting crisis after crisis, but be ready for them when they happen, and have a plan of action already prepared to meet them, e.g. 'if someone had an accident here, what would I do?'. 'If I had to take this group down there, how long would it take, could they cope, who would be the ones to watch?'.

(c) *The Habit of Checking*
   (i) That both you and your party have the necessary food, clothing and equipment before setting off. In your concern for others, beware of forgetting to check your own gear is complete. It happens sometimes.
   (ii) That any instructions you may give are heard, understood and obeyed. This is basic but often neglected, particularly in the informal, fluid circumstances that are characteristic of mountain parties. Strong winds, anorak hood up, river noises all affect the hearing for example.
   (iii) How things are going with the party. With practice this becomes a 'sense' that is always 'switched on'. If you are at the front, look back frequently. Too many leaders forge on, unaware of the mounting chaos behind them.

(d) *The Habit of Observation*
   This skill is supplementary to the habit of checking. The ability to perceive things varies greatly in people. Work to improve yours.
   (i) It is mainly by observation that you will get to know the characteristics, strengths and weaknesses of each member of your party. Although you may chat a lot with the group, it is the non-verbal signals that will tell you much of what you need to know. Mainly by observation will you become aware of signs of tiredness, boredom, low morale, tension, anxiety stresses, personality conflicts, acute discomforts, feelings of insecurity,

lack of a sense of balance, lack of powers of co-ordination, sloppy footwork, etc., etc. All these and many others you will often have to discern for yourself, for the members of your group will often tend not to want to tell you about them. The pressure of a group on the move makes many people within the group reluctant to slow it down or stop it. You may even have to find out by asking direct questions—i.e. give them an opening by making it clear their enjoyment is more important than pushing on.

(ii) Observe the environment, continuously assessing its implications for you and your party in terms of enjoyment and pleasure, danger and effort, e.g. which routes offer most interest, protection from headwinds, reasonable footing (not always footpaths which may be badly eroded), changes in weather, greasy rocks, etc.

(e) *Decision-making*

A wise leader will normally contrive to get his group participating in as many decisions as he feels he can safely allow. They should have been given the chance to say what they would like to do on a particular day. Feedback for such discussion will be invaluable to the leader. This may not be possible with some novice groups, but more experienced groups are quite likely to have ideas on the subject which should be useful. One of the difficult problems to resolve always is whether the structure of your group should be determined by the hill chosen or whether the nature of the hill to be climbed should be determined by the structure of the group (i.e. number of members and their ability). Group discussion on objectives should facilitate the resolution of this problem in the early stages of your plans. During the route there are of course many decisions in which the group should be encouraged to participate, e.g. lunch stops, where to next?, is the pace right?, should we go on?

But it is the emergency/crisis decisions that are particularly the leader's concern. If the skills and habits outlined in the preceding sections have been developed strongly enough, the business of decision-making will already be half accomplished. For the big important decisions relating to the party's safety, the relevant factors will have been already observed or anticipated. It is then a question of using past experience to assess all the factors for and against, and picking out the best course of action from a number of possible alternatives.

(f) *Conclusion*

Thus we return again to the quality of this all-important personal past experience. Learn about your own limitations before ever leading parties. First, get to know yourself in mountains. Beware against anxiety causing you imperceptibly to speed up whilst navigating in mist. Learn beforehand what it is like to be lost temporarily; what it is like to be out in foul conditions; how to handle different types of terrain in ascent and descent; what it is like to be out at night (try a planned bivouac).

There are many other skills which could be mentioned, but space does not permit dwelling on them in full here. They are mostly skills related to the human factors in the leadership situation: the art of dealing with and relating to people; the skills of communication, the relieving of tension, of using humour, of understanding the dynamics of group life and encouraging the full development of the individuals in your group, of fostering self-sufficiency, confidence and self-determination in people. Although for most of your group the aim for the day may be in getting to the top and enjoying it, it is hoped that you, as a leader, have a broader awareness of the potential of the outdoors as a marvellous medium for helping people to develop their capacities to the full. Your job is to provide the atmosphere and the setting for this to take place. Whilst your responsibilities may be the safety, comfort and enjoyment (in that order of priority) of your party, they should feel it happening in reverse order.

12 Technique on Snow and Ice

Snow has a purifying effect on mountains. At a stroke it eliminates the puny efforts of man. Artificial boundaries vanish beneath the white mantle, footpaths disappear and a general stillness contributes to a feeling that the original wilderness has returned. Lacking familiar guidelines, the traveller is thrown back on his own resources and skills to blaze his own trail through this suddenly virgin country. It is exhilarating and there are few mountaineers whose pulses do not quicken at the firstsnow fall of winter. It is also challenging and, as the depressing list of accidents each winter shows only too clearly, not everyone passes the test. The reasons for this are complex but one fundamental mistake that is made by many aspiring graduates from summer hillwalking to winter mountaineering is to underestimate the potential ferocity of conditions, particularly in the Scottish Highlands in winter. Snowfall is irregular and unpredictable and is often propelled by gale force winds into gullies and corrie headwalls where it accumulates in thick, potentially hazardous slabs topped by menacing overhanging cornices. Although temperatures rarely fall below −15°C they fluctuate within a wide range and with disconcerting rapidity, with the result that you can be wading through soft slush in the morning and cramponing on hard boiler-plate in the afternoon. High winds and zero or sub-zero temperatures are a heat-sapping combination and greatly increase the risk of exposure, particularly when coupled with exhaustion and inadequate clothing. Winter days are short; as little as 6 hours of daylight, and it is easy, even for experienced mountaineers, to underestimate the time required to overcome the difficulties of a descent in the gathering gloom when the party is tired and perhaps a little careless. A high proportion of accidents are 'slips while descending' so that this is an area of practice and experience which demands special attention. The penalty for making such a slip is likely to be far more serious in conditions of snow and ice than in summer. What could result in a grazed knee and a certain loss of dignity on a scree slope in summer could, on that same slope in winter, mean a long uncontrolled slide on hard snow with the possibility of a much more serious outcome. The demarcation between scrambling and rock climbing is far more clear than that between winter hillwalking and snow and ice climbing and, furthermore, it is easier for the winter hillwalker to stray into the realm of the climber without really being aware that he is doing so, before it is too late. Indeed, the transition may well be due to factors outside his control such as a sudden fall in temperature causing the snow to ice up. It is for this reason that the winter hillwalking leader must be familiar with those same techniques which form the bread and butter of the climber's skill: the use of the ice axe for step-cutting, cramponning, ice-axe braking, belaying on snow and so on. He must learn through experience a fine sense of what is appropriate in particular situations: when to put on the rope, what type of protection is suitable for the prevailing conditions, what line to follow to make the most of the conditions and to avoid possibly dangerous slopes. This kind of judgement is only acquired after a long apprenticeship. To quote from the syllabus for the Winter Mountain Leader Scheme: 'To lead a party into the Scottish Mountains in winter conditions is a serious undertaking. Demands are made on the leader which are far in excess of his normal responsibilities in summer.'

Equipment and Clothing

The subject of clothing has already been discussed in Chapter 2 (pages 56–58). Winter weather conditions in the British Isles, particularly in the Scottish Highlands, can provide the most searching test of the effectiveness of clothing. It goes without saying that inner warmth is essential and this is best provided by layers of wool, starting with long johns (one piece) next to the skin, followed by a long-tailed shirt and several medium weight sweaters. Various combinations are possible for the outer layers, e.g. a Goretex outer with an inner synthetic fibre liner, but it is important to be aware of the problem of overheating. Kicking steps up a long snow slope is very hard work and generates a great deal of water vapour in the form of sweat. You must be able to respond by removing one or more of the inner layers. This is particularly important if the outer layer is not vapour permeable because this can give rise to condensation, which may soak the inner clothing. When the activity ceases, cooling is accelerated by the evaporation of all this moisture. The anorak should be long enough to cover the buttocks (you do a lot of sitting on a snow climb) but not so long that it interferes with your leg movements. Some anoraks and overtrousers are potentially dangerous because they have a very smooth finish and offer very little friction against the snow in the event of a fall. Acceleration is very rapid even on quite gentle slopes. For the legs and trunk salopettes, in Helenca or ski pants material, are more practical than breeches which have a nasty habit of exposing the midriff when you least want it exposed. If woollen breeches are used they should be backed up by waterproof overtrousers which must be of a design which allows them to be put on and taken off with the minimum of fuss and bother. Overtrousers must not be worn with crampons unless they can be tucked into the gaiters which should be knee length and fit snugly round the boots and calves. Other essential items include some kind of head protection. Ski hats are popular, but they are rarely as effective as a balaclava, and a short absorbent scarf is a useful barrier against getting spindrift and ice chips down your neck. The hands are probably the most difficult part of the anatomy to protect, largely because you are continually having to use them for tasks which are much better performed without gloves. Apart from making your hands cold, continually taking your gloves off makes them wet. There is no complete answer, but for warmth wear a pair of thick woollen mitts together with waterproof overmitts and carry at least one spare pair of woollen mitts.

Boots for winter walking and climbing have to have certain characteristics to make them suitable for the job. Many accidents have been caused by people making the mistake of using their lightweight summer walking boots for a winter expedition. Unfortunately, boots for winter use do not come cheaply. The leather should be unsplit and of first quality to provide the required degree of water resistance, insulation, stiffness and general durability. The sole must be stiffened to enable the boot to be used for kicking steps in hard snow and to provide a stable platform for crampons. A mid-height boot is probably best and if you want to avoid cold feet they should not be too neat a fit. Allow plenty of room for the toes and for two pairs of stockings. Rigid plastic boots are suitable for snow and ice, but do not usually flex enough for use below the snow line.

The Ice Axe

There is probably more controversy surrounding the ice axe than almost any other item of equipment and this is in spite of the fact that it is a very ancient instrument which has remained remarkably unchanged since it was first used by shepherds in Alpine regions hundreds of years ago. It has become the basic tool of the winter mountaineer, an indispensable aid to safe progress across snow and ice covered terrain. A modern ice axe is illustrated in Fig. 144. The head is usually made in chrome molybdenum steel with a shovel-like adze at one end and a gently curved pick at the other. The head is attached to the shaft which may be of wood, metal, fibreglass or plastic. The weakest of these materials is wood so if you are selecting a shaft of this type make sure there are no knots in it and that the grain is straight and evenly spaced. The other materials, though perhaps less satisfying to handle, are considerably stronger and therefore much less likely to break under stress. The length of shaft is determined by the use to which it is to be put. If you want a walking stick then buy one, but it will

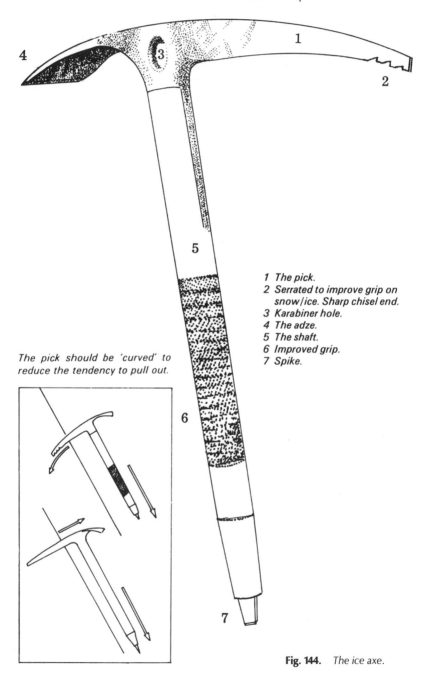

1 The pick.
2 Serrated to improve grip on snow/ice. Sharp chisel end.
3 Karabiner hole.
4 The adze.
5 The shaft.
6 Improved grip.
7 Spike.

The pick should be 'curved' to reduce the tendency to pull out.

Fig. 144.   *The ice axe.*

not be much use to you on a steep slope of hard snow or ice. Conversely, the short hammer-axe, so effective on a steep ice pitch, would be virtually useless on a moderately angled snow slope or in descent. For general winter mountaineering an axe of 70 cm is a good average length, suitable for most purposes, although your final choice will be determined by personal preference. The axe may be fitted with a wrist loop or with a longer tape threaded through the hole in the head and adjusted so that it is taut when the axe is gripped just above the spike.

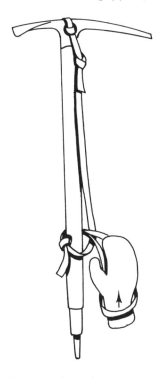

Fig. 145. *Ice axe fitted with wrist sling. The loop is gripped like a ski-stick strap.*

Advantages of wrist loop:
    Security if axe is accidentally dropped.
    Support if pulling on axe.
    Reinforces grip of gloved hand.
    Axe can be suspended from wrist, freeing hand for conventional hold, clearing powder snow, etc.
Disadvantages of wrist loop:
    Can cause problems when getting into self-arrest position.
    In the event of a fall and the axe being let go, it remains whirling round dangerously close to your body. Moral—don't let go. In this case the long sling is probably safer than the wrist loop.
    You have to change hands every time you change direction.

For more advanced climbing whether you use a sling or loop or nothing at all is a matter of personal preference. Each climber must weigh the pros and cons and adopt the method that suits him best. Whatever method is chosen it is very useful to have a holster at your waist into which an axe or hammer can be conveniently slotted.

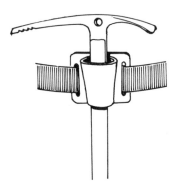

Fig. 146.   *Axe holster.*

A leather or plastic cup attached to a waist tape.

Technique on Snow

For convenience the techniques used on snow are considered separately from those used mainly on ice. On the mountain, however, these two states merge imperceptibly with one another so that it is quite impossible to say at what point one begins and the other ends. Likewise techniques which are appropriate for ice climbing may also be perfectly suitable for use on hard snow.

Carrying the Axe

It is not a matter of great moment whether you carry your axe with the pick or the adze pointing forward. What is important is to keep it out of other people's way and to have it available for support and as an aid to balance, ready to bring into use as the situation requires. Those who advocate carrying it pick forward claim that you are less likely to puncture yourself and that it is more comfortable to have the heel of your palm resting on the flat of the adze than on the narrow blade of the pick. Those who advocate adze forward point out that this is the natural position from which to move directly into the self-arrest position. Take your pick!

On Gentle Slopes

Steps are simply kicked into the snow, either straight up or in a series of zig-zags. The harder the snow the more vigorous the kick has to be and the smaller the step. Economy of effort is important because kicking a long line of steps can be very tiring, especially on the calf muscles. Swing the lower leg from the knee and allow its momentum to work for you. The step should, if possible, be large enough to take the ball of the foot and it should slope into the hill to provide a secure platform. Support and balance are obtained from the axe which is held in the walking position in whichever hand is closest to the slope.

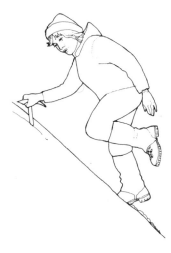

Fig. 147.   *Kicking steps using the whole axe for balance and support.*

As the slope steepens so it becomes necessary to increase your security by driving the axe shaft further into the snow. In harder snow the axe may only penetrate a short distance and in this case a two-handed grip is to be preferred, one hand on the head and the other as low down on the shaft as possible, against the snow surface, to reduce leverage.

Fig. 148.   *Two-handed grip on the axe when the snow is too hard to allow the axe to penetrate all the way.*

At this point a zig-zag ascent may be less tiring and here again the axe is driven in like a stake. A rhythm soon develops: two steps, drive in the axe, two steps and so on. The axe should be moved when the body is in a stable position, that is when the inside foot is in front and above the outside one, just as one would stand in balance on a pair of skis. To change direction turn, face to the slope, with a three step movement instead of the usual two and continue on in the new direction. On a diagonal ascent the side of the boot is used to make the step. This technique can be particularly effective on hard snow where a slash with the edge of the sole provides a small but adequate foothold. It is worth remembering that such small holds are totally inadequate if a retreat has to be made.

Fig. 149. *Kicking steps in a diagonal ascent using the axe in the brace position.*

As the slope steepens still further (45°) and especially if the snow is too hard to take more than a few centimetres of the shaft, the axe can be held across the body in the 'brace' position, outside hand on the head and the inside hand on the shaft as close to the snow as possible. This is not as secure a technique as driving the axe in vertically and quite soon you may be considering whether or not to cut steps. Your decision will be influenced mainly by the hardness of the snow and the experience of your party, but remember that you may well have to descend the same slope later in the day, in which case a line of steps might be very welcome.

Descent

On the steeper slopes this can be a daunting prospect and perhaps it is fortunate that most mountaineers tend to overestimate the difficulty of a descent. On steep firm snow face the slope, thrust the axe in as far below you as you can comfortably reach and then kick steps straight down. As the slope eases and your confidence returns, turn to face the valley and

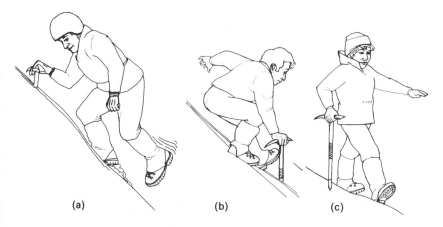

Fig. 150. *Descending a snow slope.*
(a) *On steep slopes face in and use the whole axe shaft for support.*
(b) *On intermediate slopes combine axe support with firm steps facing out and digging in the heels.*
(c) *On gentle slopes walk straight down using the heels.*

walk down. This is not a technique to be indulged in, in any half-hearted way. Lean well out so that your whole weight is brought to bear on the heel that is being driven stiff-legged into the slope below. Security is provided by reaching down and driving the axe vertically into the snow every two or three steps. As the slope eases this can be dispensed with and the axe held in the walking or self-arrest position. The commonest mistake made by newcomers to snow is to hug the slope but as with climbing a rock slab this only gives the illusion of security. As far as possible keep your body weight over your feet.

Glissading

Glissading can be great fun but, like scree running, it has to be approached with caution and common sense. The slope must be free of avalanche hazard and you must be able to see the whole of it including the run-out area which should be free of boulders and other obstacles. The danger lies in loss of control which can be caused by all sorts of things other than poor technique: a sudden change in the texture of the snow, for example. To be ready for any such emergency the axe should be held in the self-arrest position. The actual technique to be used will depend on the nature of the snow and the angle of the slope. The easiest is simply to sit down as if you were on a toboggan, controlling your speed with your feet and your body position by trailing the spike of the axe in the snow behind you. The standing glissade is much more difficult and is really a form of skiing but on very short skis! It helps to spread your arms for balance but make sure you keep a firm grip on your axe.

Fig. 151. *Sitting glissade.*

Ice Axe Braking

Since it is a relatively simple matter to slip on snow or ice and since the consequences of doing so can be serious, one of the first skills to be learned by the aspiring winter mountaineer is to be able to stop a slide. Ice axe braking or self-arrest, as it is called, is not an easy technique to master. It needs practice and beginners should be given the opportunity of doing so on the first suitable snow slope. A concave slope, free of protruding rocks and with a safe run-out, is necessary.

The basic braking position is lying facing the slope with the axe held diagonally across your body, one hand on the head of the axe in such a way that the adze is tucked in against your chest and shoulder and the pick is directed into the snow with the other hand close to the spike. Keep your elbows well in to your sides and try to get as much of your weight as possible to bear on the pick. To do this try to pull up on the axe head and arch your back over the top of it, keeping your forehead close to the snow. Keep your legs apart for stability and if you are not wearing crampons your toes can be used to add to the braking effect of the axe. Most people brake with their right hand on the axe head. It is better to concentrate on perfecting this before trying a left-handed brake.

Fig. 152. *The ice axe braking position as seen from the snow.*

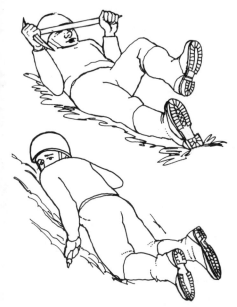

Fig. 153. *Braking with the ice axe after a feet first fall on back.*

If you fall feet-first but on your back remember to roll towards the same side as the hand that is holding the axe head and not towards the spike which could dig in and throw you. Apply pressure on the pick gradually to avoid the axe being snatched out of your grasp in your eagerness to stop.

Fig. 154.　*Braking with the ice axe after a head first fall, face down.*

Head-first falls are more difficult to control and the first action is to get into a head-uphill position from which the conventional self-arrest technique can be used. Falling head-first face down, the technique is to reach out horizontally with the pick as far as you can on the same side as the arm which is holding the axe head. Insert the pick into the snow and the braking effect on that side will cause your body to swing round past the axe into a head-uphill position. You should now be in a position with your arms at full stretch, so arch your back upwards, lift out the pick and place it below your shoulder and brake as before.

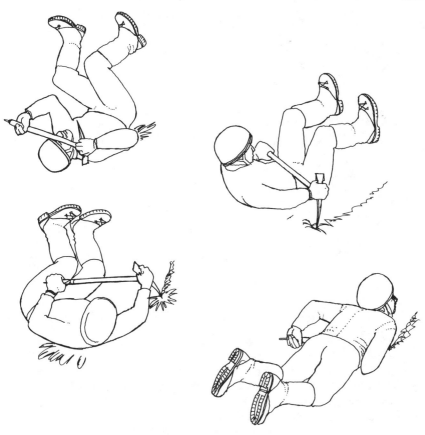

Fig. 155. *Braking with the ice axe after a head first fall on back.*

In a head-first fall on your back, the first sequence of moves is to insert the pick close to your hip and on the same side as the arm which is holding the axe head. Dig the pick in and at the same time pull yourself up on it into a sitting position. Bring your knees up towards your chest then swing your legs away from the axe head and allow them to fall through into the head-uphill position from which the normal arrest can be made.

In a tumbling fall the first priority is to stabilise your position by spreading your arms and legs as widely as possible. Once you are in a stable position you can adopt the appropriate braking method. Crampons and rucksack can cause problems.

Fig. 156. *How not to brake! The climber has rolled the wrong way, towards the arm which is holding the spike of the axe, with the inevitable result that the spike has dug into the snow.*

These descriptions and the diagrams which accompany them will make it abundantly clear that the technique of self-arrest can only be mastered as a result of determined practice. Hopefully, it may never be required in a real-life situation, but if it is, remember that you may only get one shot at it. Speed of execution is as important as technique, because of the very rapid acceleration of a falling body on hard snow.

Cornices

The formation of cornices is discussed more fully in Chapter 14 'Snow and Avalanches' (page 306). Here it is sufficient to note that they form in the lee of ridges or plateaux and that they constitute a major threat to climbers because of their unfortunate tendency to collapse and of course because they pose a final obstacle at the end of a route, by which time the prospect of retreat may be difficult to contemplate.

The collapse of a cornice is difficult to predict, but evidence may be found from neighbouring slopes. Warm conditions at any time during the winter spell danger and at these times it would be wise to steer clear of routes with menacing cornices overtopping them. The presence of a cornice indicates the accumulation of large, potentially unstable, masses of snow on the slopes below. The possibility of an avalanche must be considered and the degree of risk properly assessed.

Before attempting to break through a cornice, a solid anchor should be found well to the side and out of the way of the debris should there be a collapse. Cornices take a great variety of forms and vary widely in their hardness, but it will usually be necessary either to cut a slot in it or to tunnel through. Both require strenuous and determined effort and consume a fair amount of time. The adze of the axe should be used as a scraper although much effort can be saved by the use of a snow saw or shovel.

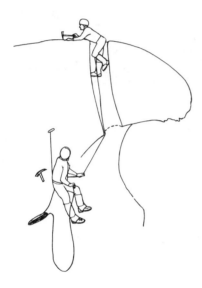

Fig. 157. *Tunnelling through a cornice.*

Techniques on Hard Snow and Ice

In the 40's it was unusual to see anyone wearing crampons in this country, even on 'The Ben' when plastered with snow and ice. Nailed boots were the order of the day and crampons were those newfangled gadgets that some people, who did not know any better, used in foreign parts. But of course the wearing of nailed boots enabled the average hillwalker to roam the mountains, if not in complete safety, at least in the confidence that he was unlikely to slip on a patch of hard snow or ice. The modern hillwalker has to get used to the fact that his footwear is not ideally suited for winter conditions. The practice of his craft calls for a keen awareness of where he may and where he may not tread. Crampons may not be an indispensable item of his equipment but without them he is inevitably restricted in the range and quality of the expeditions which are open to him.

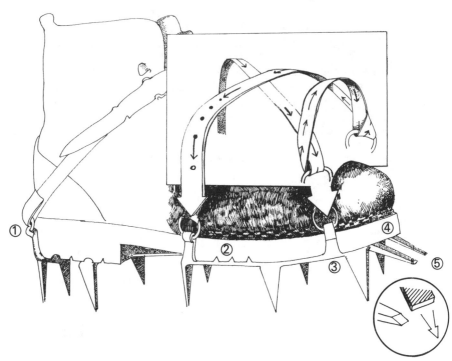

Fig. 158. *How to lace a crampon strap. Note particularly the arrangement of the strap at the toe which ensures that the top loop will not fall forward. Inset— how to sharpen the front points.*

It may seem strange but the most important thing about crampons is that they should fit your boots and be securely strapped on. The tales of crampons coming adrift at some critical stage of a route are legion. Do not let it happen to you. The crampons should be a spring fit on to your boots. In other words they should stay on without straps. The strap itself should be of waterproof material or coated to prevent the accumulation of ice. All sorts of patent straps are available but the simple binding illustrated in Fig. 158 is perfectly adequate. Note how the strap is threaded through the toe rings in a way which keeps it firmly in position. Cable bindings allow crampons to be put on and taken off very easily but do have to be used with fairly stiff boots. A wide range of crampons is available: rigid, hinged, adjustable, etc., and your choice will depend very much on how you intend to use them. However, you will certainly require 12-pointers with the two front points directed forward at an angle. Keep the points sharp using a straight grained file in the manner shown in Fig. 158.

Step Cutting

It is sometimes said that step cutting is a dying craft, and certainly with ever more climbers using crampons and modern front-point and two-handed techniques the need to cut laborious lines of steps is much less frequent. Nevertheless, there are many occasions, particularly with a party of novices, when a few well-cut steps can make the difference between success and failure, between a safe passage and unjustifiable risk. For general hillwalking without crampons it is as essential a technique as ice axe braking.

Cutting steps is a skill which improves with practice and since it involves swinging the axe with one or sometimes two hands, balance is a critical consideration. Always cut from a stable position, inside boot above and in front and try to develop a rhythm: chop two steps, thrust in the axe, move up, chop the next two steps, take out the axe and plant it higher up, move up and so on. The size and spacing of the steps will depend on the angle of the slope and the experience of the party. On snow always chop into the hole made by the previous cut (see Fig. 159).

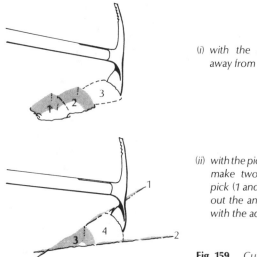

(i) with the adze—always cut away from the first chop.

(ii) with the pick—in slabby snow make two slashes with the pick (1 and 2) and then chop out the angle between them with the adze (3 and 4).

Fig. 159. *Cutting a step in snow.*

If the consistency of the snow is right, not too hard and not too soft, it is often possible to cut a slash step with a single blow of the axe, just long enough and wide enough to accommodate the side of the boot. It is much easier to develop a good rhythm with this method and a diagonal line of steps can be cut either up or down in a fraction of the time it would take to cut full steps.

If the snow is slabby, make a V-shaped slash with the pick and then chop-out inside the V. On ice the same basic rules apply though it takes more skill and effort to cut good steps with the pick. It is normal to cut steps in a series of zig-zags. On easier slopes a single line of steps will suffice but as the slope steepens it becomes difficult to bring the inside leg through and at this point two parallel lines are better, one for each boot.

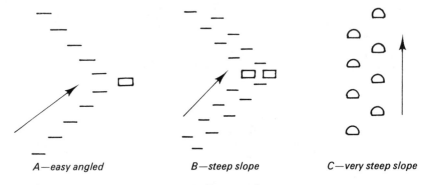

| A—easy angled | B—steep slope | C—very steep slope |

Fig. 160. *Step patterns on progressively steeper slopes.*

On the steepest slopes a direct frontal attack is best, cutting a ladder of steps straight up. Since the steps are used for both hands and feet it is helpful to fashion a small lip on each step with the adze to serve as a jug handle.

Fig. 161. *Cutting steps in descent of steep snow/ice. In this case the left leg is always moved down first, followed by the right. Then cut two more steps and so on.*

Cutting steps down can be awkward, the more so with a short axe. It is best to cut a ladder of steps directly down the slope usually one-handed, cutting two steps at a time. Face right if you are right-handed and move down in such a way that your right foot (outside leg) is always lower than your left (inside leg). In other words always step down with the lower leg first and do not attempt to step through. In the right snow conditions a single line of slash steps can be cut, one step at a time. Reach down, cut a step and move the lower foot on to it. Bring the upper foot on to the step just vacated. Repeat. On a less steep slope it is possible to descend on a diagonal line, cutting two steps at a time from a stable position (outside leg ahead and below). Support yourself with the axe while stepping through with the inside leg. On really steep or thin ice the only sensible means of descent is by abseiling.

Crampon Technique

Fig. 162. *Cramponing up an easy slope placing the feet flat on the surface and engaging all 10 points.*

Fig. 163. *Crampon techniques on moderate slopes.*

On the flat or on reasonably straightforward slopes the method is to keep your feet as flat as possible on the snow or ice so that all the points grip, except of course the front ones. Because there is a limit to how far you can flex your ankles a direct ascent must eventually give way to a diagonal one.

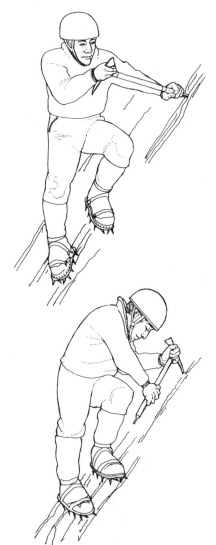

Fig. 164. *Crampon technique on steep slopes. The inside leg is being brought through. Note how the toes are pointed down the slope. The axe is in the brace position.*

Fig. 165. *Crampon technique on a very steep slope. The climber is practically walking backwards up the slope. The pick is driven in and then used for support and a certain amount of traction.*

As the slope steepens it becomes necessary to face more outwards, turning the toes more and more downhill in order to maintain the flat-footed position and ten-point contact with the snow. It also helps to bend your knees. Axe support will depend on the slope angle and will change from the walking position, to the brace position and finally, on the steepest slopes, to the anchor position.

Walking on hard snow or ice is made a good deal easier if you are wearing crampons but take care because it is easy to trip or worse still to catch a gaiter with one of your front points. To prevent snagging get into the habit of walking with your feet about 30 cm (1 ft) apart. Even walking with crampons is a precise technique, so keep alert at all times.

If the snow is damp it can cling to your boots so that the crampons become completely 'balled-up' and ineffective. Watch out for this happening and every so often hit the side of each boot with the axe shaft to dislodge the snow. If these conditions persist for any length of time it may be best to remove your crampons. An alternative suggestion is to tie polythene bags over your boots and crampons to stop them balling-up.

On hard snow or ice it will be necessary to plant the pick with a swinging blow of the axe above and ahead of you so that it can be used for support and balance while you make the next two steps. The inside hand grasps the axe head while the outside hand pulls gently out and down on the spike. It is a common mistake to rest the spike of the axe on the snow. In practice, the shaft should remain roughly parallel to the slope in order to benefit from the positive hooking angle of the pick.

There is no doubt that the 'French technique', as it is called, is difficult to master but it is worth persevering because it is a pleasing and graceful method when well executed. It is also relatively secure because of the ten-point contact and it is less tiring in the end than front pointing. It calls for constant practice and very flexible ankle joints aided by boots with softish uppers.

Front Pointing

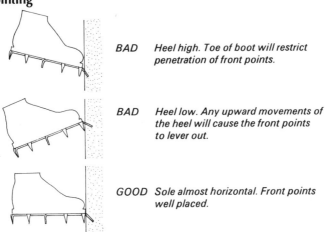

BAD   Heel high. Toe of boot will restrict penetration of front points.

BAD   Heel low. Any upward movements of the heel will cause the front points to lever out.

GOOD   Sole almost horizontal. Front points well placed.

Fig. 166. *Proper and improper use of the front points.*

Front pointing is a rather more aggressive technique, tackling the slope head on, with the result that it is physically much more demanding than the French technique. Because it is easy to learn and immediately effective many climbers adopt it to the exclusion of all other techniques. This is shortsighted because there are many situations, particularly on mixed rock, snow and ice where front pointing is not the most appropriate technique to use. However, there is no doubt that on really steep snow or ice it is the most effective method.

The front points are kicked firmly and squarely into the snow/ice with just sufficient vigour to obtain a good bite. The sole of the boot should be tilted slightly up from the horizontal and once planted, about hip width apart, the feet should remain still so that there is no tendency for the points to break out of the ice. Depending on the angle of slope the axe may be used as a dagger, thrusting the pick into the snow/ice at chest level or up to full stretch above your head. At steeper angles and on ice it will be necessary to plant the pick with a single swing of the axe, using the shaft as a hand rail as you front point up and then changing to a reverse grip on the head as you move on past.

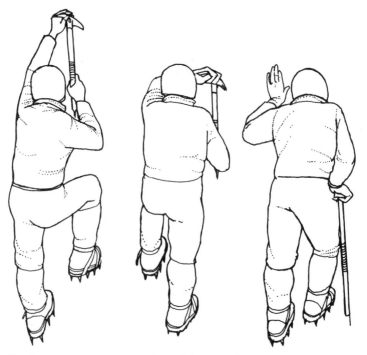

Fig. 167. *Front pointing using the pick first to pull up on and then as a push hold after reversing the grip.*

Fig. 168. *Front pointing, planting the pick with a blow of the axe. Note how the spike is clear of the slope with the shaft parallel to it.*

It is common practice now for climbers to use a second short axe or hammer-axe in the other hand. Using this two-handed technique, even overhanging ice pitches can be overcome.

The danger of front-pointing for the novice climber is that it is a deceptively easy technique to use in ascent but much more difficult to use in descent. As a consequence the overambitious beginner can be lured into a position from which escape is difficult, if not impossible, for him. The maxim that you should climb only what you are reasonably confident of being able to reverse is particularly relevant on ice.

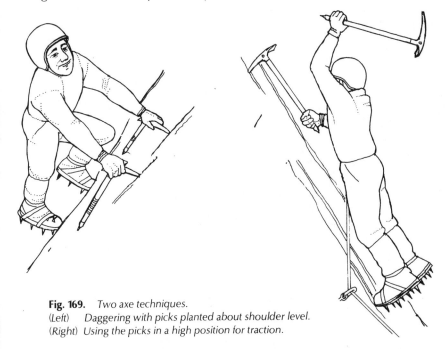

Fig. 169. *Two axe techniques.*
(Left) *Daggering with picks planted about shoulder level.*
(Right) *Using the picks in a high position for traction.*

Descending Snow/Ice

The problem about descending steep snow/ice is that it is difficult to plant the pick with a good swing of the axe. To be any good at all the pick must go in at about eye level which requires a grip about half way up the shaft. Furthermore, it is rather more difficult to ensure that the front points are well kicked in and that the boots are horizontal. As soon as possible turn sideways and follow a diagonal line of descent using the axe in the anchor position placing the feet flat on the ice with the toes turned downhill. As the angle eases it will be possible to follow a more direct line of descent facing outwards, feet well apart and flat on the ice, knees bent and with the upper body curved outwards so that all your weight is directly over your crampons. The axe can be used in whichever way gives the most positive support. This will either be the anchor position or the brace position. On a less steep slope the pick can be planted down near your feet and the shaft used as a handrail. It is very important to be positive and confident in all your movements. A tentative approach will almost certainly be repelled, possibly with dire consequences.

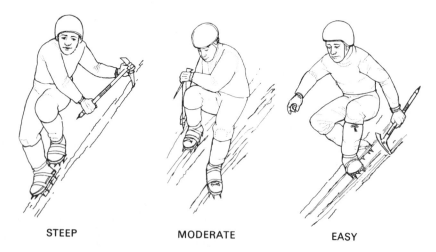

STEEP   MODERATE   EASY

Fig. 170.   *Descending snow/ice. In each case note how the feet are flat on the ice with the body weight directly over them.*

13 Security on Snow and Ice

Ice axes were not designed with belaying in mind. Primarily they were instruments for cutting steps in snow and ice. Other functions have arisen later out of necessity, without too much regard being paid to suitability for this multi-purpose role. Traditional methods of belaying placed a completely unjustified reliance on the strength of the axe shaft, often without sparing a thought for the material in which it was embedded. The modern axe is a stronger tool, but the strongest shaft in the world is useless if the snow itself is going to fracture under the expected load. Accident records show quite clearly that very often when a leader falls off on a winter climb he pulls the remainder of the party off with him. No doubt belaying on snow or ice can never match the security available on rock, but at the same time it could be a great deal safer than it is. In this chapter techniques are outlined and related to various types of snow.

Two initial hurdles must be overcome. The first is that some mountaineers tend to adopt a particular technique and use it regardless of all other factors. Many techniques are available, each one suited to particular snow conditions. The leader must be aware of these different conditions and adapt his method accordingly. The second point is that all these techniques demand very careful application. A badly placed axe, an inadequate stance, a rope in the wrong place, all can lead to disaster. The ice axe is your first and, if the worst happens, also your second line of defence. Learn through constant practice to use it instinctively so that if a slip occurs you know exactly what to do without thinking. While climbing snow your ice axe is a portable anchor available to assist and to safeguard every move. If the anchor fails or, as is more likely, the climber fails to use it properly, see to it that at least you have practised and are familiar with its use as a brake. Ice axe braking is a technique which is easy enough to understand but in the real world falls rarely occur exactly as they are described in the textbook.

Belaying on Snow

Because of the general unreliability of the snow anchor it is usually best to take an indirect belay so that the initial impact of a fall can be absorbed by

Fig. 171.   *Standing hip belay on snow.*

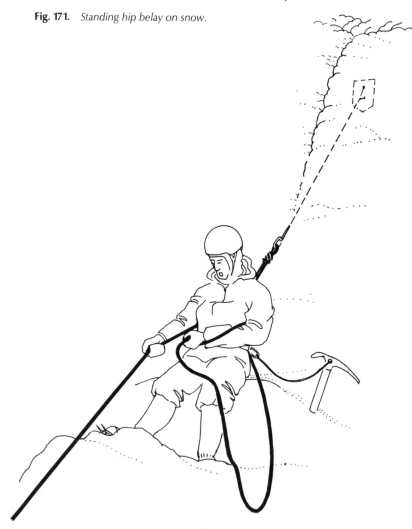

the belayer holding the rope in the conventional hip belay manner (see pages 128–130). Hopefully, the falling climber will be able to contribute to his own arrest by braking with his axe. It is important to cut an ample and stable stance in the correct position in relation to the anchor, since a pull on the anchor from the wrong direction could render it useless. A sitting position is to be preferred, with slots cut for the legs. The system for taking in the rope and holding a fall is exactly the same as described for security on rock.

Slings and Karabiners

Before discussing the subject of security on snow and ice it is necessary to introduce two items of special equipment which, although not absolutely essential, do make belaying a much more simple and effective procedure.

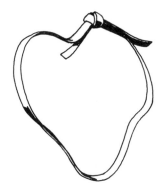

Fig. 172. *Sling tied with a tape knot.*   **Fig. 173.** *Doubled sling with karabiner.*

A sling is simply a length of nylon rope or tape tied with a double fisherman's or tape knot to form a loop (see Fig. 61). It is useful to carry several of these made from lengths of between 1·5 m and 4 m. They are normally used in conjunction with a karabiner to attach to an anchor, either to provide the main belay, or to provide additional intermediate protection, known as 'running belays'. Inspect your slings regularly for signs of abrasion or even thin cuts which can reduce their strength dramatically.

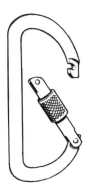

Fig. 174. *'D'-shaped karabiner with screw gate.*

Strength is the most important characteristic and in this respect the karabiner must conform to the standards laid down by the U.I.A.A. The gate is the weakest part and its design should include some arrangement for locking, in case the karabiner becomes overloaded in a fall. A locking screw across the gate itself is a common device for ensuring that the gate remains closed in use. The karabiner is a most versatile tool and is very often used in conjunction with a sling for belaying and as a waist or harness attachment. It has many other specialised uses which are beyond the scope of this book.

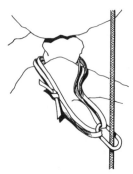

Fig. 175.   *Use of a sling and karabiner to provide a thread belay.*

A karabiner is a metal snap link, usually made out of aluminium alloy, which combines lightness with strength. A wide range of models is available, but the basic principle is the same throughout.

Ice Axe Anchor

The axe can be used to give an acceptable form of belay in certain snow conditions; basically the harder the snow the better this will be. The traditional vertical axe belay is the least secure method. The only time this should be used is in very hard snow which will prevent the axe from pivoting out. Even then there are better ways of using it.

Horizontal Axe Anchor

The basic method is the horizontally buried ice-axe. First a slot is cut across the slope to a depth of about 0·5 m. A vertical slot from about one-third the way along is then cut downslope for about 2 m. The upper end is the depth of the horizontal slot and it then tapers out to the surface. It should be wide enough to take a sling which is attached to the shaft of the axe with a clove hitch at about its balance point. This is roughly halfway in terms of surface area. The axe is placed pick down in the horizontal slot with the sling in the vertical slot. The rope is belayed in the normal manner. Care must be taken to ensure that the sling is tied to pull symmetrically on the axe and that the axe is placed hard against the front wall of the trench. It can also help to reduce swivelling if snow from above is packed into the horizontal slot round the axe, taking care not to disturb the structure of the snow below.

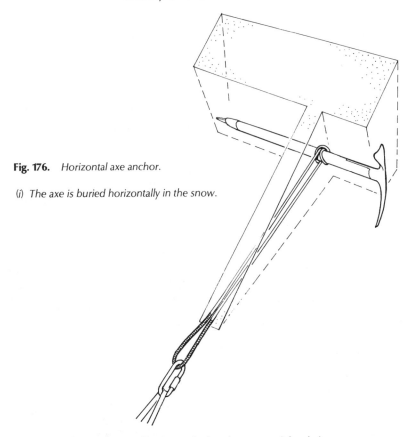

Fig. 176. *Horizontal axe anchor.*

(i) The axe is buried horizontally in the snow.

(ii) The climbing rope or a sling is attached to the centre of the shaft using a clove hitch. Turn the clove hitch so that the knot is at the back of the axe, with the free ends wrapping round the shaft, one above and one below. This ensures that the knot will tighten when the free ends are pulled.

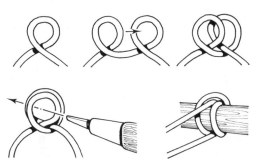

The-e are two variations of this form of belay:

Reinforced Buried Axe—An axe or hammer is driven vertically into the snow immediately in front of the buried axe and through the sling.

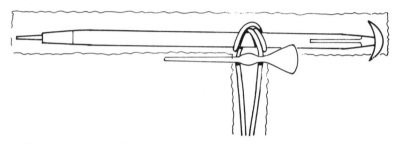

Fig. 177. *'Reinforced axe', seen in plan. In this case the belay is to the horizontal axe.*

'T' Axe—An axe or hammer is driven vertically into the snow behind the axe and in line with the vertical slot. The sling is attached to this axe by a clove hitch below the head. This runs over the horizontal placement and down the vertical slot.

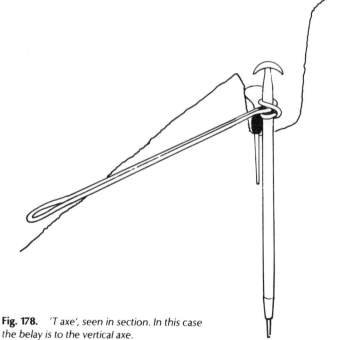

Fig. 178. *'T axe', seen in section. In this case the belay is to the vertical axe.*

The main advantage of these variations is the speed with which they can be constructed as the slots can be much shallower. They do however require a greater degree of judgement of snow conditions.

Vertical Axe

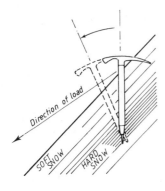

Fig. 179. *A vertical axe embedded in typical snow cover has a tendency to pivot and break out in the softer surface layer.*

Fig. 180. *Vertical axe anchor.*

This was the traditional, now largely discredited, method of belaying on snow. However, there are circumstances when the vertical axe anchor may be used to good effect. In the first place, the snow must be very hard. Secondly, it should always be used as an indirect belay or as a back-up anchor, the climber taking the initial strain with a hip belay. Thirdly, the situation, exposure, run-out, etc., may justify a less than perfect anchor in the interests of speed if the consequences of a fall are not likely to be serious. As far as the mechanics of the belay are concerned it is important to see that the rope or sling is securely attached to the shaft of the axe at the surface of the snow.

Dead Man Anchor

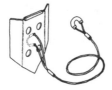

Fig. 181.   *'Dead man'.*

The 'dead man' shown in Fig. 181 is a spade-shaped alloy plate reinforced along the top with a wire or tape attached centrally. The principle is that the plate is embedded in the snow in such a way that its entire surface resists movement through the snow when a load is applied to the wire. This method has the merit of working in most kinds of snow, particularly in poorly-consolidated snow, where traditional methods offer little or no security. Careful placing of the 'dead man' to avoid pulling out is absolutely vital and it must always be tested before use. This also has the effect of bedding the 'dead man' in.

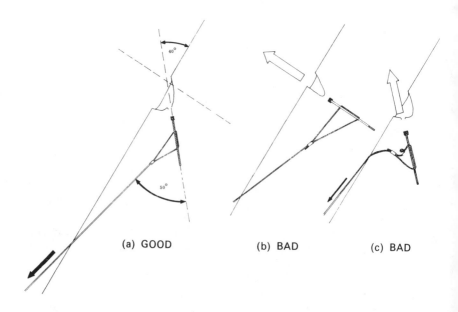

Fig. 182.   *Good and bad placement of 'dead man'.*

A horizontal slot should be cut in the snow at least 3 m (10 ft) above the stance, taking care to disturb the snow as little as possible in the immediate area. The 'dead man' is inserted at the bottom of this slot in such a way that the plane of the plate makes an angle of approximately 40° with the snow surface. A convenient way to estimate this angle is to hold your ice axe at right angles to the slope just over the slot. Bisect this angle with the plate and then tilt it back a further 5° and push it home. Some ice axes have a lip near the spike and this can be used to tap the plate into the snow to a depth of at least 30 cm (1 ft). It is necessary to clear out a passage for the wire to prevent it hooking, as in Fig. 182(c). In this illustration a sudden load on the wire could jerk the 'dead man' out of the snow.

The stance should be taken at least 3 m (10 ft) below the 'dead man'. This will ensure that the internal angle between the plate and the wire does not exceed 50°. Clearly, a high stance will result in a dangerous increase in this angle. The climber belays to the 'dead man' in the normal way, adopting a sitting position for maximum holding power, with the added benefit of reducing the 'dead man' angle.

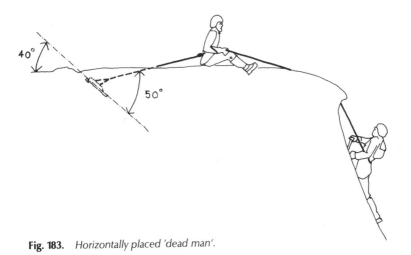

Fig. 183. *Horizontally placed 'dead man'.*

Many winter climbs finish on flat ground, on a ridge, or at the edge of a plateau. It is often difficult to provide any satisfactory belay in such a situation. The 'dead man' is just as efficient buried in a horizontal position as in any other and exactly the same rules apply for placement. The stance must be well back from any cornice and that means that the 'dead man' may be as much as 10 m (33 ft) back from the edge (Fig. 183).

Since the 'dead man' depends for its successful operation on the cohesion of the snow, it is particularly important that this is not disturbed in any way. Special care must be taken in slabby snow not to fracture the whole retaining mass of snow. The rule is that if the snow has good natural cohesion, (e.g. old snow, wind slab, wet slab), disturb it as little as possible, but if, on the other hand, it lacks cohesion, e.g. powder snow, wet snow, then the whole area should be well stamped down.

Exercise great care in placing a 'dead man' in snow which has a layered structure or icy crusts. Under load the 'dead man' can penetrate into these layers and failure can occur.

Snow Bollard

There is really no foolproof method of belaying in very soft snow. A well padded snow bollard is probably the closest you will get to finding a satisfactory anchor. It is a technique which is applicable to a wide range of snow and ice conditions and requires little in the way of equipment.

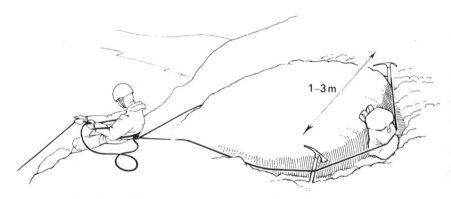

Fig. 184. *Snow bollard. The channel should be cut so that the bollard is mushroom shaped.*

The size of the bollard is determined by the hardness of the snow and will vary from about 1 m in hard snow to 3 m in soft. The channel should be approximately 30 cm (1 ft) deep but this too will vary with the nature of the snow. The rope does tend to cut in, so it helps to pad the back of the bollard with your rucksack and spare clothes. Any extra ice axes can be planted to provide additional support. If the air temperature is cold enough the groove may be warmed with the hand so that melting and refreezing reinforces the surface. In layered snow try to ensure that the rope rests in the middle of the firmest layer. A sitting stance is taken well below the bollard and the rope belayed in the normal way.

Footbrake

The footbrake is a technique which was perfected in New Zealand and is particularly suited to the situation when a party is moving together carrying coils. It can be very effective but it does require a great deal of practice and a cool head. The rope should be carried, already looped round the top of the axe shaft, so that in the event of a slip by one of the party the other can drop his coils, thrust the axe vertically down into the snow (still with the loop in position) and simultaneously stamp his boot firmly in front of the axe head as shown in Fig. 185.

IN SOFT SNOW   IN HARD SNOW

Fig. 185.   *The footbrake.*

The boot serves two purposes. It braces the top of the axe and it acts as a friction pad on the rope which is taken in a loop round the axe, across the upper of the boot and round the back of the heel. The degree of braking is controlled by the position of this rope at the heel. It is vital to understand that this is a dynamic system and that the brake must be applied gradually. Too sudden a brake will simply result in the axe being pulled out.

Belaying on Ice

Taken in isolation this is one of the most specialised aspects of mountaineering, demanding a great deal of skill and experience on the part of the climber. However, ice can be found at some time on every mountain group in the British Isles and not just on graded climbs. The mountain walker must know how to cope with a short ice pitch on an otherwise straightforward ascent. He must know how to handle ice glazed rocks and how to negotiate an icy section of ridge or an icy descent when late afternoon frost has turned the day's slush into a sheet of ice. Ice is a frequent and not always predictable element of the winter scene.

Before the invention of ice screws and pitons, one of the most favoured methods of belaying on ice was to take a direct belay to the pick of the axe driven into the ice. Nowadays such flimsy protection would be seen for what it is, a psychological belay of the most misleading kind. Occasionally, a natural anchor can be found—the base of a giant icicle, a thread belay through ice frozen rocks, a boss or flake of ice which can be fashioned into a suitable anchor. Great care is needed in working on these natural features not to fracture them through over-enthusiastic chopping with the axe.

Ice Bollards

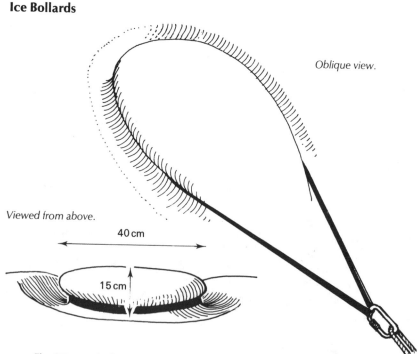

Oblique view.

Viewed from above.

40 cm

15 cm

Fig. 186. *Ice bollard.*

This is undoubtedly one of the most effective anchors on ice and its only real disadvantage is that it takes time as well as skill to make one. However, for a single difficult pitch or an abseil the security it brings to the passage may be well worth the effort. The ice bollard is really a small edition of the snow bollard, measuring approximately 40 cm (15 in) across and cut to a depth of 15 cm (6 in), with a pronounced mushroom shape at the sides and back to ensure that the rope does not ride off. Choose a site where the natural formation of the ice, such as a bulge or change of slope, makes it easier to cut. The stance must be taken well below so as to avoid any tendency to pull out on the anchor. Once again great care must be exercised in cutting out the shape. If there is the slightest sign of fracturing, discard the bollard and start again.

Ice Screws

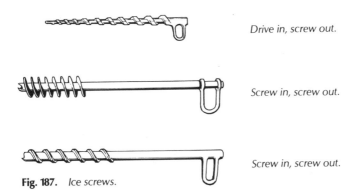

Drive in, screw out.

Screw in, screw out.

Screw in, screw out.

Fig. 187. *Ice screws.*

In general, ice screws do not make satisfactory belays, not because of any defects in design or manufacture, though undoubtedly some makes are better than others, but rather because of the inherent weakness of ice. Ice on mountains in the British Isles tends to be brittle and although a screw may appear to be solidly placed and will certainly support a steady load, under shock loading the ice may well fracture. Ice screws and pitons therefore should always be used with caution and only as a main belay when alternative methods are not practicable.

In this event two or more screws should be linked together in series to afford greater security. There are two basic types of ice screw: these are screw in—screw out and drive in—screw out. There are, of course, many variations within these broad categories and no one screw performs well in every type of ice. For this reason most climbers carry a selection, depending on the climb and the prevailing conditions.

Undoubtedly, the most versatile type of ice screw is the tubular variety which extracts a core as it is screwed into the ice. A shallow depression makes an ideal site for an ice screw which should be started in a small hole made with the pick. The screw should be tapped in with a hammer at an angle of about 10° above the perpendicular to the slope until the thread catches and it begins to turn as it is hit. It can then be screwed home using the pick or hammer as a lever if need be. The lug should lie flush with the surface but if this is not possible then a short sling should be tied to the shaft with a clove hitch hard against the surface. This greatly reduces the levering effect of a load applied to the screw.

Fig. 188. *Good placement for tubular ice screw. Clear away rotten ice—below arrow.*

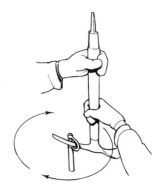

Fig. 189. *Turning an ice screw.*

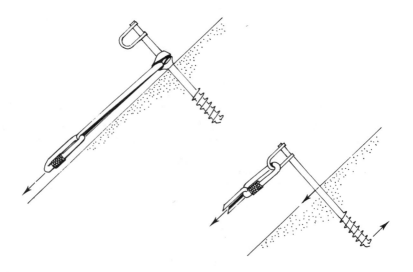

Fig. 190. *Attachment to ice screws.*
(Left) *Ice screw tied off at the surface to reduce leverage.*
(Right) *Incorrect attachment to ice screw resulting in excessive leverage.*

Experience in using ice screws and pitons will reveal their limitations. The drive in–screw out type are prone to shatter the ice on the way in, while they can also obstinately refuse to screw out. In warm conditions the ice in contact with the screw can melt, thus destroying its anchorage. In cold conditions the core extracted by a tubular screw can freeze inside making it impossible to use again until it is cleared by warming the screw and pushing out the core. 'Shattering' or 'dinner plating' are two fairly common mishaps when placing screws or pitons in ice. If this happens take it out and try again somewhere else.

Rock Belays, Chocks and Pitons

There are, in fact, very few climbs that do not have rock somewhere around which may offer an opportunity to take a natural rock belay (see pages 122–128). Such a belay is to be preferred above all others. With the additional equipment likely to be carried in winter (slings, karabiners, nuts, etc.) it should be a relatively simple and speedy matter to engineer a belay.

A sling can be used with a screw-gated karabiner to provide an anchor for the main belay. The anchor itself might be a rock spike or better still a thread of some kind where the sling is passed or threaded through some natural hole in the rock or perhaps round a stone jammed in a crack. A threaded anchor is the most effective of all because it can withstand a pull from any direction. In fact the 'nuts, chocks, and hexes', so much a part of the modern climber's hardware, are really a development from this basic idea. They are essentially artificial chockstones, admittedly of ingenious design, and they come in every conceivable shape and size. The principle of operation is simple enough, but there are one or two guidelines which may help you to find more secure placements:

Fig. 191.   *Different types of artificial chockstones, with wire, tape or rope slings attached.*
The chock may be attached to a wire, tape or rope sling. Wired chocks are easy to insert and remove and of course for its diameter, wire is much stronger than rope. However, being stiff, it can be lifted out by the movement of the climbing rope. Wire resists cutting and for this reason is preferred when there are any sharp edges around.

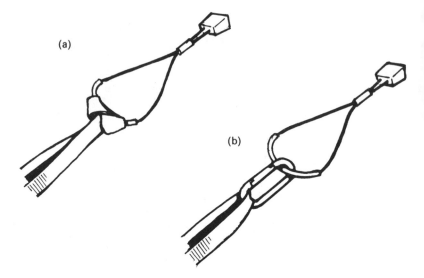

Fig. 192. *Never attach a nylon sling directly to a wired nut as in (a). Clip on with karabiner as in (b).*

Chock slings are usually short and for various reasons it may be necessary to extend them by adding another sling. Always link to a wired chock with a karabiner, never with the sling itself.

The karabiner should be clipped in in such a way that the gate will not be inadvertently opened by contact with the rock or the climbing rope. This usually means that the gate should be on the side away from the rock, with the opening at the lower end.

Fig. 193. *A hex in a perfect placement in a vertical crack.*

The ideal chock placement is at a constriction in a crack where the expected load on the sling will tend to pull the chock further into the constriction. There is a considerable art in placing chocks and many ingenious placements can be devised.

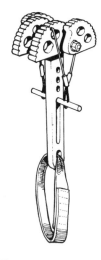

Fig. 194. *A 'Friend'. A system of spring-loaded cams for jamming in cracks.*

A 'Friend' is an adjustable jamming device using spring-loaded cams to hold it in position in a crack. It is particularly important to place it so that the expected load is in line with the shaft of the 'Friend'.

Rock Pitons

There is a welcome tendency among today's climbers only to use rock pitons as a last resort. Modern aid equipment is such that chocks and Friends and other devices yet to be invented can be used in situations which have hitherto required pitons. Even with the most careful placement and removal afterwards a piton leaves a scar and that is surely a matter of some concern. Nevertheless, from time to time there are likely to be situations where a piton is the only satisfactory anchor.

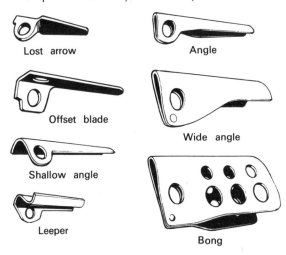

Fig. 195. *Pitons. Different types of pitons made from hard steel. A karabiner clips into the eye.*

K

Most modern pitons are of the chrome-molybdenum hard steel type and can be classified into three main groups: blades, angles, and those with a Z section called 'leepers'. Correct placement is very important to allow for the maximum mechanical advantages and torque. The piton should be placed in the crack to about half to two-thirds of its length by hand, then hammered home. The eye should be flush with the rock. If it is not, the piton should be tied-off with a short loop of tape using a clove hitch. It may also have to be tied-off if there is any possibility of the karabiner acting as a lever against the rock. Do not overdrive pitons. Both the resistance to the hammer and the rising ring of the piton as it is struck gives an indication of when to stop.

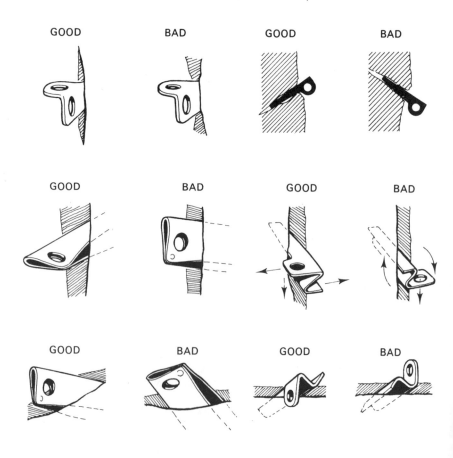

Fig. 196.   *Good and bad placement of pitons.*

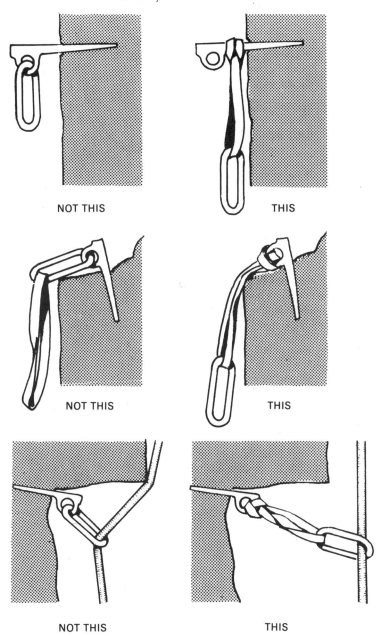

Fig. 197. *Some Do's and Don'ts about tying on to pitons.*

Belay Plates

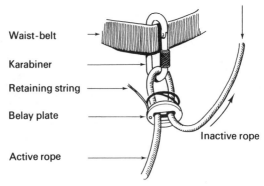

Waist-belt →

Karabiner

Retaining string

Belay plate

Active rope

Inactive rope

Fig. 198. *Belay plates.*

In many situations, belay plates may be a suitable, or even preferable, alternative to the waist belay. To use the plate a bight of rope is taken through the slot and put into a screw-gate karabiner which is attached to the front of the waist-belt. As in the waist belay the active rope is the one which goes directly to the person climbing. To pay out the rope the active hand simply pulls the rope through the plate while the inactive hand keeps a grip of the inactive rope. This is easier if the ropes are held parallel.

(a)

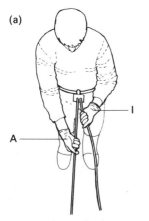

A

I

(b)

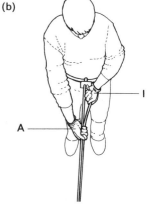

A

I

I moves forward taking rope through plate. A allows rope to run.

A grips both ropes. I slides back to plate, grips inactive rope and returns to A, pulling more rope through the plate.

Fig. 199. *Taking in, using a belay plate.*

To make (a) easier, hand A can pull back as I moves forward, but it then must return to forward position to hold ropes for (b).

To take in the rope the hands are worked as in a waist belay, i.e. the inactive hand pulls forward parallel to the active rope, the active hand then holds both ropes, the inactive hand then returns to above the plate and takes another length of rope. Again the inactive hand must never lose contact with the rope.

To brake, the inactive hand is pulled back towards the side of the waist at the same time allowing the rope to run so that the braking effect is applied gradually.

The advantage of the plate is that it is normally convenient to use and very safe. It saves the trouble of putting the rope over the rucksack as in the waist belay. However, it can be awkward to use with an iced-up rope and it takes a lot of practice to let the rope slide intentionally through the plate in the event of a fall. For this reason it should only be used when the anchor is absolutely sound and capable of withstanding the sudden impact of a fall.

The figure-of-8 descendeur can also be used in this manner but besides being bulky it tends to kink the rope.

Moving Together

If you are the most experienced member of a party it will be your responsibility to decide when to rope up. If there is a risk of serious injury to anyone as a result of a slip then it is certainly time to put on the rope, but you must be quite clear about the level of security it offers. If you take a belay at every pitch then you may be able to safeguard the party adequately. If for any reason this is not practicable then the rope is only likely to ensure that if one falls, all fall. Moving together roped is a recognised technique on glaciers and on terrain when it is possible to respond quickly to an emergency by improvising a direct belay or by using one of the belaying methods particularly suited to these circumstances. There are of course many expeditions when the rope is required intermittently and it may be sensible and save a lot of time to keep it on for the easy in-between sections.

14 Snow and Avalanches

Snow Structure

Introduction

Mountains + Snow = Avalanches. It seems a simple enough equation, but it is one which has taxed some of the best scientific minds in those countries which possess the two basic ingredients of mountains and snow. At best, avalanche forecasting is an inexact science. It is simply not possible to say that a particular slope will avalanche at a predicted time, and it probably never will be. Avalanche forecasting is about probabilities and is based on information derived from a variety of sources. One of the most important of these is the local mountain rescue team or ski patrol, whose intimate knowledge of their own area can make a vital contribution to the accuracy of the forecast. Rescue teams, by the very nature of their work, are exposed to severe conditions, which demand an understanding of the development of the snowpack and the effect of storms on the avalanche cycle.

Not all the features described in this section occur in Scotland because snow conditions here differ in some respects from those in areas where most snow studies are carried out. As far as possible, examples in the text are chosen from those most usually found in Scotland.

Snow Crystals

Snow crystals form in the atmosphere. Although the basic habit of the crystal is hexagonal, the detailed form is infinitely varied and is determined by the temperature and degree of vapour saturation at the time of formation. Much has been written about the process of crystallisation, but from a practical point of view it is sufficient to know that the crystal form will have a profound effect on the subsequent changes which take place within the snow cover and on its propensity for avalanching. The behaviour of a layer of Graupel (hail), for example, in which the individual crystals lack any cohesion, will be markedly different from a layer of Stellar crystals whose delicate and complex structure is highly sensitive to change. Some of the main families of crystals are illustrated in Fig. 200.

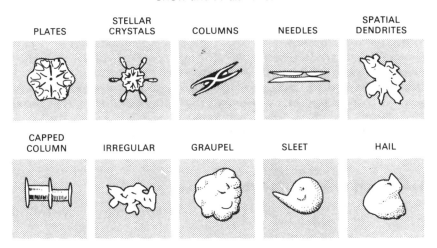

PLATES STELLAR CRYSTALS COLUMNS NEEDLES SPATIAL DENDRITES

CAPPED COLUMN IRREGULAR GRAUPEL SLEET HAIL

Fig. 200. *The basic forms of solid precipitation.*

Metamorphism

No sooner have they formed than snow crystals start to undergo certain changes. These may take place as the snowflake falls through the atmosphere, drastically altering the original shape, such as by the addition of rime as the crystal falls through a moist layer, or they may take place as the snow accumulates on the ground. The nature and speed of these changes, which are collectively known as metamorphism, is determined by the prevailing temperature and pressure.

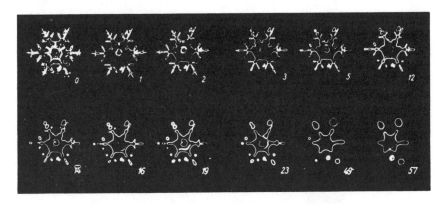

Fig. 201. *Equitemperature (ET) metamorphism in a single stellar snow crystal maintained at a constant temperature of −5°C for a period of 57 days. Note the gradual simplification and rounding off of the crystal form.*

Equitemperature (ET) Metamorphism

In the normal course of events this leads to a simplification of crystal structure with the establishment of strong bonds between individual crystals and a shrinking of the whole snow layer. This process is known as 'equitemperature (ET) metamorphism' or, in common parlance, 'settling' and it is accelerated as snow temperature rises towards melting point. It is clearly a process which has a stabilising influence on the snow pack resulting ultimately in the formation of a single compact layer of homogeneous ice crystals.

Temperature Gradient (TG) Metamorphism

Under certain conditions, usually in cold regions or at high altitudes where there is intense radiative heat loss from the snow surface, a steep temperature gradient exists between the relatively warm base layers in contact with the ground and the much colder surface layers exposed to the atmosphere. Under the influence of this gradient, water vapour moves upwards through the snow cover recrystallising at favourable localities within the snowpack.

The end product of this process of 'temperature gradient (TG) metamorphism' is depth hoar, sometimes known as 'sugar snow' because the individual crystals are totally lacking in cohesion. Such layers are extremely fragile and may give rise to devastating avalanches when overloaded beyond their strength. Furthermore, because they are buried deep within the snow pack they can only be detected by digging a snow pit to ground level or by careful examination of the early winter weather records in order to identify those conditions which encourage their growth. In Scotland, depth hoar is virtually unknown because it is rarely cold enough for long enough to permit the crystals to form.

Fig. 202. *A single crystal of depth hoar magnified twenty times, the product of temperature gradient (TG) metamorphism. Note the hexagonal symmetry and cup like crystal form with characteristic striations.*

Melt/Freeze Metamorphism

In spring, the temperature of the whole snow cover may be just below freezing level. Because of radiation heat loss at night, the snow alternately freezes and thaws and this gives rise to the third process of change known as melt/freeze metamorphism. The effect of this is that the larger crystals grow at the expense of the smaller and that there is a very marked difference in the strength of the snow, depending on whether it is in the melt or freeze phase of the cycle. The danger lies in the melt phase when water (rain or melt water) percolates through the snow till it reaches the ground or an impermeable crust. Flowing at this level, it may completely undermine the anchorage of the snow to the underlayer, whether that be the ground surface or older snow, and provide an effective lubricant for any subsequent avalanche. It is important to distinguish this type of occurrence from the avalanche which results from a rapid thaw following a fall of fresh snow. In this case there is a genuine melting of the crystal fabric which precipitates a wet surface slide.

These then are the three fundamental processes of metamorphism which determine the nature of the snowpack and which give rise to the infinite variations of its physical and mechanical properties.

Snowfall

What is it that causes snow to avalanche? Well, first of all there has to be enough snow. The more there is and the faster it accumulates the more likely it is to avalanche and the larger that avalanche will be. Even 25 cm of snow can form an impressive slide. Most avalanches occur during or immediately after a heavy fall of snow, so this is a time to be particularly careful in the mountains. Evidence suggests that the rate of precipitation is as important as the total amount of snow which falls in a single storm. Precipitation intensities in excess of 2 mm/hr (water equivalent) are usually regarded as hazardous. This is roughly equivalent to a fall of 2 cm of fresh snow per hour. It will be appreciated that precipitation intensity is a measure of the rate at which a slope is loaded. New snow adds to the burden on the layers below and this can cause a failure in them. Indeed, the most common avalanche trigger is a fall of fresh snow.

The correlation between new snowfall and avalanching can be seen in the following figures from Switzerland:

New snow added in 3 days	Observed avalanches
Up to 10 cm	Rare avalanches, mostly of loose snow.
10–30 cm	Very occasional slabs, frequent sloughs.
30–50 cm	Frequent slabs on slopes 35°.
50–80 cm	Widespread slabs on slopes down to 25°.

(De Quervain, 1975)

Angle of Slope

The slope must also be sufficiently steep to allow the snow to slide. Generally speaking, the steeper the slope, the more likely it is to avalanche, but on very steep slopes, say over 60°, the snow rarely gets a chance to accumulate, so avalanches on such slopes are infrequent. The most dangerous slopes are therefore those of intermediate angle, between 30°–45°.

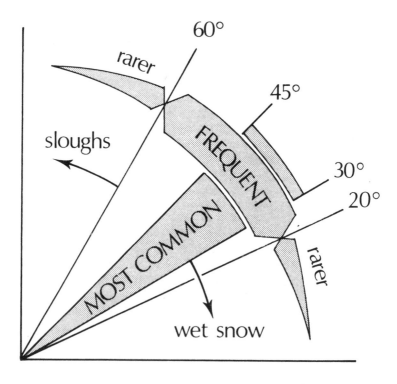

Fig. 203. *The frequency of avalanches in relation to slope angle. The most frequent and devastating avalanches occur on slopes of between 30° and 45°.*

Strength v. Stress

These two factors of weight of snow and angle of slope are the main stress factors tending to move the snow downhill. They are resisted by the strength of the snow which, in simple terms, can be regarded as a function of the cohesion of the individual crystals and the adhesion of the various layers to each other and to the surface of the ground below. Theoretically, at least, when the stress factors exceed the strength of the snow, failure will occur. In practice affairs are a good deal more complex. Providing the overloading is not too sudden the snow may adjust by internal deformation (creep) or by the sliding of the whole snow layer along the ground (glide). These phenomena are well seen in the spring when the whole snow cover may become buckled and warped as a result of the plastic response of the snow to downslope pressure. It is the absence of such a response which allows the tension to build up to the point where slab fracture is the only way of restoring equilibrium to the system.

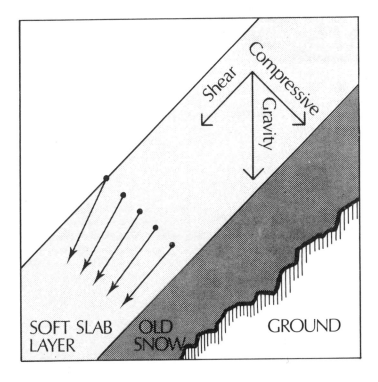

Fig. 204. *The forces at work in an inclined slab of snow. The force of gravity can be resolved into shear and compressive components. When shear stress exceeds shear strength slab failure may occur. In response to shear pressure the snow creeps and glides downslope. The higher the temperature the more rapid the deformation. The arrows represent the movement of a snow crystal at different depths within the snow layer.*

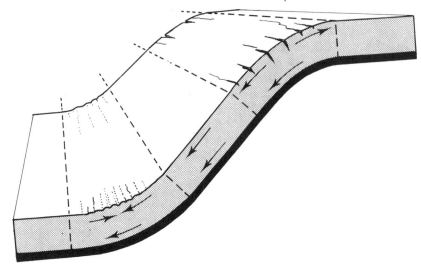

Fig. 205. *The tendency for the snow to creep and glide downhill under the influence of gravity creates an area of compression at the bottom of the slope where it is concave and an area of tension at the top where it is convex. It is in the convex part of the slope that an avalanche is most likely to be released.*

Slab Avalanches

Slab avalanches constitute by far the greatest potential hazard in the mountains in winter and they are, more often than not, quite impossible to identify merely by a surface inspection. Dangerous slabs can result from a variety of conditions but it is in the attachment of the slab to the layer below that we must look for the underlying cause. In extreme cases there may be no attachment at all, the underlayers having contracted away leaving the slab completely unsupported over a considerable area. This situation makes it easier to understand the often hair-trigger sensitivity of slabs.

More commonly, there will be some discontinuity between the slab and the layer below. This may take the form of a crust, or perhaps an intervening layer of weak unconsolidated snow or in Alpine regions it may be that an earlier firm anchorage has been destroyed by the growth of a layer of depth hoar. In the spring the attachment of the whole snow cover to the ground becomes of increasing significance. Smooth surfaces such as rock slabs or long grass offer little support.

Probably the greatest single factor in promoting the development of slabs is the wind. Under its influence, snow is transported and packed into 'windslabs' which can vary in hardness from no more than firm powder (soft slab) to a consistency more akin to concrete (hard slab). The latter is associated with high windspeeds in excess of 30 m.p.h.

Snow Profiles

It was stated earlier that avalanche forecasting is an inexact science. It is clear that much can be inferred from the careful observation of recent and prevailing weather conditions and from a knowledge of local terrain and the location of avalanche paths. Nevertheless, it is only by a detailed examination of the whole snow cover from surface to ground that its various characteristics can be positively identified and an attempt made to estimate the likelihood of an avalanche. Snow pit analysis is an essential tool of the forecaster whether he be a research worker at the Institute for Snow-Avalanche Research or the leader of a ski mountaineering expedition. The difference lies in the degree of sophistication of the measurements. Even in extreme conditions it is usually possible to expose the surface layer and examine its attachment to the layer below. This is no token exercise, since the majority of avalanches are surface slides involving only the uppermost layer of the snow cover.

The standard procedure is to dig a pit to the ground in a location as typical as possible of the avalanche prone slopes within the forecast area. Temperature measurements should be taken first, before the snow has had time to adjust to the sudden exposure to atmospheric temperature. Readings are normally taken at 10-cm intervals using dial thermometers. The back wall of the pit is then examined to pick out the different layers, crusts, etc., and to identify the dominant crystal type and degree of metamorphism. A hand lens and plastic snow card marked in square millimetres facilitates the task. The hardness and the humidity of each layer can be estimated using a series of simple tests. The density of the snow can also be measured with the aid of standard cylinders and a spring balance. The information obtained in this way can be plotted graphically, as shown in Fig. 206.

It is almost universal practice in Forecasting Stations to use an instrument known as a ram penetrometer to provide additional information about snow strength. This is a rod which is driven down through the snow, overcoming the variable resistance of the different layers. The plot resulting from these measurements is also shown in Fig. 206. The hatched area on the left of the profile represents the penetration resistance.

Snow Profile Analysis

The plot should be examined together with the snow pit profile to identify any weak layers, such as a buried layer of dry unconsolidated powder or a

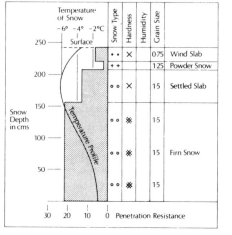

KEY:

Snow Type—   (International Snow Classification symbols)

+++   *New snow—most usually dendrites (star-shaped crystals)*
ᐱᐱᐱ   *Powder snow*
• • •   *Small granules—ET metamorphism complete*
□□□   *Angular crystals—first stage of constructive metamorphism*
∧∧∧   *Depth hoar—these, and the crystals below, are final stages in TG metamorphism*
△△△   *Filled cup crystals*
○ ○ ○   *Firn snow—large ice granules formed after repeated thawing and freezing*
V V V   *Surface hoar*

Hardness—   Humidity—

| | *Very soft—no resistance to gloved fist* | | *Dry—lacks cohesion*

| / | *Soft—flat hand can be pushed in* | I | *Damp—can make snowballs*

| X | *Medium hard—finger can be pushed in* | II | *Wet—makes compact snowballs*

| // | *Hard—pencil can be pushed in* | III | *Very wet—water can be squeezed out*

| ※ | *Very hard—knife blade can be pushed in* | IIII | *Free water running through snow*

Crystal size—
                              Quoted in millimetres.

Fig. 206. *A profile taken at the fracture line of the surface slab avalanche in Coire Cas on 19 February 1969 in which 39 people were involved, 9 of whom were injured. Note the slab resting on an unconsolidated powder snow base.*

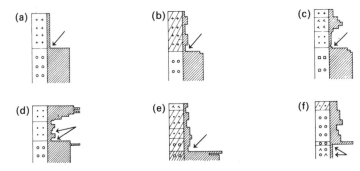

(a) Surface avalanche of loose, dry powder snow,
(b) Surface avalanche of loose, fresh snow getting wet,
(c) Surface avalanche of soft dry slabs,
(d) Surface avalanche of hard dry slabs,
(e) Surface avalanche of soft slabs from old, wet firn snow,
(f) Full depth avalanche of hard dry slabs from old firn snow gliding on depth-hoar bottom-layer.

N.B. Arrows indicate weakest stratum and/or gliding surface. (From Zimrú nebezpečí v horách—Houdek and Vrba.)

Fig. 207. *Principal types of avalanche situations as revealed by their resistance profiles.*

At the top of the chart seven snow profiles are shown, taken at various times between January and May 1970 (see Fig. 208).

Penetration Resistance: The shaded area on the left of each profile represents the resistance of the snow, as measured by a ram penetrometer. The greater the resistance (hardness), the more extensive the shaded area.

Snow Type and Humidity: The two columns on the right of each profile represent snow type and humidity. Five grades of humidity are recognised: the higher the humidity, the more vertical lines appear in the column.

Temperature, Hardness and Crystal Size: These are not included on the chart, but are mentioned elsewhere in the text. Temperature is recorded every 10 cm from the snow surface to the ground. Hardness is estimated by hand and is closely related to the penetration resistance.

Avalanches: The occurrence of avalanches is noted by arrows at the top of the chart. These should be compared with snow conditions as indicated by the preceding profile and with weather conditions summarised below. Notice how the three avalanches in the second fortnight of March follow a period of heavy snowfall, accompanied by strong, persistent winds from the south-west.

An examination of these relationships over a period of years can lead to a better understanding of the conditions which give rise to avalanches in this area.

Furthermore, the profiles themselves provide a record of the behaviour of the snow throughout the winter. The complete life cycle of each layer of snow A, B, C, D, E can be followed from its formation to its eventual disappearance. Again, over a period of years certain recurring features may be identified and lead to a better understanding of snow conditions.

layer of wet snow. It is especially important to look for any sharp discontinuities in the strength characteristics of adjacent layers. These represent boundaries where the adhesion between the layers is low and consequently they are the likely focal planes for avalanches. Fig. 207

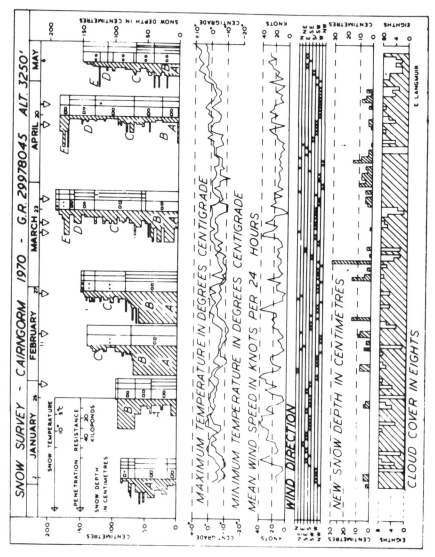

Fig. 208. *A snow and weather survey carried out on Cairngorm during the winter of 1969–70.*

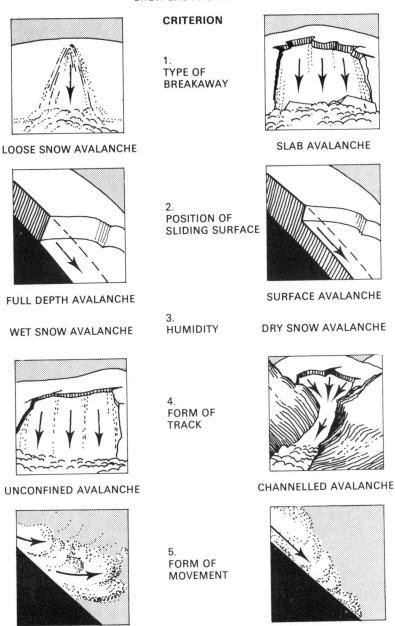

CRITERION

1.
TYPE OF
BREAKAWAY

LOOSE SNOW AVALANCHE

SLAB AVALANCHE

2.
POSITION OF
SLIDING SURFACE

FULL DEPTH AVALANCHE

SURFACE AVALANCHE

3.
HUMIDITY

WET SNOW AVALANCHE

DRY SNOW AVALANCHE

4.
FORM OF
TRACK

UNCONFINED AVALANCHE

CHANNELLED AVALANCHE

5.
FORM OF
MOVEMENT

AIRBORNE POWDER

FLOWING AVALANCHE

Fig. 209. *Avalanche classification system.*

shows a representative series of ram profiles, all of which have marked discontinuities indicating a high degree of avalanche hazard. Quite apart from their immediate contribution to the forecast, snow profiles, if taken at regular intervals throughout the winter, can provide a record of the development of the total snow cover and the progress of individual layers within it. If this record is coupled with the careful recording of all observed avalanches it may be possible to establish patterns of association which will assist in the recognition of dangerous conditions in future years. Such a composite record is shown in Fig. 208.

Types of Avalanche

An avalanche is a complex dynamic phenomenon which is not easily pigeon-holed into one category or another. Many of the larger ones defy classification comprising, as they do, a series of consecutive events each one triggered by its predecessor and involving one layer after another until the whole snow cover could be on the move. Nevertheless, it is possible to describe most avalanches by reference to a set of five criteria. This simple system, recognised internationally, is illustrated in Fig. 209.

Within this system it is possible to identify a number of recurring types which merit some further consideration.

Dry 'Powder' Snow Avalanches

This is the most common type of avalanche in cold, dry conditions. At such times slopes, especially north facing ones, may be dangerous for weeks until the snow has settled. Windward slopes may settle after a few days of good weather, although it must be remembered that wind transported snow may form dangerous slabs elsewhere. The higher the altitude the greater and more prolonged the hazard.

Features

Most, so-called, 'powder' avalanches in fact start off as soft slabs. Gathering momentum and material on the way they produce a fast moving mass of powder snow in part flowing along the ground and in part airborne. Travelling at speeds in excess of 45 m/sec (100 m.p.h.) accompanied by a vicious air blast such avalanches can cause widespread destruction. The inhalation of snow dust is a common cause of death among victims of this type of avalanche.

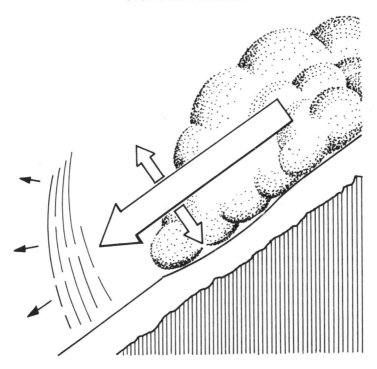

Fig. 210. *A large airborne powder avalanche may cause impact pressures from 5 to 50 tons/m². The expanding snow cloud may travel at speeds up to 125 m/sec (280 m.p.h.) and is preceded by a powerful air blast.*

Indications

As little as 20 cm (8 inches) of snow in the starting zone can pose a threat although, as mentioned previously, the precipitation intensity is also of critical importance. As a rough guide, an accumulation rate in excess of 2 cm per hour is a dangerously high value. Typical circumstances include: new snow falling on a surface crust or on a layer of surface hoar, or new snow falling after a period of cold weather.

Soft Slab Avalanches

These are the most common of winter avalanches and are associated with the rapid accumulation of fresh snow on lee slopes under the influence of winds of 10–30 m.p.h. After heavy falls the danger may not be confined to lee slopes and all slopes should be treated with suspicion until the snow settles. This may occur in a matter of hours or it may take several days if conditions remain cold. Extensive small surface slides are a sure sign that settlement is taking place.

Features

Although it may be released as a unit, the soft slab, by definition, pulverises in motion and if it is large enough may develop into a mixed powder avalanche—see above. Initially, it involves only the surface layer of snow, although its release may trigger off other weaknesses within the snow cover. It is as well to remember the dictum that most soft slab avalanches are released by their victims.

Indications

Soft slabs are most easily recognised by reference to the weather conditions which favour their formation. Since they are surface phenomena it is usually possible in the field to dig through the surface layer and examine the attachment to the underlayer. In a suitable test location the slab will often respond to a kick with a boot or ski by breaking away in straight-edged pieces. The same kind of practical test on a larger scale involves 'test skiing' in safe locations, but which have a similar exposure to the avalanche prone slopes. It is important to remember that in the absence of fresh snow, drifting alone can build up soft slabs on lee slopes.

Hard Slab Avalanches

The hard slab presents one of the greatest hazards in the mountains, not because of its frequency, but because its deceptively solid surface gives a false sense of security to those passing over it. The combination of high winds (30 m.p.h.) and low temperatures favour the formation of hard slabs on lee slopes. If it remains cold, the danger can persist for some time and may be obscured by subsequent snowfalls.

Features

Release is much the same as for soft slabs and may be accompanied by a sharp cracking noise. In this case however the slab breaks up into a jigsaw of angular blocks many of which remain intact on the journey down the slope. It need hardly be said that a large hard slab avalanche possesses enormous destructive power.

Indications

Hard slab has a dull, chalky appearance and occasionally emits a booming noise when walked upon. A lack of adhesion to the underlayer is characteristic of all hard slabs and indeed in some cases it is not attached at all over a considerable area. Such circumstances give rise to sudden local subsidence which can be most alarming, even on the flat. In Alpine areas hard slabs are frequently associated with steep temperature gradients and a consequent build up of depth hoar. A dangerous slab exhibits an almost hair-trigger sensitivity and may be released by the passage of a climber or skier.

Climax Avalanches

So called because they are the result of changing characteristics deep within the snow cover over a prolonged period of time. They could be described as 'delayed action' avalanches caused by the failure of some weak layer overloaded beyond its strength. The overloading is almost invariably caused by a fall of new snow. It will be clear that such avalanches usually involve the entire snow cover and for this reason can reach devastating proportions.

Indications

Surface indications are useless. The only sure way of recognising the danger of a climax avalanche is to dig a snow pit to ground level or to take a profile using the ram penetrometer.

Reference to the weather records for the early winter may reveal the existence of conditions which would be conducive to the formation of depth hoar, such as a prolonged cold spell, lasting perhaps several weeks when the snow cover is relatively thin and subject to a steep temperature gradient.

In Scotland climax avalanches may be caused by prolonged cold spells following snowfall with maximum temperatures below $-4°C$ for 10 days to 2 weeks. A significant number of slabs are released without any loading, sometimes triggered by a sudden rise in temperature of a degree or two. R. Ward found that 40% of all slabs were primed by a week to 10 days of cold weather and then set off by a snowfall or drifting.

Wet Avalanches

Common in spring and following thaw conditions at any time during the winter, wet avalanches result from water weakening the bonds between crystals or lubricating some potential sliding surface within the snowpack.

Obviously, they can only occur when the snow temperature is close to the melting point. Depending on the degree of saturation they can start on shallow angled slopes (20° and occasionally less than that). The danger is especially great after a heavy snow storm which starts cold and finishes warm. The cold snow is light and dry forming a weak substratum for the warmer and more dense snow above and a poor anchorage to the old snow surface below.

Features

Wet avalanches may be loose or slab in form. They travel at relatively low speeds and can sometimes be outrun by a competent skier or occasionally by making a fast exit on foot out of the avalanche path. Great turbulence is set up as the avalanche flows down the slope, producing snow boulders which gouge long grooves in the bed surface. A big wet slide acts like a giant bulldozer picking up a mass of debris on the way (trees, shrubs, rocks, etc.), all of which add to the very considerable destructive force. In a channelled avalanche the debris sets like concrete immediately on stopping and this greatly reduces the chances of survival of anyone caught in it, as well as impeding the rescue effort. These avalanches can be very big with debris accumulating up to 30 m (100 ft) deep.

Indications

This is possibly the easiest hazard to anticipate because of the conditions which initiate a wet avalanche cycle; namely a rapid temperature rise after snowfall, usually late in the winter and often in damp, overcast weather. Rain, wet snowfalls, warm winds and melting are all contributory factors. A snowpit may reveal layers of wet snow on top of crust, or a layer of surface hoar which may be dangerously weakened by percolating water. There is likely to be little, if any, temperature gradient between the bottom and top of the snow cover. Local small scale avalanching, cracks in the snow, large snowballs rolling down the slope are some of the visible warning signs.

Ice Avalanches

Ice or glacier avalanches are the direct result of glacier movement. At the present state of knowledge they are quite unpredictable and can fall at any hour of the day or night. They vary from the fall of an individual serac to the collapse of a whole mountain side. In 1962 the collapse of a hanging glacier on Huascaran (6,768 m) in Peru released 3 million tons of ice which travelled 10 miles in 15 minutes and wiped out five villages killing 4,000 people and 10,000 head of livestock.

Features

Large blocks of ice and often masses of earth and rock. Additional debris may be brought down by avalanches triggered off by the first one. It may be accompanied initially by a cloud of pulverised ice but in its later stages becomes a flowing river of mud, rock and ice.

Indications

Overhanging ice, seracs, etc., are obvious danger spots. Large sections of ice above cliff tops or ridges. Heavy rain entering crevasses and lubricating the undersurface of the ice may accelerate ice movement and therefore increase the danger.

This brief résumé of the changes which take place in snow crystals and the processes which lead to the establishment of stable or unstable conditions is of general relevance. Scottish conditions are different from those in the Alps or North America, so that although the basic processes are the same in all three areas the frequency and speed with which they occur can be very different. The scale too, is of a different order so that generally speaking avalanches in this country are smaller, less damaging to life and property, and confined to the higher mountain country.

Avalanche Hazard Evaluation

Whoever exposes himself to the danger of an avalanche without it being absolutely necessary is without doubt very stupid; however, in practice people expose themselves to this danger more often than they think; for snow can start to slide even on slopes with an incline of 30°. This means that virtually every mountain excursion presents a certain danger. Should one therefore give up wonderful trips into the mountains? Of course not, but one must try to act after consideration in order to reduce the risk to a minimum. Nevertheless, even experts will be surprised again and again by avalanches.

André Roch

Winter Climate and Snow Conditions

The maritime climate of the British Isles in winter gives rise to conditions in the mountains which are in some important respects quite different from those prevailing in the Alpine regions of mainland

Europe. Precipitation levels, taken over all, are greater here than in the Alps, but of course a much smaller proportion of this falls as snow, even on our highest mountains. Higher average temperatures and dramatic variations in temperature within a very short space of time ensure a relatively rapid settling and stabilisation of the snow cover and, indeed, thaws may be sufficiently protracted to remove the snow cover entirely from some mountain areas. If it were not for the wind which blows almost continuously above 600 m (2,000 ft) in winter time, redistributing the snow and piling it into gullies and lee slopes, skiing and snow and ice climbing would be practically non-existent in this country. Thanks to the wind these thick localised deposits withstand the denuding effects of periodic thaws and provide high quality skiing and climbing well into the spring. By this time what remains of the winter's snow is coarsely crystalline and compact. Improved weather with clear night skies favours continuing melt/freeze metamorphism giving superb conditions for the late skier and climber—provided he makes an early enough start!

Such unique snow conditions suggest that there should be equally marked differences in the frequency of particular types of avalanches and this is indeed the case. The most important fact is that conditions do tend to stabilise quickly, the period of acute danger being during the snow storm itself and in the 24 hours immediately following. Rapid settling means that full depth avalanches are rare except in the spring when melting water destroys the attachment of the snow cover to the ground. Such late avalanches are usually confined to locations where the terrain consists of smoothly inclined rock slabs. It also means that the next snowfall frequently accumulates on a hard undersurface which may provide a poor anchorage, particularly if the snow is cold and dry at first, warming up later on. The freeze–thaw cycle together with the surface hardening effect of the wind gives rise to numerous icy crusts and these, too, provide potential sliding surfaces for subsequent snow layers. By far the most common type of avalanche is the surface slab, wet and dry, which is released from lee slopes during and after snowfall. Wind transported snow can give rise to substantial accumulations of 'wind slab' in the complete absence of fresh snow. As previously stated the danger period is usually quite short, a matter of 24 to 48 hours, but this can be prolonged by cold weather.

Cornices are an ubiquitous feature of cliffs and corrie head walls and may be regarded as exaggerated extensions of the slopes below, with similar characteristics and tendencies. They undergo the same metamorphic processes and respond in the same way to the freeze–thaw cycle. Because they extend outwards above the scarp face, pressures are generated which deform the cornice and which may eventually cause it to collapse. This often happens in the late winter when melting weakens the strength of the whole structure. It is not uncommon for the collapse of a cornice to be the trigger which releases an avalanche in the slope below.

Substantial falls of cold dry snow are rare, particularly in the windless conditions which set the scene for the powder snow slides of Alpine areas. Prolonged cold spells with the temperature remaining below −10°C for several weeks are unusual and for this reason depth hoar, the product of a steep temperature gradient within a relatively shallow snow cover, is practically unknown in Scotland. Climax avalanches of this type are therefore also unknown. Remember that in Scotland after a week to 10 days of cold weather the danger from climax releases due to brittle failure becomes serious.

Assessing the Risk

It has already been stated that avalanche forecasting is about possibilities and occasionally probabilities, but rarely, if ever, about certainties. The mountaineer must do the best he can, selecting relevant information from a host of factors, weighing one against another, constantly updating himself in an attempt to arrive at a realistic evaluation of snow stability and the likelihood of avalanches on one slope as against another. It is a daunting task and yet not an impossible one. A systematic approach to the subject is a great help and it should start before you even set foot on the hill. Avalanche forecasts are now available on a daily basis in the Cairngorms, Glencoe and Lochaber.

Past Weather

Find out what the weather has been like, particularly in the previous week or so, noting any heavy snowfalls, strong winds and likely accumulation slopes for soft and hard slabs. Note also the temperature profile for the period and consider how this will have affected the settling process in the snow cover. From this historical information draw what inference you can about the present state of the snow in the general area of your proposed route. Your enquiries may reveal, for example, that there has been 15 cm (6 in) of fresh snow in the valley four days previously and that since then the weather had been cold, −6°C, with clear night skies and 5–10 knot winds from the East. It would be reasonable to assume that the winds at 600 m (2,000 ft) would be at least 10–20 knots and that it has redistributed the snow on to SW–NW facing slopes where soft to medium hard slabs may be expected. Cornice collapse may trigger slabs below. The cold weather will have delayed settling so that these slabs are likely to remain in an unstable condition. The hard surface of the old snow layer is unlikely to provide a secure anchorage. The snow profile may look something like this:

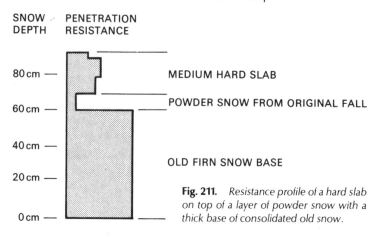

Fig. 211. *Resistance profile of a hard slab on top of a layer of powder snow with a thick base of consolidated old snow.*

Terrain

If you do not know the area it is common sense to talk to someone who does and discuss your plans and intended route. In particular find out if there are any peculiarities of terrain which might affect your choice of route, e.g. known avalanche paths, safe approach routes and so on.

On the Mountain

Once on the hill you should be subconsciously adjusting your assessment in the light of conditions as you actually find them. Clearly these will be changing as you gain altitude and you must make allowances for a fall in temperature of approximately 1·5°C for every 300 m, as well as for a likely increase in wind speed. Assess the prevailing weather conditions and how they are going to influence the situation. You have three main factors to consider: snowfall, wind and temperature and the effect that each of them may have on the old snow pack as well as on the accumulation of the new.

Snowfall

80–90% of avalanches are due to excessive loading caused by new snowfall. As a very rough guide, new snow depth in excess of 25 cm (10 in) can create a serious avalanche risk in itself. The faster it accumulates the more serious the risk and rates of 2 cm (1 in) per hour or more should be considered potentially dangerous. The more dense and compact the snow, the greater the loading in relation to snow depth and the greater the hazard. The maximum loading of course comes from rain and a wet avalanche cycle and extensive cornice collapse can be expected following a rain storm.

Wind

Wind has two important effects on snow. In the first place it erodes and transports it from exposed slopes and ridges and deposits it, often very unevenly, in sheltered gullies, hollows and lee slopes. In the second place, the snow crystals are broken up in transit so that when they are redeposited they accumulate in a much more compact mass with a distinctly layered structure. These accumulations are known as 'wind slabs' and vary in hardness from almost the consistency of powder snow to rock hard deposits of marble-like quality. Huge amounts of snow may be transported in this way, the stronger the wind, the greater the volume of snow transported and the harder the resulting slabs. Slabs constitute the greatest avalanche hazard in mountains so it is of vital importance to recognise both them and the conditions which give rise to them.

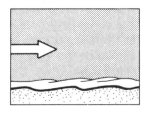

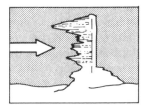

(i) *Wind rippled surfaces —drifting snow:*

(ii) *Sastrugi—wind carved features:*

(iii) *Rime deposits:*

Fig. 212. *Indications of wind direction.*
  (i) *Ripples in the snow surface formed by drifting snow. The shallow slope of the ripples faces into the wind and the steep face away from it.*
  (ii) *In harder, wind-packed snow, strong winds carve out sastrugi which present their steep faces to the wind.*
  (iii) *Rime is deposited by moist winds on upstanding features such as cairns, fence posts, pylons, etc. The deposit grows into the wind so that it points in the direction from which the wind has come.*

Temperature

It is difficult to estimate air temperature, partly because of the increased chill experienced when there is any wind at all and also because of the superficial warmth of direct sunlight. Nevertheless, indications can usually be found as to whether the air temperature is above or below 0°C. As we have seen, temperature plays a crucial role in the development of the snow cover. Sustained cold retards settling and prolongs the danger period. Cold new snow lacks cohesion and provides an unstable base for subsequent falls. By contrast, relatively warm air, above 0°C, accelerates the stabilisation of the snow cover and moist new snow tends to adhere to its underlayer.

On the other hand low temperatures can stabilise earlier surface layers of slush, at least till the next thaw. If the temperature is above freezing, wet sloughs of new snow can be expected immediately, but conditions quickly stabilise as the snow settles down. A continuing thaw will cause melting in older snow layers with the possibility of setting off a cycle of wet snow avalanches and cornice collapse. This is most common in the Spring, particularly after a succession of cloudy days which greatly restricts the amount of heat which can be lost by long wave radiation.

There are two types of surface deposit to look out for. Surface hoar is a coarsely crystalline but fragile deposit on the surface of the snow formed by the sublimation of water vapour in the atmosphere, usually overnight. It gives the snow a characteristic sparkling appearance as sunlight is reflected off the large, striated, crystal faces. Surface hoar provides a very weak foundation for further snow layers. Once buried it is extremely difficult to identify, even in snow pit observations. The condition must be detected while the crystals are still on the surface. The second type of deposit is caused by the freezing of water droplets carried by the wind on to solid objects in its path; rocks, fence posts, ski-lift pylons and so on. The deposit 'grows' into the wind and so is a useful indicator of earlier wind direction as well as signalling humid and relatively warm air. It is known as rime or fog crystal.

Be Observant

The most urgent warning of avalanche danger is an avalanche. Look around you. Are there any signs of avalanche activity? If so, can you tell

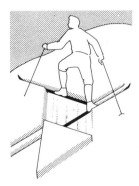

Fig. 213. *A small slab breaking away as the skier makes a turn. This is a clear warning of serious avalanche risk, especially on lee slopes where the snow will have accumulated to greater depth.*

how recent? What type are they? Where are their starting zones and what is their general orientation? This information can provide invaluable guidance as to which slopes are vulnerable and which safe.

Practical Tests

Digging a Snow Pit

Up till now your assessment of snow conditions has been almost entirely indirect, based on assumptions and deductions from historical information and from superficial observations of present weather and snow conditions. It makes very good sense before you venture on to a potentially hazardous slope to put your deduction to the test and to examine the profile of the snow *in situ*. This exercise need take no more than a matter of a few minutes since it is normally only necessary to excavate the surface layer with your ice axe to expose its junction with the layer below. The objective is to establish the depth of the surface layer and thus the seriousness of a possible surface slide and to identify any weaknesses either within the layer itself or in its attachment to the underlayer. In Scotland because of rapid settlement there is nearly always a distinct discontinuity between the new and recent snowfall(s) and the older snow underneath. Just the same principles apply to the examination and interpretation of the surface pit as to the more sophisticated version described earlier (pages 295–300) save that the measurements are much more crude and that it is unusual to have the means to take snow temperatures. Choose a spot which has a similar aspect to the suspect slope but is itself free from avalanche danger.

What to Look For

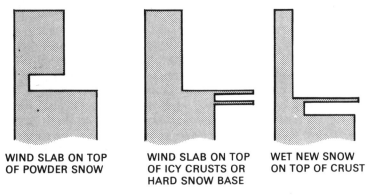

| WIND SLAB ON TOP OF POWDER SNOW | WIND SLAB ON TOP OF ICY CRUSTS OR HARD SNOW BASE | WET NEW SNOW ON TOP OF CRUST |

Fig. 214. *What to look for. An inspection of the surface layer and its attachment to the underlying snow will provide vital information about the condition of the surface layer and its tendency to avalanche.*

Be on the look-out for any sudden variation in any of the physical characteristics of the snow, particularly in hardness because this is the easiest property to recognise and also because it reflects an extremely important characteristic of snow, its strength. You will usually find that a marked difference in one characteristic is also reflected in others. Where you find such variations, usually between the surface layer and its base, then the slope must be rated as a high avalanche risk. In addition to hardness check also for humidity and crystal type.

Axe Test

An even quicker alternative to the surface pit, which can tell you a great deal about the surface layers, is to thrust your axe into the snow perpendicular to the surface. It is best to do this with a repetitive tamping action, applying the same amount of pressure on the spike of the axe each time. The axe will penetrate the snow a little further each time and any sudden variations in hardness will be apparent by an equally sudden difference in the extent of penetration. If this is the case, investigate by digging a surface pit. The safest profile would be indicated by a gradually increasing resistance with depth with no sudden variations. Obviously, this test is only valid in surface layers which are shallower than the length of the axe. A further limitation is that it may fail to show up very thin weak layers sandwiched between layers of similar hardness.

Shovel Test

It may well be that the surface pit or axe test has revealed a potential sliding surface. It is often possible to confirm this by making a simple practical test. Dig a pit at least as deep as the surface layer with a vertical back wall. Cut away a chimney about 30 cm (1 ft) deep on one side of the wall and make a V-shaped slot on the other side so that you leave an isolated block of snow between, also about 30 cm (1 ft) wide. This is your test block and you must take care not to disturb it in any way.

Now thrust the axe, or better still a shovel or the heel of a ski, down the back of the isolated block of snow and holding on with both hands pull gently outwards, exerting as little leverage as possible. If the surface layer has poor adhesion to the layer below the block will suddenly shear along the contact face. Sometimes shearing will take place just by the action of inserting the axe, indicating a highly unstable condition. This is a field test and it is not appropriate to apply too rigid an interpretation. Nevertheless, with experience, it is possible to evaluate the degree of risk in a general way (see Fig. 215).

(a) *A bench is cut into the snow to expose the surface layer and the top of the underlayer.*

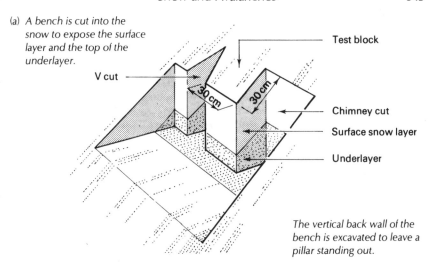

V cut

30 cm 30 cm

Test block

Chimney cut

Surface snow layer

Underlayer

The vertical back wall of the bench is excavated to leave a pillar standing out.

(b) *A shovel (or an ice axe or the heel of a ski) is carefully inserted at the back of the pillar. A gentle pull is then applied to the shaft in a horizontal direction until the pillar of surface snow separates from the underlayer.*

The ease of separation is a measure of the adhesion of the surface layer to the layer below and provides useful first hand evidence of the likelihood of a slab avalanche.

Degree of risk	Indication
Very high risk	Surface slab slides off when axe or shovel is inserted.
High risk	Light pressure releases slab.
Some risk	Moderate pressure releases slab. In this case other evidence should be carefully evaluated before making a decision.
Low risk	Sustained pressure required to release slab.
No risk	Surface slab cannot be released by sustained pressure.

Fig. 215. *The shovel test.*

Route Finding

It is unusual, though not unknown, for a party of mountaineers to be caught in an avalanche which they did not themselves trigger-off. Most avalanche accidents are caused by their victims. This is a thought to bear in mind when selecting a route through avalanche country. No matter how critical the risk of avalanche there is almost always a safe route to be found somewhere. Unfortunately, the decision to follow it is not always easy to make, partly because it is rarely possible to be absolutely sure of your evaluation of the degree of risk and partly because other factors tend to complicate matters. The safe route, for instance, might mean a substantial detour which you have neither the time nor the energy to accomplish. It is an inescapable fact that many avalanche accidents occur when circumstantial pressures have forced a party to ignore or minimise the obvious warning signs and 'take a chance'.

Your choice of route will be very much influenced by your assessment of snow conditions and how these might change in the course of your journey. The predominance of the lee slope slab in the Scottish mountains makes it essential to avoid these slopes during and immediately after heavy snowfall or drifting. Although avalanches have been known on slopes as shallow as 11°, the main danger lies within the range 30°–50°. Avoid bulging convex slopes where the snow cover is stretched under tension and favour concave shapes such as bowls and hollows where compressive forces tend to hold the snow in place. Given the choice, stick to ridges and the high ground above the avalanche paths and if you have to cross suspect slopes do so as high as possible so that, although you may be more likely to trigger a slide, you will be close to or right at the fracture line and therefore much more likely to remain on top of the debris or escape it altogether. Following a valley route may well be a safe option but bear in mind that an avalanche can flow out across a valley floor for a considerable distance. Small gullies and valleys with steep side walls are particularly dangerous, even although the total amount of snow involved may be relatively small.

Snow can accumulate to considerable depths on the lee side, often topped by a cornice. If a slide is released, the debris can only pile up on top of the unfortunate party below. An open slope is much to be preferred to a confined one and, if there is a degree of risk, always work out what is likely to happen in the event of a slide.

A knowledge of the terrain is obviously a great advantage in working out a safe route since the places most exposed to avalanches can be avoided. Occasionally, the evidence of previous avalanche activity is clearly to be seen by its effect on the vegetation: a swathe cut through the forest, trees and bushes permanently bent downslope, and so on. It must

Fig. 216. *Danger in a narrow confined valley.*
Danger above! This party is walking into a potential death trap. Strong winds have deposited heavy masses of snow on the slopes above. There is no escape should an avalanche be released. Even quite small valleys can be extremely hazardous in these conditions.

be said though that few avalanches reach the timber line in this country. The presence of trees, particularly thick forest, do provide a measure of protection, but often a good deal less than many assume. An avalanche is unlikely to start on a forested slope but the presence of trees is no guarantee of protection from an avalanche released from the slopes above.

Crossing a Suspect Slope

The first question to ask yourself when faced with the crossing of a suspect slope is, 'do I have to?'. A number of factors must be weighed in the balance and every possible alternative considered before making the decision to cross. Usually, it is not possible to choose the time of your crossing, but this is a factor which should be borne in mind when planning your route. A slope on which there is every likelihood of a wet avalanche may be frozen solid and perfectly safe in the early hours of the day before the sun has had a chance to do its work.

L

Having decided to cross, the next question to ask is, 'where?' Where is the slope likely to fracture and where is the best crossing point? As we have seen, the fracture is likely to be across an area of tension in the slope and if at all possible you want to be above this area.

It is quite common for the upper fracture to follow a line connecting islands of stability on the slope, such as a group of rocks or trees. Such islands can provide useful anchor points if it becomes necessary to use the rope to safeguard a particularly exposed section. If you do elect to use the rope, the belayer should not be tied on to the same rope as the person crossing since a big avalanche would simply result in both being swept away. Try to visualise what will happen if the slope does go and work out what your escape options will be. Brief your party.

Before you embark on the slope there are certain basic precautions to take. Make sure that any encumbrances can be shed at a moment's notice. Undo your rucksack waist belt and at least one shoulder strap, take off the axe wrist loop, zip-up your clothing, put on gloves and pull on your anorak hood, securing it over your mouth and nose if possible. Skiers should cross on foot, but if on skis ensure that safety straps are untied and wrist loops free. If you are carrying safety beacons make sure they are all switched to 'transmit' and carried inside the clothing (see pages 321–323). A less effective alternative is to trail an avalanche cord. This is a 20–30 m length of brightly coloured nylon tied to the waist at one end and left to trail behind you on the snow. Should you be taken by the avalanche it is possible that some part of this light cord will be thrown up on the surface, even if you are not. The cord has metal tags crimped on at 2 m intervals with an arrow and the number of metres to the end of the cord (in the direction of the arrow) marked on. Just make sure you tie on to the right end of the cord!

The crossing should be made one at a time, if possible following a descending line which avoids too sudden an undercutting of the slope above. The others should keep a sharp look-out for anything higher up and be prepared to plot the progress of the victim should the worst happen. It has too often been a fatal mistake to assume that because one person, or even a whole party, has crossed a suspect slope in safety then it is safe for others to do so. Frequently, the earlier crossings simply bring the slope into a critical state of equilibrium ready to be released by the next person to cross.

Avalanche Search and Rescue

The rather depressing news conveyed by Fig. 217 is that the chances of survival in an avalanche dwindle rapidly after $1\frac{1}{2}$ to 2 hours even when the

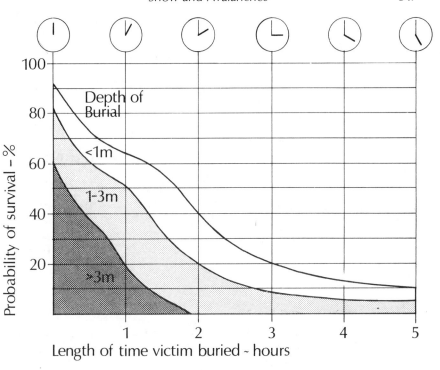

Fig. 217. *Probability of survival for avalanche victims as a function of time, showing also the effect of depth of burial. In Switzerland, the survival rate for completely buried victims is 19%. (From a study of avalanche accidents by de Quervain.)*

victim is buried close to the surface. It also shows that the deeper the victim is buried the shorter the time he will survive.

Speed is therefore of paramount importance in any avalanche search operation. The chances of survival are greatly reduced as the burial time increases. Few victims are brought out alive after 2 hours or more in the snow. The operation may be considered in three phases:

1. A preliminary search by the survivors of the avalanche.
2. An advance party search carried out with the men and equipment that can be got to the site without delay.
3. A systematic search using probes, dogs and other methods of detection.

Search by Survivors

It is remarkable how it is possible on many avalanche incidents for witnesses to follow the course of the victims during their descent, right up until their final burial. It is vitally important that the position of the victims when engulfed and when last seen be clearly marked with a stick, etc. The line connecting these two positions acts as a pointer to the likely burial area. This area and indeed the whole of the debris should be examined as closely as time permits for any sign of the victim, his clothing or equipment. A reversed ski stick, an ice axe, or a stick with the basket removed makes a simple probe to test likely spots.

Obviously, the amount of time devoted to this preliminary search depends on the location of the accident and the number of survivors. However, this surface search is absolutely essential and half an hour to an hour is suggested as being of the right order.

Swiss records for the period 1960–1974 show that of the 777 people buried in avalanches and found alive, 371 freed themselves, 282 were found by members of their own party and only 124 by an organised rescue party. This is no reflection on the efficiency of the rescue organisation but serves to underline the importance of the preliminary search by those who witness an accident.

Advance Party Search

An advance party must be sent immediately and with all speed to the site of the avalanche. They should take with them only what is immediately available in the form of first aid, shovels and sounding rods or sticks. It is the job of this party to follow up the preliminary search and concentrate their attention on the most likely area of debris. Some rescue posts in the Cairngorms and elsewhere carry a supply of probes, shovels and other equipment required for avalanche work.

Systematic Search

A great many people may be involved in this phase and a high degree of accuracy and co-ordination is essential. For these reasons the search must be conducted with military precision and must be under the direct control of an experienced rescue co-ordinator.

In spite of all the scientific advances in this field, the two oldest methods of search remain the most effective, namely the use of sounding rods or probes and the use of dogs. One of the most important reasons for this is the fact that neither method requires that the victim should be carrying some special device, such as a magnet or radio. They depend for their operation on natural and permanent properties of the human body and can therefore be employed with a good chance of success on all buried victims.

Danger of Further Avalanches

There is more than a grain of truth in the statement that the safest place to be after an avalanche is in its track, but it is a statement which has to be qualified. Obviously, that particular avalanche will not fall again, at least not until after the next snowfall, but other avalanche paths may feed into its track and a sharp look-out must be kept against such a possibility.

Use of Sounding Rods

These come in a variety of forms but are normally jointed metal rods up to 4 m (13 ft) in length. The rescuers are arranged in an extended line across the debris and advance up the slope probing at set. intervals and to a predetermined depth. An area once searched in this way should be clearly marked with flags or sticks.

Fig. 218. *Probing with an avalanche rod to detect a buried victim. Rocks or even lumps of snow may deflect the probe making it difficult to strike a deeply buried person.*

It is normal to probe to a depth of 2 m (6 ft) even although the depth of the debris may be considerably greater. The saving in time far outweighs the slim chance of finding a victim alive at a greater depth. Even with a team of 20–30 people the business of probing takes a very long time and here again a saving can be made by adopting a wide spacing between probes. Rescuers stand with their feet 0·5 m (20 in) apart and separated from their neighbours' feet by a distance of 0·25 m (10 in).

For coarse probing the rods are driven in between the feet. The whole line then advances by one 0·70 m pace and the process is repeated. In this way each square metre of debris is probed twice. With this method 20 men can search an area of 1 hectare (100 m × 100 m) in 4 hours with a 76% chance of finding the victim.

For fine probing the rods are driven in at both toes and also centrally. The line then advances by 0·30 m (1 ft) and the process is repeated. Using this method each square metre is probed 13 times and it would take 20 men 20 hours to search 1 hectare with 100% chance of success.

The great disadvantage of sounding, effective though it is, is the length of time it takes to cover the ground, even with large numbers of rescuers. It is for this reason that a well trained dog is worth its weight in gold for it can search a given area in a tenth of the time that it would take a team of 20 men.

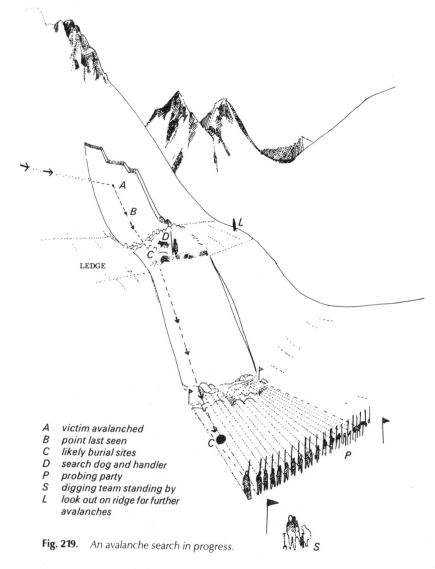

A   *victim avalanched*
B   *point last seen*
C   *likely burial sites*
D   *search dog and handler*
P   *probing party*
S   *digging team standing by*
L   *look out on ridge for further avalanches*

Fig. 219.   *An avalanche search in progress.*

Use of Avalanche Trained Dogs

Details of the Search and Rescue Dog Association have been given on pages 227–228. The success of trained dogs in the search for buried victims is well documented. They will find all buried persons still alive or those who died shortly before, normally regardless of the burial depth and nature of the snow. The speed of search varies with the tenacity and stamina of the dog as well as with the prevailing conditions, but on average a trained dog will search an area of 1 hectare in about half an hour.

If dogs are to be used they should be brought to the site of the accident as soon as possible. There is no reason why the search should be delayed till their arrival, provided the area is cleared 10–15 minutes before they are set to work. The rescuers must of course move off downwind of the area.

Trenching

If these methods fail to locate the victim trenches must be dug into the debris. These trenches should be approximately 1m wide and spaced at intervals of 3 m. The walls of the trenches should then be probed horizontally.

Other Methods

Many other ingenious methods of detection have been devised. They can be divided roughly into those which require the victim to carry some device such as a VHF transmitter or a magnetic disc and those which depend on some natural function or property of the body. The latter offers the best hope for development since it is always difficult to persuade people to carry extra equipment, no matter how compact. However, for organised groups and search parties, pocket transceivers are now available which greatly improve the chances of being found for those who carry them.

Avalanche Beacons

There is no doubt that the most effective insurance against being killed in an avalanche is to carry an avalanche beacon. This is a small portable transceiver which transmits a signal which can be picked up by other sets operating on the same frequency. Each member of the party should carry a beacon which is kept in the 'transmit' mode while in avalanche country. In the event of someone being buried in an avalanche the search is conducted by the remaining members of the party who switch their sets to the 'receive' mode. An increase in signal strength indicates an approach to the victim's set.

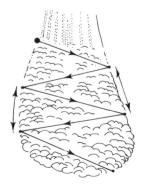

Fig. 220. (a) An avalanche beacon or 'bleeper';

Fig. 220. (b) Search technique using a single beacon. The distance apart of the turning points down each side should be just within the maximum range of the beacon;

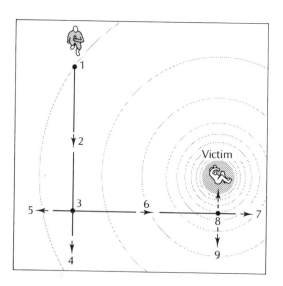

Fig. 220. (c) Technique to be adopted after the first signal has been received from the buried beacon.

It is unfortunate that there is not as yet an agreed international frequency although strenuous efforts are being made in this direction. Check that your sets are compatible with those in general use in the area of your expedition. The cost, though not prohibitive, is beyond the means of many modestly financed expeditions. However, it is often possible to hire equipment for limited periods at favourable club rates.

Although the principle of operation and use is simple enough, the actual technique of searching requires a bit of practice. It is usually possible to pick up a signal at 50–100 m range and to move fairly rapidly towards the victim. It is in the final 5 m or so that some difficulty is normally experienced.

It is very important to test all beacons in both modes before setting out. Replace used and partly used cells and carry a spare set in your pocket. Never carry beacons in your rucksack but attach them to your body in the recommended manner. All sets should be switched to 'transmit' at the start of the day and kept in that mode until your return.

First Aid

In about 80% of fatal avalanche accidents the cause of death is suffocation. If the victim is alive he may be suffering from shock, exposure, frostbite and other mechanical injuries to the body. If necessary, mouth-to-mouth resuscitation and/or external cardiac massage should be given immediately (remember that the mouth is likely to be full of snow). Great care should be exercised in taking the victim out of the snow so as not to aggravate any injuries. He should be placed in a casualty bag in the head-low position and the treatment continued as discussed in Chapter 8, page 197.

It should be remembered that a buried casualty is likely to be extremely cold and if unconscious may easily be mistaken for dead. Respiration and pulse may be undetectable. Always assume that the patient is alive until a doctor confirms otherwise.

What to do if Caught in an Avalanche

This is the sort of advice which is easy to give but which may be quite impossible to follow. Nevertheless, it is the distillation of the experience of many victims over a period of years. There are, of course, a number of physical variables, to say nothing of human ones, and the best course of action depends to a large extent on them. For instance, what may be a number one priority in a powder snow avalanche may be of little importance in a wet slab.

Remove rucksack and skis (these should already be in the quick release position if there is any risk of avalanche). A good skier, may of course, be able to traverse or schuss out of danger. Do not be too hasty in throwing away your ice axe until it is clear that it is likely to do more harm than good.

Make a quick assessment of the avalanche; whether you are at the top, bottom, middle, or to one side; what type it is (wet, dry, etc.) and where your best line of escape lies. If you have already made a proper evaluation of the risk and considered the emergency options you will be much more likely to find the appropriate response if and when the need arises.

Delay your departure as long as possible by thrusting your ice axe into the stable underlayer and hanging on with all you have got. The more you let past you at the start the less is likely to bury you at the finish.

It may be advantageous to work out to the side of the avalanche and escape in that direction possibly by swimming or rolling.

If swimming movements are possible, then a sort of double-action back stroke seems to be the most effective, with the back to the force of the avalanche and the head up. Obviously, if you are in danger of being struck by blocks and slabs of snow then your arms will have to be used to protect your head and face. There is no cut and dried procedure here—ride it out as best you can and save your great effort for the last few seconds.

Keep your mouth shut! In a powder avalanche cover the mouth and nose with the top of your sweater or anorak or your rucksack if you have not already disposed of it.

A supreme effort should be made in the last few seconds as the avalanche loses its momentum and begins to settle. This may be the only time that you are able to obtain some purchase on the moving debris. Two things are paramount: an air space; and a position as near to the surface as possible. The chances of survival are greatly reduced if deeply buried.

Don't panic!

Avalanche Protection—a summary

Precautions Before Leaving

Consult local expert advice and find out the recent weather history and snow conditions. Obey avalanche warning notices.
Carry first aid kit and basic rescue equipment, including shovels, in the party.
Carry avalanche beacons set to 'transmit' and be practised in their use.

Never expose more than one of the party to risk at any given moment.
Do not assume that the passage of another party is proof that a slope is safe.
Never go alone.
Know how to improvise a rope or ski stretcher.

Weather Indications

Lee slopes are particularly prone to soft slab avalanches. Keep clear of accumulation areas during and immediately after a snow storm. Know which way the wind has been drifting the snow.

Low temperatures prolong avalanche risk.

Any sudden increase in temperature after snowfall, especially with a dry wind, creates avalanche danger.

Rain on unconsolidated snow gives rise to wet avalanches, especially where the underlayer offers poor attachment.

Powder avalanches are rare in Scotland, but occasionally occur after 30 cm (1 ft) or more of new snow in cold weather. Slopes take 2–3 days to settle and longer if cold and out of the sun.

Things to Watch for in the Topography

Most avalanche accidents are caused by their victims. Keep high and on the ridges and avoid being the trigger which releases a slide.

Avoid cornices and the slopes below them after drifting or during a thaw.

Avalanche slopes which run out into gullies where the debris can pile up are especially dangerous.

The most dangerous slope angles are between 30° and 45°.

Fracture commonly takes place on the convex part of the slope.

Thin forest offers no protection.

Things to Watch for in the Snow

The most reliable indication of unstable conditions are signs of recent avalanches in the neighbourhood.

Be on the look out for other warning signs: large snowballs (sunballs) rolling downslope, sudden collapse of snow cover under weight, hollow feeling and noise of slabs, cracks appearing in the snow, mini slabs released from boots or skis, signs of melting etc., etc.

The attachment of snow layers to each other is of fundamental importance. Assess this by digging a small pit or by probing with axe or ski stick. Adjoining layers which differ markedly in hardness are likely to be poorly attached to each other. Note particularly any weak layers and crusts.

The deeper the snow, the greater the danger. An accumulation rate in excess of 2 cm (1 in) per hour can lead to avalanche hazard.

15 Cold Injury

Frostbite

Frostbite is a condition which is fortunately relatively rare in this country. When it does occur, it is usually associated with emergency situations involving forced bivouacs or with fractures or other injuries. Nevertheless it is very important to be able to give the right treatment in the field, to avoid permanent damage or loss of tissue. The condition is closely related to mountain hypothermia, previously described (Chapter 8), since one of the body's reactions to general cooling is to reduce the supply of blood going to the extremities in order to conserve heat in the core. This is done at the expense of a greatly increased risk of frostbite since a sluggish circulation is stage one of the frostbite process. It is unusual, therefore, to have simply a frostbite problem to deal with. It must be appreciated that frostbite normally reflects a more serious general condition of body cooling and that both must be dealt with simultaneously. If for any reason this is not possible, then treatment for hypothermia must take precedence. As in other things, a knowledge of avoidance is paramount, coupled with early recognition and treatment before irrevocable damage is done.

Frostbite is the freezing or partial freezing of parts of the body, usually the face and extremities, the hands and feet. Provided blood circulation to these parts is adequate and tissue remains warm and nourished there is no danger of frostbite. Excessive surface cooling, almost invariably exacerbated by faulty clothing or a condition of exhaustion, shock or general cooling of the whole body, leads to a progressive reduction of circulation in the exposed part. Once circulation becomes negligible the tissue freezes. The initial stage of the process is known as 'frostnip'. This is speedily reversible provided action is taken in time. Keep a watch out for white nose, cheeks or ears on your companions and rewarm immediately. It is not possible to watch the hands and the feet as these are normally covered, but cessation of feeling or even a feeling of warmth following cold, are danger signs which must not be ignored. It should be noted that local cold injury is possible at temperatures above freezing, usually following a period of prolonged exposure to wet cold conditions.

While it is fairly easy to rewarm the hands, it takes a great deal of will-power in a difficult situation to go to all the trouble of removing gaiters and boots to warm up the feet. However, if these warning signs are ignored, true frostbite may be the result, with a long and painful period of recovery and perhaps the risk of permanent tissue damage or even loss.

Treatment

'Frostnip' should be treated immediately by thawing the exposed part on some warm part of the anatomy. Fingers can be warmed under the armpit, ears by the hands, and feet on the belly of a companion. The important thing is to recognise this first stage of frostbite, especially in the feet, and rewarm immediately.

Frostbite may be superficial or deep. Superficial frostbite is confined to the skin and surface tissues which take on a greyish-white appearance, frozen hard on the surface, but resilient underneath. With proper treat-ment a full recovery is likely with no loss of tissue. Deep frostbite, on the other hand, affects not only the surface tissues, but involves the deeper structures of muscle, tendon and bone. Recovery is a slow and painful process almost inevitably resulting in some permanent loss of tissue.

The preferred treatment is active rewarming, but once rewarming has taken place, the greatest care is absolutely essential to protect the injury from further cooling or physical damage. For this reason it is best to head for home or for a base where adequate protection can be guaranteed. It is considerably less damaging to walk out on a frozen foot than a thawed one and in the likely circumstances a great deal safer for all concerned. In this country in almost every case the rule must be immediate evacuation to a place where professional medical help is available. In a situation where the victim is immobilised by other injuries and may have to wait some considerable time for rescue, treat for exposure by providing shelter, warmth and nourishment, but do not attempt to rewarm the frostbitten part by exercise or by any other means.

> Do not rub with snow or, for that matter, anything else.
> Do not give alcohol or cigarettes.
> Do not apply direct heat to injury from hot water bottle or stone.
> Do not apply traction to fractures.
> Do not pick or burst blisters.

This treatment or, more accurately, non-treatment ensures the maximum chance of recovery later. Fractures should be treated with a well padded splint (not inflatable) and periodic checks made as to the state of the extremities. Footwear must be removed gently and the foot carefully padded with spare socks and sweaters and placed inside a rucksack.

It is highly unlikely that in this country it should ever be necessary to do more than is outlined above. The treatment at base would normally be supervised by a doctor or carried out in hospital. Experts on cold injury are agreed that immediate rapid rewarming for 20 minutes in a hot bath at 42°C–44°C offers the best hope of recovery and minimal loss of tissue. In the field when speedy evacuation is not possible, as on a major expedition abroad, this treatment should be administered at base camp.

Whether rewarming is induced or spontaneous, as could happen if the victim was evacuated to a warm tent at a low level or indeed if any early diagnosis of the injury has not been made, it is important to realise that further exercise or use of the frostbitten part is out of the question. In the case of a frostbitten foot the victim must be regarded as a stretcher case and evacuated accordingly. Everything must be done to prevent further damage or cooling. A dry, loose cotton wool dressing is all that is required after the injury has been gently cleaned by dabbing with warm (not hot) soapy water. Pads of wool may be required to separate the fingers or toes. A cage of some sort must then be improvised to prevent accidental contact and the pressure and drag of sleeping bag or blankets. On no account touch or prick blisters or interfere in any other way with the injury.

Prevention

Frostbite is inextricably related to the general temperature balance of the whole body, and the preventative measures previously recommended (see Chapter 8) to combat hypothermia are equally valid to give protection from frostbite. Basically a party that is fit, well fed, clad and watered, and in good spirits has little to fear. This assumes that the equipment and clothing worn, particularly on the hands and feet, will give adequate insulation from the cold. Boots must be roomy and allow for the wearing of one or two pairs of warm socks or stockings (of wool and preferably loop stitched). A fitting which allows socks to wrinkle up under the heel or at the toes creates local pressure points which may become the focal point of frostbite injury. Do not wear wet socks or mitts (which, incidentally, are much superior to gloves as far as insulation is concerned), and carry spares of both. Change into dry socks at night and, if there is a risk that your boots might freeze up, put them into a polythene bag and keep them with you inside your sleeping bag.

The temperature of deep powder snow may be many degrees below the ambient temperature so that your feet may be much colder than the rest of your body. Gaiters not only provide additional insulation but they prevent snow from getting into your boots, a sure recipe for frostbite. In very cold weather avoid touching or handling metal with bare hands (you are liable to stick to it) and do not let your hands get wet with stove fuel or other liquids which freeze below 0°C.

In cold weather keep a watch on your companions' faces for any sign of frostnip (local pallor on nose, cheeks or ears). Stop and rewarm immediately. Rewarming the feet is a time-consuming business, but impress on everyone the importance of taking action before it is too late. A feeling of numbness or even warmth following chill are warning signs which are ignored at your peril. Remember, too, that an exposed or injured person is much more liable to frostbite and, finally, that the 'freezing power' of the environment depends on wind as well as temperature (see Wind Chill Chart, Fig. 128). The effect of a 40 m.p.h. wind at −7°C is exactly the same as that of a 2 m.p.h. breeze at −20°C.

Non-Freezing Cold Injury

Immersion Foot is due to prolonged exposure of the extremities to water and is characterised by painful, swollen feet or hands and, in more severe cases, by muscle damage, ulcers and gangrene. It is not known to what extent the condition occurs among mountaineers but there is no doubt that the early stages of the injury are occasionally encountered among inexperienced hillwalkers taking part in expeditions lasting two or more nights, where the feet may be wet or damp more or less continuously for the whole period. Two distinct types are recognised due to warm water (tropical) and cold water immersion. It is the latter which concerns us here.

While the main cause is exposure to water for a period in excess of 48 hours, contributory factors show a striking similarity to those which lead to mountain hypothermia: general chilling of the body, exhaustion, dehydration, lack of proper nutrition, etc. More specific factors include constricting clothing and footwear which tend to restrict the circulation in the extremities.

The condition may develop insidiously over a long period of time and early symptoms such as numbness or pins and needles and slight swelling may well be ignored. Removal of the boots results in increased swelling, tingling and sometimes severe pain. Later on the skin may turn yellow, blue or black and may remain in this condition for several hours or even days. This is followed by a stage which lasts 1–10 weeks, where the feet become red, hot and dry and blisters may develop as in frostbite. The patient experiences burning and shooting pains accompanied by a bounding pulse. In the most severe cases there may be muscle wastage and the development of ulcers and superficial gangrene.

Rest in a horizontal position is the best treatment with the feet kept cool by exposing them to the air. Analgesics should be given to reduce pain. In most cases recovery is complete within 2–5 weeks, although severe cases may take considerably longer. The patient may be left with some after effects, such as increased sensitivity to cold.

Preventative measures are obvious. Keep your feet dry or if that is not possible, make sure that you change into a dry pair of socks as soon as practicable. The quality and fit of socks or stockings is of crucial importance in minimising the risk of cold injury. Well fitting loop-stitched or woollen stockings are helpful in preventing the condition.

Snow Blindness

This has been referred to earlier when considering the effects of heat. Snow blindness is an extremely painful and debilitating condition brought about by exposure to intense ultraviolet radiation. Symptoms may not appear for 8–12 hours after exposure and by that time the damage has been done. This radiation increases with altitude. Snow reflects about 90% of ultraviolet light, so that it is not enough merely to shield the eyes from direct sunlight. Goggles, or glasses with light shading all round the lenses are required and, in addition, they must filter at least 90% of the ultraviolet radiation. In an emergency glasses can be improvised by cutting a horizontal slit in a piece of cardboard. It is a common error to believe that eye protection is not required on dull, overcast days, and this has resulted in a number of unnecessary cases of snow blindness. The situation is aggravated by internal reflection from the cloud base, which has a multiplication effect on the ultraviolet radiation.

The eyes initially feel simply irritated or dry, but later they feel as though they are full of sand. Moving or blinking the eyes becomes extremely painful. Even exposure to light may cause pain. Swelling of the eyelids, redness of the eyes and excessive watering may occur. A severe case of snow blindness may be completely disabling for several days.

Snow blindness heals spontaneously in a few days; however, the pain may be quite severe if the condition is not treated. Cold compresses applied to the closed eyes, and a dark environment may give some relief. The patient must not rub his eyes. Local anaesthetic agents should not be used since they rapidly lose their effectiveness and may lead to damage of the delicate corneal surface.

Readers are reminded that over-exposure to ultraviolet radiation can also result in painful and, occasionally, serious sunburn. Reliable preparations which effectively filter this should be applied to all exposed areas, particularly the nose and cheeks, the lips and the underside of the chin and ears.

16 Snow Shelters

There are two quite distinct sets of circumstances under which snow shelters might be used. The first is in an emergency situation arising from an accident or from an error of judgement where a party is forced to spend a night in the open without the benefit of camping or bivouac equipment. In snow conditions it may be that the only possible form of shelter available would be that provided by a snow shelter of some kind. Obviously, every effort should be made to get off the exposed tops and down to a more sheltered location and it may well be that the time and energy spent in constructing a shelter might be better spent in getting off the mountain. Nevertheless, circumstances can and do arise when a bivouac is inevitable and there is no doubt that lives have been saved as a result of a prompt decision to dig in before darkness and storm dictated their own terms. Time is likely to be short with darkness already falling and the resources available to the party may be limited to that which would normally be carried on a winter walk: ice axes, rope, rucksack, emergency rations, spare clothing and so on. What can be achieved will depend very much on the physical condition and morale of the party, the nature of the terrain and snow cover and the weather conditions.

The second set of circumstances is quite different and arises from a deliberate decision taken in advance to spend the night in a snow shelter. Special equipment can be carried to aid in the construction of a shelter, such as a snow saw and shovel and to make living conditions more comfortable, e.g. sleeping bag, insulation mat, stove, food, etc.: in fact all the gear that would normally be carried for an overnight stop. Under these controlled circumstances, sufficient time can be allowed to build a much more elaborate and spacious form of shelter. The value of such an exercise should not be underestimated. Snow shelters have been used to great advantage in polar regions and on expeditions to mountainous areas in all parts of the world.

A well designed snow shelter affords complete protection from the wind. It is well insulated by the snow, which is a poor conductor of heat and is, therefore, quickly heated by body warmth alone. It is quiet, easily lighted and adaptable. Unfortunately, it is time-consuming work. It takes approximately $1\frac{1}{2}$ hours per man sheltered to build and for that reason it is wise to seek a suitable location well before dark.

M

A number of different types of shelter are discussed in this chapter, each suited to particular snow and weather conditions. In Scotland the snow cave is the most reliable, since it is the only one with the structural strength to withstand sudden and devastating thaws. It is normally possible to construct some kind of snow shelter, provided there is sufficient snow. This is not likely to be found on exposed ridges or plateaux. Seek out the deeper drifts in more sheltered locations lower down. Some of these present a steep face on the lee side into which it is possible to tunnel and quickly gain a degree of protection from the elements.

It is quite common for large cornices to contain hollows where the snow has canopied over the top. In dire emergency they are certainly worth investigating for possible enlargement into a snow hole. Any investigation should be carried out on a rope secured from above and under no circumstances should a cornice or lee slope site be used if there is any likelihood of an avalanche, remembering that such sites are among the most sensitive trigger points.

The most useful tool for digging is a broad, short-handled shovel which, together with a special saw for cutting blocks, can make relatively light work of moving quantities of snow. Anyone who has had to use an ice axe for making a snowhole will vouch for the fact that it is far from being the ideal tool for the job. However, in an emergency it may well be all that is available and for this reason it is sensible to get some practice in using it for this purpose. If possible, to save time and energy, blocks should be quarried above the site of the shelter using the snow layer which has the most suitable consistency. Windblown snow usually provides excellent building material.

Precautions

Certain precautions need to be taken when using snow shelters to ensure maximum safety and comfort.

Only dry clothing and sleeping bags will keep you warm during the night. In addition, there is always the danger of wet clothing freezing: therefore every care should be taken to see that they are kept dry and the following points need to be borne in mind: —

Digging snow is warm work. Strip off to avoid making clothes damp with sweat which may freeze later.

Ensure adequate ventilation at all times—see below.

All equipment must be brought inside.

Remove any wet clothes before settling in and place them in a rucksack.

If it is freezing hard, wrap your boots inside a polythene bag and take them into your sleeping bag.

Brush off all particles of snow clinging to clothing before entering the shelter. These may melt in the warm atmosphere, wetting clothing.

Water vapour given off during cooking may condense, wetting clothes also. If possible, avoid having liquids boiling or simmering. Increase ventilation.

Use a torch instead of candles, or if this is not possible, use only one candle.

Insulate the body from beneath as much as possible. Avoid sleeping on polythene or other slippery material, or you are liable to find yourself suddenly outside the cave.

Take a shovel or digging implement into the shelter with you in case you have to dig yourself out.

Leave a light on in the shelter if you have to leave it for any reason during the night. It may help you to find it when you come back.

If there are several snow shelters in use connect them up with a climbing rope firmly secured inside the entrance of each. This will ensure that communications can remain open even during the most severe drifting and that the shelters can be quickly located afterwards.

Ventilation

Nearly all the recorded accidents in snow shelters have been caused by carbon monoxide (CO) poisoning. It cannot be stressed too strongly that ensuring adequate ventilation is the most important single precaution which must be taken. Normal stove burning produces little CO. However, if the flame touches a cool surface, such as a billy filled with melting snow, combustion is not completed and considerable unburnt CO is produced. The danger can be lessened by avoiding direct flame contact with the billy, but increased ventilation, both at the door and above the stove, is the only safe procedure. If you get a headache after cooking, it is a clear sign that the ventilation is inadequate.

In a freshly built shelter there will always be a certain amount of air movement through the walls. This will be reduced in time, as glazing takes place on the inside. In these circumstances it is quite possible for the supply of oxygen to become exhausted. This means that even if there is no burning stove or candles, additional ventilation must be provided. The door, or at least a section of it, should be left open at all times and if drifting occurs, it should be cleared out every 2 hours, or more often if drifting is fast.

Ventilation is also necessary to prevent overheating and melting. If the external temperature is below −10°C there should be no problem. At higher temperatures, which are common in this country, some dripping is inevitable and close to freezing point the structure itself may be in danger of collapse. In this event the door should be kept fully open and if the shelter has been in use for some time, the roof can be skimmed to a thickness of a few inches to increase heat loss. A ventilation hole in the roof greatly improves the through draft.

Snow Cave

The best location for a snow cave is in a drift of snow with a fairly steep face $> 30°$. This will ensure that there is sufficient depth of snow and that it can be easily disposed of down the slope. It also means that shelter can be obtained reasonably quickly and that the snow is likely to be in good condition for cutting. It is relatively easy to make and, for Scottish conditions and emergencies, probably the most dependable type of shelter. There are many variations between the elaborate snow palace and the simple burrow which would normally have to suffice in an emergency. The classic snow cave is constructed as follows (see Fig. 221).

Mark the top of the projected cave with a ski stick, axe, etc. Otherwise you may have unexpected company dropping in through the roof.

For the maximum insulation and structural stability the walls and ceiling should be at least 60 cm thick.

Although the final entrance should be small, for ease of working it is best to make this larger to start off with and fill it in later. Dig a deep slot into the drift, high and wide enough to allow you to work upright. Blocks should be cut with a saw or shovel when possible and loose snow can be removed on a polythene bag, or anorak.

Excavate the snow on either side of the slot to create an open living area. The roof should taper from head to feet so that you are sleeping in the warm air created by your own body and not underneath it.

Smooth off the roof to remove dripping points.

Reduce the entrance to a size which will allow access by crawling. A sack or polythene bag filled with snow makes an excellent door.

Make a ventilation hole in the roof. This is often in the thinnest part of the cave wall which is most likely to remain relatively unaffected by drifting. It may be the best escape route in the event of a complete drift-in.

Igloo

There is a good deal of fun and interest in building an igloo but it is not a suitable type of shelter for conditions in the British Isles. The design has been developed by the Eskimo for use in the Arctic where sub-zero temperatures persist for months on end. Even in the Cairngorms the likelihood is that thawing or near-thawing conditions would cause an igloo

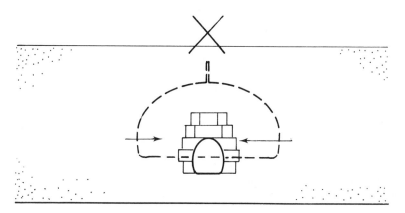

(a) Vertical section parallel to front of drift

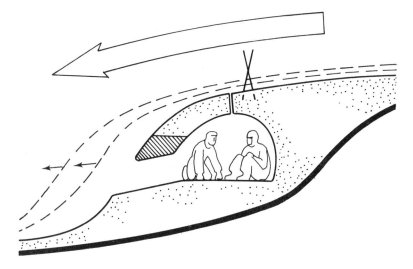

(b) Vertical section at right angles to front of drift

Fig. 221. *Snow cave in a drift.*

to buckle and collapse. However, there are occasions when it is possible to build an igloo-like extension to a snow cave, using material cut from the cave, so that an understanding of the technique is not without relevance. Wind-packed snow provides the best building material because it can be conveniently cut into blocks of just the right size and shape. Although it is possible to do without, a snow saw greatly assists construction.

To build an igloo, proceed as follows:

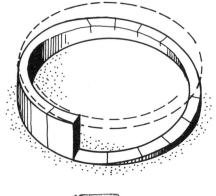

Fig. 222.   *Starting to make an igloo. The first course of blocks are in place. A single ring of full sized blocks is laid and then cut to form a ramp.*

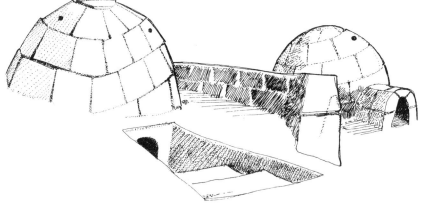

Fig. 223.   *Igloos showing alternative entrances and wind break.*

Select a safe site close to a source of good building snow. The way the
   blocks are mined is determined by the layering, but if possible, cut
   the blocks with their largest surface vertical.

Mark out a circle, the diameter of which will be dictated by the number
   of people to be accommodated. As a guide, a diameter of 2 m (7 ft)
   should be allowed for one person, plus 0·3 m (1 ft) for each additional
   person. Thus, a two man igloo will have a diameter of 2.30 m (8 ft).
   Since, for stability, the igloo must approximate to a hemisphere,
   anything with a diameter greater than 3 m would not be practicable.

The blocks should be as large as can be handled, the thickness being
   determined by the conditions. The bigger the blocks the quicker the

igloo will be made. Do not spend too much time trimming the blocks to the exact shape. This can be done when they are in position by running the snow saw back and forth along the joints.

Fig. 222 explains the method of construction. The builder stands inside, placing the blocks in an inward leaning spiral and making sure that each one has three points of contact with the previous one. To do this, the bottom and the end faces in contact may be made slightly concave. As the igloo rises and closes in, there comes a time when the blocks have to be passed in through a temporary opening cut in the side. The final opening in the roof is sealed by passing a block through, end on, and then lowering it into position. Before closing the roof, smooth off the inside of the igloo and throw out any loose snow.

All the small holes in the igloo can be filled in with pieces of broken blocks and the whole structure should be covered with loose snow.

The door should be placed at right angles to the prevailing wind and may be cut at floor level or as a trench. A straightforward opening with a short tunnel, somewhat larger than the door, would seem to be the best answer. An air vent should be opened in the roof.

If high winds are expected a low wall should be built to windward to protect the base of the igloo against erosion.

If the igloo is on a slope, a level floor should be excavated first and the wall built up until it is level. A ramp can be cut and the igloo continued as before.

Furnishings and fittings can now be added, the last word in luxury being a slab of clear ice inserted as a window!

Snow Pit

This is not a satisfactory shelter and should only be used when no other alternatives are possible. The actual construction is simple enough except

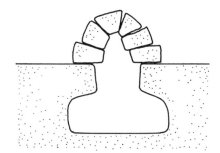

Fig. 224. *Snow pit.*

Dig a pit big enough to work in comfortably, at least 1 m (3 ft 4 in) × 0·75 m (2 ft 6 in) by 1·5 m (5 ft) deep. Enlarge the bottom to provide an area wide enough to sit or lie in. Roof over the top of the pit with snow blocks.

that all the material has to be thrown out of the pit. It follows much the same pattern as the Snow Cave and indeed it can be regarded as a variant of it.

Soft Snow Mound

This unusual design of shelter originated in the USA where it has been successful in areas of shallow snow cover, below the timberline. When snow is disturbed it undergoes a process known as age hardening. It is this process which is used to consolidate shallow, loose masses of powder snow, which are later excavated to provide a shelter.

Fig. 225. *Soft snow mound excavated to provide simple shelter.*

Snow is collected and shovelled into a mound, 3·5 m (11½ ft) in diameter and 2 m (6½ ft) high. Do not pack it down by patting or tramping since this causes uneven hardening. If necessary the snow can be reshovelled to accelerate the age hardening process. The mound should be as close to a hemisphere as is possible.

When the mound has reached the required height it should be left for at least 1 hour, preferably longer, to consolidate. Considerable shrinkage will take place overnight, even in cold weather and due allowance must be made for this.

After consolidation, dig into the centre of the mound. The finished product looks very much like an igloo, complete with door and air vent.

Snowball Shelter

In heavy damp snow it is possible to make various types of shelters from giant snowballs. These can be rolled together, preferably to a gathering area at the foot of a slope and then used as they stand, or cut into blocks to make a crude form of igloo.

Combination Shelters

All sorts of combinations between the various types of shelters mentioned in this chapter are possible. The choice will be determined by the terrain and the snow condition. There is considerable scope for the fertile imagination in the ultimate design. However speed is often a vital safety factor and that must always be considered. It is quite likely that in a real emergency some sort of combination shelter will be the most appropriate and some suggested designs are given in Figs. 226 and 227. The choice of site is all important and advantage should be taken of the natural configuration of the snow, using drifts, cornices, half-buried rocks, etc., to save time and energy. Blocks can be cut with the pick of the ice axe, snow can be shifted with a dinner plate, while a 'dead man' can double up as a shovel. Even the wire can occasionally be put to good use, rather in the manner of a cheese-cutter.

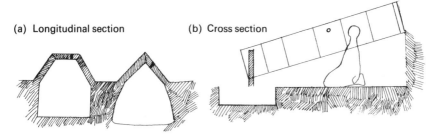

(a) Longitudinal section   **(b) Cross section**

Fig. 226.   *One man emergency snow shelter.*

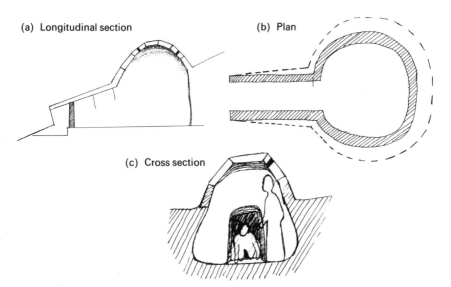

(a) Longitudinal section   **(b) Plan**

(c) Cross section

Fig. 227.   *Two man emergency snow shelter.*

The one and two man shelters shown in Figs. 226 and 227 can be built very quickly given reasonable snow and for this reason they are recommended as Emergency Shelters.

One final word of warning. It is very easy to lose small items of equipment in a snow shelter and for this reason a methodical approach pays dividends. It is also a temptation to leave behind waste food and unwanted packaging and other bits and pieces under the illusion that they will somehow remain out of sight. They will only remain out of sight until the spring thaw reveals the full extent of the thoughtlessness of those who have found shelter in the snow.

Bibliography

This bibliography has been compiled to help those who are seeking to improve their total mountaineering knowledge. Mountaineering has a rich literature and candidates for leadership awards are encouraged to read as widely as possible. Books out of print may often be obtained second-hand or from libraries. This is a practical guide and is not intended to be comprehensive. For instance, the vast Alpine and Himalayan literature is not represented at all. In addition to the books mentioned here, E. P. Publishings's 'Know the Game' Series and the Spurbooks Venture Guides Series provide cheap and elementary treatments of most of the topics covered. The principal UK distributor of outdoor literature is Cordee Books, 3a De Montfort Street, Leicester LE1 7HD.

MOUNTAINEERING TECHNIQUE—MODERN WORKS

British Mountaineering Council (1990) *Crampons*.
British Mountaineering Council (1988) *Knots*.
British Mountaineering Council (1987) *Ropes*.
Fyffe, A. and Peter, I. (1990) *The Handbook of Climbing*. Pelham Books.
Livesey, P. (1989) *Rockclimbing*. Springfield Books.
Long, J. (1989) *How to Rock Climb: (USA)*. Chockstone Press (Cordee).
March, B. (1984) *Modern Snow & Ice Techniques*. Cicerone Press.
March, B. (1985) *Modern Rope Techniques in Mountaineering*. Cicerone Press.
Moran, M. (1988) *Scotland's Winter Mountains*. David & Charles.
Peters, E. (1985) *Mountaineering: The Freedom of the Hills*. Mountaineers' Books: USA (Cordee).

HISTORIES AND REFERENCE BOOKS

Brooker, W. D. (1989) *A Century of Scottish Mountaineering*. Scottish Mountaineering Club.

Hankinson, A. (1984) *First Tigers: Early History of Rock Climbing in the Lake District.*

Humble, B. H. (1986) *The Cuillin of Skye.* The Ernest Press.

Jones, T. and Milburn, G. (1986) *Welsh Rock.* Pic.

Jones, T. and Milburn, G. (1988) *Cumbrian Rock.* Pic.

Neate, J. (1987) *Mountaineering Literature: A Bibliography of Material Published in English.* Cicerone Press.

BIOGRAPHIES AND OTHER NARRATIVES

Bell, J. H. B. (1989) *Bell's Scottish Climbs.* Gollanz.

Brown, H. M. (1980) *Hamish's Mountain Walk.* Paladin.

Mill, C. (1987) *Norman Collie.* Aberdeen Univ. Press.

Murray, W. H. (1979) *Mountaineering in Scotland/Undiscovered Scotland.* Diadem.

Murray, W. H. (1984) *Mountaineering in Scotland.* Diadem.

Oppenheimer, L. J. (1988) *Heart of Lakeland.* The Ernest Press.

Perrin, J. (1983) *Mirrors in the Cliffs.* Diadem.

Pilley, D. (1989) *Climbing Days.* Hogarth Press.

Sansom, G. S. (1982) *Climbing at Wasdale Before The First World War. The Mountain Journal of an Edwardian Gentleman.* Castle Cary Press.

Simpson, J. (1988) *Touching the Void.* Pan.

Smith, R. (1981) *The Winding Trail.* Diadem.

Tasker, J. (1982) *Savage Arena.* Methuen.

Tilman, H. W. (1985) *The Seven Mountain Travel Books.* Diadem.

Wilson, K. (1978) *The Games Climbers Play: Anthology of Mountaineering Articles.* Diadem.

GUIDEBOOKS

This section lists only guidebooks written for the general mountaineer and a handful of the better illustrated guidebooks. There is a huge literature of specialist rock and ice climbing guidebooks (available from climbing shops rather than bookshops) and, lately, a bewildering profusion of 'walkers' guides' of very mixed quality.

General Guides

Butterfield, I. (1986) *The High Mountains of Britain and Ireland.* Diadem.

Gilbert, R. (1990) *Richard Gilbert's 200 Challenging Walks.* Diadem.

Wilson, K. (1989) *Classic Rock. Great British Rock Climbs*. Diadem.
Wilson, K. and Gilbert, R. (1980) *Big Walks. Challenging Mountain Walks and Scrambles in the British Isles*. Diadem.
Wilson, K. and Gilbert, R. (1982) *Classic Walks. Mountain and Moorland in Britain and Ireland*. Diadem.
Wilson, K. and Gilbert, R. (1988) *Wild Walks*. Diadem.
Wilson, K. and Alcock, D. (1983) *Cold Climbs*. Diadem.

Scottish Guides

Andrew, K. M. and Thrippleton, A. A. (1972) *The Southern Uplands*. Scottish Mountaineering Club.
Bennet, D. (1989) *The Munros*. Scottish Mountaineering Club.
Bennet, D. (1986) *The Southern Highlands*. Scottish Mountaineering Club.
Bennet, D. and Johnstone, G. (1990) *The Corbetts & Other Scottish Hills*. Scottish Mountaineering Club.
Bennet, D. and Strang, T. (1990) *The Northwest Highlands*. Scottish Mountaineering Club.
Bull, S. P. (1986) *Black Cuillin Ridge: Scramblers' Guide*. Scottish Mountaineering Club.
Donaldson, J. C. and Brown, H.M. (1981) *Monro's Tables and Other Tables of Lesser Heights*. Scottish Mountaineering Club.
Hodgkiss, P. (1984) *The Central Highlands*. Scottish Mountaineering Club.
Murray, W. H. *West Highlands of Scotland*. Collins.
Murray, W. H. (1987) *Scotland's Mountains*. Scottish Mountaineering Club.
Watson, A. (1975) *The Cairngorms*. Scottish Mountaineering Club.

English Guides

Allen, B. (1988) *On High Lakeland Fells*. Pic.
Hannon, P. (1989) *80 Dales Walks*. Cordee.
Harding, M. (1986) *Walking the Dales*. Michael Joseph.
Poucher, W. A. (1988) *Peak and the Pennines*. Constable.
Poucher, W. A. (1984) *Lakeland Peaks*. Constable.
Rawson, J. and Redfern, R. (1990) *From Bleaklow to Dovedale*. Diadem.
Wainwright, A. *Pictorial Guides Lakeland Fells: 7 Vols*. Westmoreland Gazette.

Irish Guides

Herman, D. (1979) *East Region*. Gill & Macmillan.
Herman, D. (1989) *Hill Walkers Wicklow*. Herman.
Lynam, J. (1988) *The Mountains of Connemara*. Cordee.
O'Suilleabhain, S. and Lynam, J. (1978) *South-west Region*. Gill & Macmillan.
O'Suilleabhain, S. (1978) *Irish Walks: South West*. Gill & Macmillan.
Rogers, R. (1980) *North-east Region*. Gill & Macmillan.
Rogers, R. (1980) *Irish Walks: North East*. Gill & Macmillan.
Simms, P. and Foley, G. (1979) *North-west Region*. Gill & Macmillan.
Thee, B. (1987) *The Hills of Cork & Kerry*. Gill & Macmillan.
Whilde, T. (1978) *West Region*. Gill & Macmillan.
Whilde, T. (1978) *Irish Walks: West*. Gill & Macmillan.

Welsh Guides

Gillham, J. and Greaves, V. (1989) *Snowdonia to the Gower*. Diadem.
Marsh, T. (1987) *Mountains of Wales*. Hodder & Stoughton.
Poucher, W. A. (1987) *The Welsh Peaks*. Constable.

MAPS

The Ordnance Survey publishes 1:50,000 maps and 1:25,000 maps covering the whole of the U.K. Special 'leisure' maps now cover the main climbing grounds in England and Wales and the Cuillin of Skye, Torridon and the Cairngorms in Scotland. The Irish Ordnance Survey publishes a series of maps at 1:100,000 and are introducing 1:50,000 sheets for mountain areas. Useful independent map-publishers are Bartholomews, Harvey Mountain Recreation and the Scottish Mountaineering Trust (for Skye).

NAVIGATION

Cliffe, P. (1986) *Mountain Navigation*. Cordee.
Keay, W. (1989) *Land Navigation*. Duke of Edinburgh's Award.
McNeill, C. (1989) *The Skills of the Game*. Crowood Press.
Ministry of Defence (1989) *Manual of Map Reading and Land Navigation*. HMSO.
Porteous, B. (1978) *Orienteering:* Oxford Illustrated Press.

CLIMATE AND WEATHER

Barton, L. R. and Wright, D. (1985) *A Chance in a Million*. Scottish Mountaineering Club.

Epp, M. and Lee, S. (1987) *Avalanche Awareness*. Wildside (Cordee).

Holford, I. (1985) *Looking at Weather*. Weather Publications.

Pedgley, D. E. (1979) *Mountain Weather. A Practical Guide for Hillwalkers and Climbers in the British Isles*. Cicerone Press.

Watts, A. (1985) *Instant Weather Forecasting*. Adlard Coles.

ACCESS CONSERVATION AND AMENITY

Acts (1949) *National Parks and Access to the Countryside Act;*
   (1967) *Countryside (Scotland) Act;*
   (1968) *Countryside Act (Chapter 41);*
   (1981) *Wildlife and Countryside Act;* HMSO.

British Mountaineering Council (1988) *Tread Lightly.*

Clayden, P. and Trevelyan, J. (1983) *Rights of Way: A Guide to Law and Practice*. Open Spaces Society and Ramblers' Association, 25A Bell Street, Henley-on-Thames, RG9 2BA.

Fedden, R. and Joekes, R. (1989) *The National Trust Guide*. National Trust.

Fuller, R. J. (1982) *Bird Habitats in Britain*. Poyser.

Gardner, J. F. (1989) *Rights of Way and Access to the Countryside*. Longmans.

Gillmor, D. A. (ed) (1979) *Irish Resources and Land Use*. Institute of Public Administration, Dublin.

Green, B. (1985) *Countryside Conservation*. Allen & Unwin.

McEwen, J. (1980) *Who Owns Scotland? A Study in Land Ownership*. Polygon Books.

Mountaineering Council of Scotland; Scottish Landowners' Federation (1988) *Heading for the Scottish Hills*. Scottish Mountaineering Trust.

Nethersole-Thompson, D. and Watson, A. (1981) *The Cairngorms: Their Natural History and Scenery*. Melvin Press.

Pearsall, W. H. (1972) *Mountains and Moorlands*. Collins New Naturalist.

Rickwood, P. (1982) *The Story of Access in the Peak District*. Peak Park Joint Planning Board.

Rothman, B. (1982) *The 1932 Kinder Trespass. Personal View of the Kinder Scout Mass Tresspass*. Willow Publishing.

Shoard, M. (1980) *The Theft of the Countryside*. Maurice Temple Smith Ltd.

Stamp, L. D. (1970) *Britain's Structure and Scenery*. Collins New Naturalist.

Tansley, A. G. (1939) *The British Islands and their Vegetation*. Vol. I and Vol. II. Cambridge University Press.
UK Parliament (1981) *Wildlife and Countryside Act 1981*. Chapter 69 of Public General Acts and Measures. HMSO.

CAMPING AND BACKPACKING

Fleming, J. (1985) *The Well Fed Backpacker*. Random House.
Gunn, C. (1988) *The Expedition Cookbook*. Chockstone (Cordee).
Hunter, R. (1982) *Winter Skills*. Constable.
Manning, H. (1987) *Backpacking One Step at a Time*. Sierra Club (Cordee).
Robinson, D. (1982) *Backpacking*. EP Publishing Ltd.
Walker, K. (1990) *Wild Country Camping*. Constable.

JOURNALS AND MAGAZINES

(Annual) *Irish Mountaineering*. I.M.C.
(Annual) *The Climbers' Club Journal*. C.C.
(Annual) *The Alpine Journal*. A.C.
(Annual) *Scottish Mountaineering Club Journal*. S.M.C.
(Annual) *The Fell and Rock Climbing Club Journal*. F.R.C.C.
(Bi-monthly) *Mountain*. Mountain Magazine Ltd.
(Monthly) *High*. David Green Publications.
(Monthly) *Climber and Hillwalker*. Holmes McDougall.
(Monthly) *The Great Outdoors*. Holmes McDougall.

OUTDOOR EDUCATION AND MOUNTAINEERING

Chambers, J. (1988) *A Challenge to the Individual*. (Award Scheme for people with disability). Duke of Edinburgh's Award.
Croucher, N. (1981) *Outdoor Pursuits for the Disabled*. Woodhead Faulkner.
Department of Education and Science (1989) *Safety in Outdoor Education*. HMSO.

MOUNTAIN RESCUE AND FIRST AID

Bollen, S. (1990) *First Aid on Mountains*. British Mountaineering Council.
British Red Cross Society (1988) *Practical First Aid*. Dorling Kindersley.

Hackett, P. (1986) *Mountain Sickness (Altitude)*. American Alpine Club (Cordee).

McInnes, H. (1984) *International Mountain Rescue Handbook*. Constable.

Mountain Rescue Committee. *Mountain and Cave Rescue Handbook*.
  Pugh, L. G. C. E. (1966) *Hypothermia in climbers*. British Medical Journal, 1, 123-129. Article.

Steele, P. (1989) *Medical Handbook Mountaineering*. Constable.

Ward, M. (1974) *Frostbite*. British Medical Journal, 1, 67-70. Article.

Wilkerson, J. (1987) *Hypothermia & Frostbite*. Mountaineer Books (Cordee).

Wilkerson, J. (1987) *Medicine for Mountaineering*. Mountaineer Books (Cordee).

OUT OF PRINT

Kirkus, C. F. *Let's Go Climbing*. (last edition 1960; Nelson).

Shipton, E. E. *Upon that Mountain*. (last edition 1956; paperback; Pan).

Styles, S. F. *Blue Remembered Hills*. (last edition 1965; Faber).

Weir, T. *Highland Days*. (last edition 1984; Gordon Wright).

Young, G. W., Sutton, Noyce. *Snowdon Biography*. (last edition 1957; Dent).

Out of print books can be obtained through the Public Library system, and the books listed above are readily available from second-hand book dealers.

Contacts for Access and Conservation Information and Advice

National Parks of England and Wales

Brecon Beacons National Park
Information Officer
National Park Office
Glamorgan Street
Brecon
Powys LD3 7DP
Brecon (0874) 4437

Dartmoor National Park
Youth and Schools' Liaison Officer
Dartmoor National Park Office
Parke
Haytor Road
Bovey Tracey
Newton Abbot
Devon TQ13 9JQ
Bovey Tracey (0626) 832093

Exmoor National Park
Assistant Visitor Services Officer
Exmoor National Park
Exmoor House
Dulverton
Somerset
Dulverton (0398) 23665

Lake District National Park
Youth and Schools' Liaison Officer
Lake District Special Planning Board
National Park Centre
Brockhole
Windermere
Cumbria LA23 1LJ
Windermere (09662) 3467

Northumberland National Park
Youth and Schools' Liaison Officer
Northumberland National Park and Countryside Department
Eastburn
South Park
Hexham
Northumberland NE46 1BS
Hexham (0434) 605555

North York Moors National Park
Assistant Information Officer
North York Moors National Park Information Service
The Old Vicarage
Bondgate
Helmsley
North Yorkshire YO6 5BP
Helmsley (04392) 657

Peak District National Park
Youth and Schools' Liaison Officer
Peak National Park Study Centre
Losehill Hall
Castleton
Derbyshire S30 2WB
Hope Valley (0433) 20373

Pembrokeshire Coast National Park
Youth and Schools' Liaison Officer
Pembrokeshire Coast National Park
County Offices
Haverfordwest
Dyfed SA61 1QZ
Haverfordwest (0437) 4591

Snowdonia National Park
Youth and Schools' Liaison Officer
Snowdonia National Park Office
Penrhyndeudraeth
Gwynedd LL48 6LS
Penrhyndeudraeth (0766) 770274

Yorkshire Dales National Park
Information Officer
The Yorkshire Dales National Park
Colvend
Hebden Road
Grassington
Skipton
North Yorkshire BD23 5LB
Grassington (0756) 752748

Mountaineering and Rambling Associations

Addresses and telephone numbers are provided for those organisations with a permanent office and professional staff. The up-to-date details for those organisations with voluntary officers should normally be available through the Countryside Commission(s) or Sports Council(s).

British Mountaineering Council
Crawford House, Precinct Centre, Booth Street East, Manchester M13 9RZ
Tel: 061-273 5835

Role —Representative body for mountaineers in England and Wales
Work —Work on access to open country and rock climbing areas
Membership—Clubs, associate organisations, individuals
Publications —*High*, monthly magazine

Mountaineering Council of Scotland

Role —Representative body for mountaineers in Scotland
Work —Access to mountain areas and conservation
Membership—Clubs, individuals
Publications —*Newsletter*, 3 times a year

Federation of Mountain Clubs of Ireland

Role —Representative body for mountaineers in Northern Ireland and Eire
Work —Access to mountains and conservation
Membership—Clubs
Publications —*Mountain Log*, newsletter 3 times a year

Ramblers' Association
1/5 Wandsworth Road, London SW8 2LJ
Tel: 01-582 6878

Role —Representative body for ramblers in England, Wales and Scotland

Work   —Protection of public rights of way, access to the
                 countryside, conservation
Membership—Local groups, individuals
Publications —*Rucksack*, magazine 4 times per year

Open Spaces Society
25a Bell Street, Henley-on-Thames, Oxon RG2 2BA
Tel: Henley (0491) 573535

Work   —Commons, rights of way and open country access and
                 conservation
Membership—Local authorities and organisations, individuals
Publications —Journal, 3 times per year

National Conservation Bodies

Council for the Protection of Rural England
4 Hobart Place, London SW1W 0HY
Tel: 01-235 9481

Work   —Planning, land use and conservation issues
Membership—Associate organisations and individuals
Publications —*Countryside Campaigner*, 3 times per year

Council for the Protection of Rural Wales
31 Broad Street, Welshpool, Powys SY21 7JP
Tel: Welshpool (0938) 2525

Work   —Planning, land use and conservation issues
Membership—Associate organisations and individuals
Publications —*Rural Wales*, 3 times per year

Association for the Protection of Rural Scotland
14A Napier Road, Edinburgh EH10 5AY
Tel: 031-229 1898

Work   —Planning, land use and conservation issues
Membership—Associate organisations and individuals
Publications —Annual Report

Council for National Parks
4 Hobart Place, London SW1W 0HY
Tel: 01-235 0901

Work   —Concerned with land use, economics, conservation,
                 recreation and administration in National Parks
Membership—Member organisations, individual 'Friends'
Publications —*Tarn and Tor*, twice-yearly newsletter

Scottish Wildland Group
Work   —Protection of wild land in Scotland
Membership—Individuals
Publications —*Wild Land News*, twice-yearly newsletter

Regional/Local Conservation Organisations

Friends of the Lake District
Gowan Knott, Kendal Road, Staveley, Kendal, Cumbria LA8 9LP
Tel: Kendal (0539) 821201

Work   —Protection of the natural beauty and amenity of the Lake
               District
Membership—Affiliated organisations, individuals
Publications —Spring and Autumn newsletters; *Conserving Lakeland*,
               magazine twice-yearly

Snowdonia National Park Society
Capel Curig, Betws y Coed, Gwynedd
Tel: Capel Curig (06904) 234

Work   —Protection of natural beauty and amenity of Snowdonia
Membership—Affiliated organisations, individuals
Publications —Annual Report

North-East Mountain Trust
PO Box 142, Aberdeen

Work   —Planning, land use and conservation issues in North-East
               Scotland
Membership—Clubs and organisations
Publications —*Tak Tent*, newsletter, 8 times per year

Personal and Group Clothing and Equipment for Hillwalking and Camping Expeditions

Notes

It is the Leader's responsibility to see that his party is adequately clothed and equipped.

See that individual loads do not exceed one-third of the body weight of the individual and in no case more than 30 lb.

The delineation between LOW and HIGH level is taken to be approximately 500 m (1,640 ft) above sea level.

Clothes not worn must be carried in the pack. A spare set of clothing must also be carried in a polythene bag and used only for night wear.

Ideally each member of a party should carry a personal map, compass, watch and whistle, plus a torch in winter.

It is not intended that these lists should be slavishly followed in every detail. They are offered as a guide or check list from which appropriate items may be chosen.

Individual Equipment

SUMMER

Low Level Walk	Low Level Camp	High Level Walk	High Level Camp
Day rations	Day rations	Map	Map
Whistle	Whistle	Day rations	Day rations
Boots	Rucksack	Compass	Compass
Stockings	Boots	Watch	Watch
Trousers	2 Stockings	Whistle	Whistle
Shirt	2 Trousers	Boots	Rucksack
Sweater	2 Shirts	Stockings	Boots
Anorak	2 Sweaters	Trousers	2 Stockings
*Cagoule	Anorak	Shirt	2 Trousers
First Aid	Cagoule	2 Sweaters	2 Shirts
Overtrousers	First Aid	Anorak	2 Sweaters
	Toilet requisites	*Cagoule	Anorak
	Sleeping bag plus	*Gloves	Cagoule
	inner	First Aid	Gloves
	K.F.S. mug	Large polythene	First Aid
	Polythene bag	survival bag	Toilet requisites

354

Low Level Walk	Low Level Camp	High Level Walk	High Level Camp
	Overtrousers	Overtrousers	Sleeping bag plus
		Hat	inner
			K.F.S. mug
			Polythene bags
			Overtrousers
			Hat
			Karrimat
			Torch

* Optional equipment depending on conditions and aim of expedition.

WINTER

Low Level Walk	Low Level Camp	High Level Walk	High Level Camp
Day rations	Day rations	Map	Map
Whistle	Whistle	Compass	Compass
Boots	Boots	Watch	Watch
Stockings	Rucksack	Whistle	Whistle
Trousers	2 Stockings	Torch	Torch
Underclothes	2 Trousers	Day Rations	Day Rations
Shirt	2 Underclothes	Boots	Rucksack
2 Sweaters	2 Shirts	2 Stockings	Boots
Anorak	2 Sweaters	Trousers	2 Stockings
Cagoule	Anorak	Overtrousers	2 Trousers
*Balaclava	Cagoule	Underclothes	Overtrousers
Gloves	Balaclava	Shirt	2 Underclothes
*Overmitts	Gloves	2 Sweaters	2 Shirts
*Light Scarf	*Overmitts	Anorak	2/3 Sweaters
Gaiters	Light Scarf	Cagoule	Anorak
First Aid	Gaiters	Balaclava	Cagoule
	First Aid	Gloves	Balaclava
	Toilet requisites	Overmitts	Gloves
	Sleeping bag plus	Light scarf	Overmitts
	inner	Gaiters	Light Scarf
	K.F.S. mug	Ice Axe	Gaiters
	Polythene bag	Goggles or	Ice Axe
	Karrimat	Sunglasses	Goggles
		Crampons	*Crampons
		First Aid	First Aid
		Large polythene	Toilet requisites
		bag	4 Season Sleeping
			bag
			K.F.S. mug
			Polythene bag
			Karrimat

* Optional equipment depending on conditions and aim of expedition.

Common Equipment: Shared

SUMMER

Low Level Walk	Low Level Camp	High Level Walk	High Level Camp
Map 1:2	*Torch 1:2	Rucksack 1:3	Mountain tent
Compass 1:2	Map 1:2		Stove
Watch 1:2	Compass 1:2		Fuel and bottles
Rucksack 1:4	Watch 1:2		Billies
	Stove		Rations
	Fuel and bottles		Water carrier
	Billies		Tin opener
	Rations		Matches
	Water carrier		Brillo pads
	Tin opener		Toilet paper
	Matches		Shovel
	Toilet paper		
	Shovel		
	Tent		

* Optional equipment depending on conditions and aim of expedition.

WINTER

Low Level Walk	Low Level Camp	High Level Walk	High Level Camp
Rucksack 1:4	Torch 1:2	Rucksack 1:3	Mountain tent
Compass 1:2	Compass 1:2	Thermos flask	Stove
Whistle 1:4	Whistle 1:4		Fuel and bottles
Torch 1:4	Stove		Billies
	Fuel and bottles		Rations
	Billies		Water carrier
	Rations		Tin opener
	Water carrier		Matches
	Tin opener		Toilet paper
	Brillo pads		Shovel
	Toilet paper		
	Shovel		
	Tent		

Additional Equipment for Leader

SUMMER

Low Level Walk	Low Level Camp	High Level Walk	High Level Camp
First aid kit	First aid kit	30 m (9 mm) nylon rope First aid kit Bivi or survival bag Sleeping bag Emergency ration	30 m (9 mm) nylon rope First aid kit Bivi or survival bag

WINTER

Low Level Walk	Low Level Camp	High Level Walk	High Level Camp
First aid kit	First aid kit	120 ft (9 mm) nylon rope First aid kit Red flare Emergency ration Sleeping bag Torch, Batteries (extra) Large bivouac tent	120 ft (9 mm) nylon rope First aid kit Red flare Emergency ration Large polythene bag Torch, Batteries (extra)

First Aid Kit

It is emphasised that the list of items given below is a suggested First Aid kit to be carried by the leader of a party of up to 10 people walking or climbing on the mountains of the British Isles and absent from medical services for a period of less than three days. A First Aid kit is a very personal thing and it is quite impossible to produce a pack which will satisfy everybody. However, most people would agree with the general principles on which this list of items has been based. These are:

1 It should be simple and avoid offering alternative treatments.
2 It should contain readily available and reasonably cheap items.
3 It should be light in weight and small in bulk.
4 As far as possible single items should be able to be used for a number of functions.
5 It should be effective and comprehensive within the above limitations.

I am greatly indebted to Dr Peter Steele and Dr Neil Macdonald for their advice and comments on the contents of this kit.

Item	No.	Use	Carried by individual
Bandaid strip 6 cm × 30 cm	1	Quick cover for cuts and grazes	
Dumbel sutures	4	Wound closure in place of stitches, finger dressings, awkward places	2
Zinc Oxide plaster 2.5 cm × 5 m	1	Holding gauze dressings in place to secure bandages	1
Bandages 10 cm × 4.5 m crepe	2	Elasticity for support/absorbent for bleeding	1
Triangular (compressed)		Arm sling/head bandage, etc.	
Dressing Melolin gauze squares 10 cm × 10 cm 5 cm × 5 cm	2	Non-stick absorbent cover	1
Plain gauze squares 10 cm × 10 cm	1		
Wound dressing (compressed gauze)	1	To stop bleeding in large wound	1
Antiseptic, sachet or cream	2	For dirty wounds	
Scissors, blunt/sharp	1		

Item	No.	Use	Carried by individual
Forceps, oblique end	1	For splinters	
Scalpel blade	1		
Safety pin (nappy)	1		
Luggage label pencil (wax and plain)	4	For written messages	1
Aspirin/Paracetamol	24	For pain	
Calamine cream	1	For sunburn/itching	
Insect repellant	1	Mosquitos/midges, etc.	Op.
Suncream, lip salve	1	Optional—should filter U.V.	Op.
Wintergreen cream	1	Optional—aching muscles, sprains	Op.
Steristrip plaster		In place of stitches	
Chiropody felt		For blisters	

Training of Mountain Leaders

Purpose

The purpose of the Mountain Leader Training Scheme is to ensure the safer enjoyment and understanding of the hills by young people. This is done by providing training and assessment in the technical skills required by those who wish to lead groups of young people in the mountains and moorlands of the British Isles. There is a Summer Award and a Winter Award.

Since its introduction in 1964, the Scheme has achieved widespread recognition by authorities responsible for the welfare of young people in hill and mountain activities, including Education Authorities and Youth Organisations, parents and individuals.

Operation

The Scheme is operated by the Mountain Leader Training Boards of the UK which approve training and assessment facilities and develop syllabus content. Joint arrangements exist for the co-ordination of the work of the National Boards.

Limitations

The Mountain Leader Training Scheme must be seen for what it is—the opportunity to gain minimum technical competence for leading parties in the hills. It does not provide a professional qualification.

The Scheme provides training and assessment in technical and party management in the hills in a variety of testing conditions. It seeks to integrate training, experience, and assessment.

The Summer award specifically excludes training or assessment in the skills required to cope with the special hazards of winter conditions, particularly ice and snow. Specific training for winter conditions is provided by the Mountain Leader Award operated by the Scottish MLTB.

The completion of a training course alone is in no way a qualification in itself.

Qualifications for Entry

Candidates are expected to be committed and experienced hillwalkers or mountaineers prior to registering for the Scheme.

The Scheme is not intended as a first introduction to mountaineering. There are other courses run by L.E.A.'s schools and colleges, voluntary organisations and clubs which are more suitable for the beginner.

Candidates should have a genuine practical interest in party leadership.

Responsibility of Employers and Organisers

It is the responsibility of the employer or organiser to decide whether a leader possesses the personal attributes needed for leadership—e.g. consideration, responsibility, empathy and understanding of young people.

It is the combination of technical skills, wide experience and personal qualities which forms the basis for effective leadership.

It is not intended that the adoption of the Mountain Leader Scheme by organising authorities or employers should exclude from party leadership those highly competent walkers and mountaineers who are known to possess the necessary qualities but do not hold the Mountain Leader qualification.

While Mountain Leader training may well be of positive benefit to leaders among lesser hills which do not pose potential hazards of objective dangers or remoteness, it would be contrary to the purpose of the Scheme for employers to insist on the Mountain Leader Scheme as necessary training for leaders in such terrain.

The employment of a holder of the Mountain Leader qualification in no way absolves the employer from his responsibility to ensure the suitability of his staff for party leadership.

The Mountain Leader Scheme and the Mountain Environment

Mountains mean freedom, adventure, beauty and solitude, as well as the opportunity to earn a living from the land. Therefore, whilst pursuing their own ends and fostering a love of the hills, leaders of parties of young people have a responsibility to ensure due regard for other hill users and to encourage an understanding of the problems of mountain conservation, access and erosion. Consideration of these aspects is vital if the ethics and traditions of mountain life are to be preserved.

Information

Full information, syllabus, registration forms, etc., are available from the joint publishers of this book.